FOGHORN OUTDOORS

SOUTHERN CALIFORNIA
CABINS &
COTTAGES

FOGHORN OUTDOORS

SOUTHERN CALIFORNIA
CABINS &
COTTAGES

Great Lodgings with Easy
Access to Outdoor Recreation

Ann Marie Brown

AVALON
TRAVEL

FOGHORN OUTDOORS:
SOUTHERN CALIFORNIA
CABINS & COTTAGES
First Edition

Ann Marie Brown

Published by
Avalon Travel Publishing
5855 Beaudry Street
Emeryville, CA 94608, USA

Please send all comments, corrections,
additions, amendments, and critiques to:

FOGHORN OUTDOORS:
SOUTHERN CALIFORNIA
CABINS & COTTAGES
AVALON TRAVEL PUBLISHING
5855 BEAUDRY ST.
EMERYVILLE, CA 94608, USA

email: atpfeedback@avalonpub.com
website: www.foghorn.com

Printing History
1st edition—April 2002
5 4 3 2 1

ISBN: 1-56691-446-9
ISSN: 1538-0548

Editor: Marisa Solís
Series Manager: Marisa Solís
Proofreaders: Emily Lunceford and Mia Lipman
Research Assistant: Julie Sheer
Graphics Coordinator: Susan Snyder
Production Coordinator: Alvaro Villanueva
Designer: Alvaro Villanueva
Cover Designer: Jacob Goolkasian
Map Editor: Olivia Solís
Cartographers: Chris Folks, Suzanne Service, Mike Morgenfeld
Indexer: Vera Gross
Icon Designer: Barrett Cox

Cover photos: © The Simpson House Inn, Santa Barbara

Distributed by Publishers Group West

Printed in the United States by R.R. Donnelley

CONTENTS

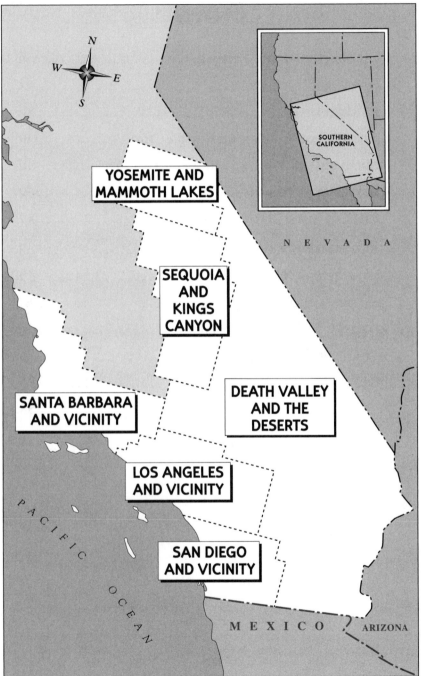

YOSEMITE AND
MAMMOTH LAKES

SEQUOIA
AND
KINGS
CANYON

SANTA BARBARA
AND VICINITY

DEATH VALLEY
AND THE
DESERTS

LOS ANGELES
AND VICINITY

SAN DIEGO
AND VICINITY

SOUTHERN
CALIFORNIA

NEVADA

PACIFIC OCEAN

MEXICO   ARIZONA

© AVALON TRAVEL PUBLISHING, INC.

MAPS

DEFINING
CABINS AND COTTAGES

The foremost purpose of this book is to provide a hearty resource of cabins and cottages for a successful overnight or weeklong getaway. The secondary goal is to provide enough information about nearby outdoors attractions to jump-start your interest in beachcombing for sea shells, hiking a summit trail, fishing for trout, or soaking in mineral hot springs. This book therefore caters to those who welcome outdoor recreation by day *and* a roof over their head by night—whether that roof is constructed of pine logs, canvas, or fiberglass.

. . . *Fiberglass?* Yes, you read right. The range of materials used to construct the "cabins and cottages" featured in this book is due to our broad definition of a cabin: a self-contained, stand-alone lodging. That is why the cabins and cottages that fill this guidebook range from rustic tent cabins to luxurious vacation home rentals. They may be part of a resort, lodge, ranch, campground, or rental company. Each lodging is a separate building or unit, and would be suitable for couples, families, or singles who want more privacy and personality than a typical hotel or motel room provides.

Each lodging in *Foghorn Outdoors: Southern California Cabins & Cottages* is located in or near a major outdoor recreation area, including seven national parks: Joshua Tree, Death Valley, Mojave, Devils Postpile, Yosemite, Sequoia, and Kings Canyon. Also included are cabins and cottages along the length of the Southern California coast from San Diego to San Simeon, and throughout the southern and central Sierra Nevada mountains. Because these cabins and cottages are located near major recreation areas, general information on nearby outdoor activities, such as hiking, fishing, snow skiing, and bicycling, is provided.

Foghorn Outdoors: Southern California Cabins & Cottages provides everything you need for an enjoyable weekend getaway or a week-long vacation centered around outdoor recreation and a cabin or cottage (or yurt, chalet, or yacht) that's right for you.

HOW TO USE THIS BOOK

Foghorn Outdoors: Southern California Cabins & Cottages is divided into six chapters: Santa Barbara and Vicinity, Los Angeles and Vicinity, San Diego and Vicinity, Yosemite and Mammoth Lakes, Sequoia and Kings Canyon, and Death Valley and the Deserts. Although that is a lot of territory to cover in one book, navigating this guide can be done easily in two ways:

1. If you know the name of the lodging facility you want to stay at, or the name of the surrounding geographical area or nearby feature (town, national or state park or forest, mountain, lake, river, etc.), look it up in the index beginning on page 253 and turn to the corresponding page.

2. If you know the general area you want to visit, turn to the map at the beginning of that chapter. You can then determine which cabins are in or near your destination by their corresponding numbers. Opposite the map will be a chapter table of contents listing each lodging in the chapter by map number and the page number it's profiled on. Then turn to the corresponding page for the cabin you're interested in.

ABOUT THE CABIN PROFILES

Each featured cabin profile includes an introduction to the lodging facility and what it has to offer. This usually includes an overview of the grounds, units, facilities, and amenities. There is also a discussion of the recreation opportunities available on-site or within a short drive. These range from horseback riding to kayaking and from hiking to fishing. The practical information you need to have an enjoyable trip is broken down further into the following categories:

Facilities — This section conveys the number of cabins or cottages available, whether kitchen facilities are available, and whether private or communal bathrooms and showers are available. Amenities inside the cabins (such as fireplace, hot tub, and air-conditioning) as well as on the property (such as swimming pool, restaurant, and picnic area) are also mentioned here.

Bedding — This section tells whether linens and towels are provided, and if not, what you should bring to sleep comfortably.

Reservations and rates — This section notes whether reservations are required or recommended. It also discusses the rates for each cabin, which often range due to cabin size, amenities, time of week, and time of year. If there are additional fees for extra persons or pets, that will also be noted here. If there are package deals, that will also be noted. If a cabin is open during part of the year, those dates will be mentioned.

Directions — This section provides mile-by-mile driving directions from the nearest major town.

Contact — This section provides an address, phone number, and website address, if available, for the featured cabin.

ABOUT THE ICONS

The icons in this book are designed to provide at-a-glance information on activities that are available on-site or nearby a cabin. Some icons have been selected to also represent facilities available or services provided. They are not meant to represent every activity or service, only the ones that the majority of our readers would be interested in.

 — Hiking trails are available.

 — Biking trails or routes are available. Usually this refers to mountain biking, although it may represent road cycling as well. Refer to the text for that cabin for more detail.

 — Swimming opportunities are available.

 — Fishing opportunities are available.

 — Boating opportunities are available. Various types of vessels apply under this umbrella activity, including motorboats, canoes, kayaks, sailboats, personal watercrafts, and row boats. Refer to the text for that cabin for more detail, including mph restrictions and boat ramp availability.

 — Beach activities are available. This general category may include activities such as beachcombing, surfing, and volleyball. Refer to the text for that cabin for more detail on what's allowed.

 — Winter sports are available. This general category may include activities such as downhill skiing, cross-country skiing, snowshoeing, snow mobiling, snowboarding, and ice skating. Refer to the text for that cabin for more detail on which sports are available.

 — Hot or cold springs are available.

 — Pets are permitted. Lodging facilities that allow pets may require a deposit, nightly fee, or for the pet to be on a leash. Cabins may also restrict pet size. Refer to the text for that cabin for more specific instruction or call the cabin in advance.

 — The cabin or cottage is especially popular with families. Typically that is because it has activities nearby that are suitable for children. These include a playground or play area, swimming pool, ocean beach, lake with a wading or swimming beach, or family-oriented skiing or snow play. At these kid-friendly cabins, you won't have to travel far to keep the kids entertained.

 — Wheelchair access is provided. Not all cabins at a facility may be wheelchair accessible, but if at least one is, the cabin will receive this icon. Refer to the text for that cabin for more detail or call the cabin in advance.

ABOUT THE RATINGS

Every lodging option in this book is rated on two scales.

Luxury rating — This scale of **1** to **5** rates the comfort level of the cabin. We expect that users of this guidebook will have different requirements for cushy living, but in general, a place with more amenities will get a higher ranking. For example, a tent cabin without bathrooms or running water may receive a **1** or **2**. That doesn't mean that you can't have the perfect vacation here. All it means is you might have to carry your water from a nearby fountain and be prepared to use chemical toilets. Likewise, a cottage with fireplace, hot tub, king-size bed, and down comforters will probably rank 4 or 5. But, that doesn't guarantee the perfect vacation; the cabin may be close to a noisy highway, the management may not be friendly, or the recreation options may be an hour's drive away.

Recreation rating — This scale of **1** to **5** rates the accessibility of on-site or nearby activities. We expect that users of this guidebook are interested in the outdoors and seek a cabin experience that is coupled with recreation opportunities. This scale does not rate the number of activities available, nor the level of expertise needed to participate in them. Rather, it rates how *accessible* they are. For example, if you can access a trailhead or launch your boat within a two-minute walk of your cabin, the recreation rating will likely be a 5. On the other hand, if fishing or downhill skiing requires a one-hour drive, the cabin may be rated a 1. That doesn't mean you can't have the same quality vacation . . . it just means you'll need more than your feet for transportation.

THIS CABIN RANKS . . . — Each cabin and cottage that appears in this guide are carefully selected from myriad options, so we like to think that each of the cabins profiled in this book is special. But those places that are extra-special may receive a ranking in one or more of the "Best of Cabins and Cottages" categories. For the complete list of the categories and the cabins that have made it to the top ranks, turn to page xv.

ABOUT THE MAPS

Each chapter in this book begins with a map of the area. Every cabin profile in the chapter is noted by a number on the map. These points are placed as precisely as possible, but the scale of these maps often makes it difficult to pinpoint a cabin's exact location. We advise that you purchase a detailed map of the area, especially if it is new to you.

INTRODUCTION

Over and over, traveling around California teaches me to be flexible and adaptable. It's a lesson for which I'm grateful, because these seem to be critical life skills. In travel writing, as in the rest of life, things just don't always go as you plan.

In the course of researching this book, for example, a major rainstorm on the Central Coast closed the cabin where I was scheduled to stay. But a series of detours on a flooded road took me to another cabin resort—one I never would have found otherwise. With a fire roaring in the fireplace and rain splashing on the windowpanes, I spent a cozy, wonderful night in a place I would ordinarily have passed by.

On another occasion, noisy neighbors in the cottage next door caused me to give up my attempt at slumber and go for a drive before dawn. At four in the morning, I stopped my car along a Mojave desert highway and was awestruck by a horizon-to-horizon sky blanketed with glittering stars.

Yet another day, I drove many miles from my rental cabin to hike a peak in the San Gabriel Mountains. When I arrived at the trailhead, I found the trail was closed due to a forest fire. Sorely disappointed, I settled for hiking to the summit of another peak instead. As I neared the mountaintop, I saw my first bighorn sheep close-up. He was only a few feet ahead of me on the trail, displaying remarkable spiraling antlers.

During my travels for this book, there were days when it snowed in the middle of the desert, or rain poured down just after the day had dawned clear and blue. But each time, what seemed like an obstacle turned out to be a blessing in disguise. I wound up making new friends, discovering new places, or witnessing a sight I would have otherwise missed.

Kurt Vonnegut Jr. wrote that "peculiar travel suggestions are dancing lessons from God." If you travel around Southern California and stay at any of this book's cabins, cottages, ski huts, fire lookouts, boat-and-breakfasts, or guest ranches, you'll probably learn to dance. At the very least, you'll have a great time trying.

—Ann Marie Brown

QUESTIONS TO ASK WHEN RESERVING A CABIN

The majority of these questions are addressed in the cabin and cottage write-ups that follow. But resort owners change, policies change, and times change, so it's wise to ask a few questions. The best advice: Know before you go.

- How many people does the cabin accommodate, and is there any extra charge for additional people?
- Are pets allowed in the cabin? Is there any extra charge for pets?
- Does the cabin have a private bathroom and shower, or do I use a shared bathroom facility on the grounds?
- Does the cabin have electricity and heat? Should I bring flashlights and lanterns?
- Does the cabin have a fireplace or woodstove? Should I bring my own firewood?
- Does the cabin have a kitchen, and are all dishes, pots, pans, and utensils provided? What about paper towels, toilet paper, soap, trash bags, and cleaning supplies?
- Does the cabin have a barbecue or fire grill where I can cook outside?
- Is there a grocery store nearby, or should I bring all my own food?
- Is there a restaurant or café nearby?
- Does the cabin have all linens provided, or should I bring sleeping bags, pillows, and towels?
- Is the cabin a single unit or duplex-style? Is it situated very close to other cabins, where I might hear my neighbors?
- Is the cabin close to the road, so I might hear road noise?
- Does the cabin have a view?

ABOUT THE NATIONAL FOREST ADVENTURE PASS

Beginning in 1997, a fee policy was instituted in Angeles, San Bernardino, Cleveland, and Los Padres National Forests as a way of raising revenue to cover the costs of recreation on national forest land.

The policy is as follows: Any vehicle that is parked in the Angeles, San Bernardino, Cleveland, and Los Padres National Forests must display a national forest adventure pass. You are free to drive through national forest land without a pass, but if you park your car, you must display one. The cardboard pass hangs from your rearview mirror.

Passes are available for a fee of $5 per day or $30 per year, and the same pass is valid in all four national forests. When you purchase a yearly pass, you receive an extra pass for use on a second vehicle, such as a motorcycle or trailer. Passes can be purchased at all Angeles, San Bernardino, Cleveland, and Los Padres National Forest visitor centers and ranger stations. They are also available at many commercial establishments, such as grocery stores and mini-marts located on or near national forest land.

Note that there are a few gray areas to the fee policy. In some regions, such as Crystal Lake Recreation Area in Angeles National Forest or Santa Ynez Recreation Area in Los Padres National Forest, a concessionaire runs the developed services—campgrounds, picnic areas, restrooms, etc. In those areas, a national forest adventure pass is not valid. You must pay a fee directly to the concessionaire.

TRAVELING WITH PETS

Many of the cabins and cottages in this book allow pets in some or all of their units. Look for the 🐕 symbol to easily identify these places. However, before packing your pet's suitcase, please alert the resort's management of your intentions. At many places, dogs are permitted only in some cabins; you'll need to reserve one of these dog-friendly cabins in advance. Also, some resorts charge a nightly fee for dogs, while others insist on a one-time fee or a doggy cleaning deposit. If you have more than one dog with you, the fee is usually per dog. Find out the specifics before you go.

Also, most cabin and cottage owners agree that dog owners must not leave their dogs unattended. That means that if you leave your cabin or cottage, your dog goes with you, even for short stints like meals or drives to the store. It's unfair to your dog to leave him or her alone in a strange place, and it's even more unfair to other cabin or cottage guests who get stuck listening to an upset, barking dog. If you bring your dog to a cabin or cottage resort, be prepared to have him or her at your side at all times. And it goes without saying that when you're around other people (as you will be at any resort), your dog must be leashed, no matter how well-behaved he or she is.

Please remember that in general, if you are vacationing in or near a national or state park, your dog will not be allowed to hike on trails with you. Dogs are permitted on roads and in picnic areas and campgrounds in these parks, but not on hiking trails. However, if you are vacationing in or near national forest land, your dog will be allowed to hike with you on most trails. Before you leave on your trip, contact the parks where you are heading for updated information regarding dog policies.

BEST CABINS AND COTTAGES

Of the hundreds of cabins and cottages in this book, here are my favorites in the following categories:

BEST FOR HIKING

Grant Grove Lodge, Sequoia and Kings Canyon, p. 206. These cabins provide ready access to dozens of trails in King Canyon and Sequoia National Parks and Giant Sequoia National Monument.

Silver City Resort, Sequoia and Kings Canyon, p. 221. The only cabin resort in Mineral King, Silver City gives you the chance to explore the spectacular high country of Sequoia National Park without sleeping in a tent at night.

Bearpaw High Sierra Camp, Sequoia and Kings Canyon, p. 216. You have to hike 11 miles to reach this tent cabin camp, and once you're there, many more day trips are possible.

Rock Creek Lakes Resort, Yosemite and Mammoth Lakes, p. 169. These cabins are only one mile from the Mosquito Flat Trailhead at 10,300 feet in elevation, with trails leading into spectacular Little Lakes Valley and Mono Pass.

Yosemite High Sierra Camps, Yosemite and Mammoth Lakes, p. 134. The High Sierra Camp loop allows you to stay at five tent cabin camps spaced 5.7–10 miles apart, the perfect distance for day hiking.

Tuolumne Lodge, Yosemite and Mammoth Lakes, p. 136. These 59 tent cabins are located within 100 yards of the John Muir Trail and the Pacific Crest Trail, and within a stone's throw of the trailheads at Tuolumne Meadows.

BEST FOR FISHING

Bishop Creek Lodge, Sequoia and Kings Canyon, p. 201. This resort makes no pretenses; it's a base camp for anglers heading to South Lake or Sabrina Lake to catch trout all day.

Parchers Resort, Sequoia and Kings Canyon, p. 203. Located only one mile from South Lake in Bishop Creek Canyon, these 10 cabins are perfectly situated for rainbow and brown trout fishing.

Alpers Owens River Ranch, Yosemite and Mammoth Lakes, p. 148. At this fly-fishing ranch near Mammoth, you can choose between a trophy trout pond, the Owens River, and Alpers Creek—all within a few feet of your rustic cabin.

Hot Creek Ranch, Yosemite and Mammoth Lakes, p. 164. For dedicated fly fishers, Hot Creek Ranch offers luxurious cabins along a stretch of Hot Creek in the Owens River Valley.

Convict Lake Resort, Yosemite and Mammoth Lakes, p. 166. Fishing for brown and rainbow trout is the main task of vacationers staying at Convict Lake's 23 cabins.

Lake San Antonio South Shore Resort, Santa Barbara and Vicinity, p. 6. Just steps from these 17 cabins, you can fish for striped bass, largemouth bass, catfish, crappie, and bluegill; don't be surprised if you catch up to 100 bass per day.

BEST FOR HORSEBACK RIDING

Circle Bar B Guest Ranch, Santa Barbara and Vicinity, p. 19. Ride Old Paint through the coastal hills of Santa Barbara after a good night's rest in one of Circle Bar B's seven cabins.

Bonnie B Ranch, Sequoia and Kings Canyon, p. 187. Rent this 3,000-square-foot ranch house and the 440 acres surrounding it, then ride the ranch's horses for a week.

Rankin Ranch, Sequoia and Kings Canyon, p. 233. A taste of old California, Rankin Ranch is all about cowboys, cattle ranching, hayrides, and horseshoes.

Golden Trout Wilderness Pack Trains Cabins, Sequoia and Kings Canyon, p. 225. Saddle up and ride into the Golden Trout Wilderness after a night in these rustic cabins.

Hunewill Guest Ranch, Yosemite and Mammoth Lakes, p. 122. At this Bridgeport ranch, 120 horses are waiting to be ridden, so pack up your cowboy boots and a bag of apples and carrots.

Red's Meadow Resort, Yosemite and Mammoth Lakes, p. 158. Stay at these rustic cabins in Devils Postpile and take guided rides into the John Muir and Ansel Adams Wilderness Areas.

BEST FOR BOATING & WATER SPORTS

Lake San Antonio South Shore Resort, Santa Barbara and Vicinity, p. 6. The Paso Robles foothills heat up in summer, which makes long and narrow Lake San Antonio an obvious choice for waterskiing and boating.

The Forks Resort, Sequoia and Kings Canyon, p. 184. Bass Lake is the Sierra foothills' most popular water-skiing lake, and the Forks Resort provides easy access to it.

Miller's Landing, Sequoia and Kings Canyon, p. 185. These cabins are located right across the road from Miller's Landing Marina at Bass Lake, where you can rent patio boats, ski boats, Waverunners, fishing boats, kayaks, and canoes.

Shaver Lake Lodge, Sequoia and Kings Canyon, p. 188. Twenty cabins overlook Shaver Lake, where sailors, water-skiers, and jet skiers share the water with anglers and kayakers.

Lakeshore Resort, Sequoia and Kings Canyon, p. 195. These Huntington Lake cabins give you easy access to waterskiing, fishing, and especially sailing; this lake is considered the premier high-altitude sailing lake in the United States.

Shore Acres Lodge, Los Angeles and Vicinity, p. 55. This cabin resort on the shore of Big Bear Lake is near Holloway's Marina, where you can rent personal watercrafts as well as boats for sailing, waterskiing, and fishing.

BEST FOR WINTER SPORTS

Giant Oaks Lodge, Los Angeles and Vicinity, p. 51. Located only five miles from Snow Valley Ski Resort and a half-hour from San Bernardino, Giant Oaks Lodge makes a weekend ski trip simple.

Our Secret Garden Mountain Retreat, Los Angeles and Vicinity, p. 61. Take the "back" way to the lifts at Big Bear's Snow Summit and Bear Mountain ski areas from this cabin resort.

Tamarack Lodge Resort, Yosemite and Mammoth Lakes, p. 159. Cross-country ski and snowshoe right from your cabin door on more than 45 kilometers of groomed track.

Pinecrest Chalet, Yosemite and Mammoth Lakes, p. 117. The closest lodging to Dodge Ridge Ski Area, Pinecrest Chalet's 23 cabins and townhouses provide easy access to skiing and snowboarding.

Tioga Pass Resort, Yosemite and Mammoth Lakes, p. 128. The road to the resort isn't plowed in winter, but if you're willing to ski in six miles, you'll have a warm cabin in a private winter wonderland.

Mammoth Mountain Chalets, Yosemite and Mammoth Lakes, p. 156. These A-frame chalets are literally across the street from the chairlifts at Mammoth Mountain Ski Area.

Rock Creek Lodge, Yosemite and Mammoth Lakes, p. 170. Founded in the 1920s as one of the first ski resorts in America, Rock Creek Lodge is the perfect base camp for a cross-country skiing vacation.

Snowcrest Lodge, Los Angeles and Vicinity, p. 44. Located a half mile from the chairlift at Mount Baldy, the six rustic cabins at Snowcrest Lodge are a throwback to the 1930s.

BEST FOR FAMILIES

Montecito Sequoia Lodge, Sequoia and Kings Canyon, p. 210. This resort is run like a High Sierra Club Med for families, with nonstop organized activities for kids.

Rankin Ranch, Sequoia and Kings Canyon, p. 233. If your children are budding cowboys or cowgirls, take them on a cabin vacation at Rankin Ranch.

Rancho Oso Guest Ranch, Santa Barbara and Vicinity, p. 20. Spend the night in the "Saloon" or in one of 10 covered wagons at this campground in the Santa Ynez Mountains.

Pinecrest Lake Resort, Yosemite and Mammoth Lakes, p. 116. This resort caters to families, with nightly movies, paddle boat rentals, guided nature hikes, and two- and three-bedroom housekeeping cabins near Pinecrest Lake.

Virginia Creek Settlement, Yosemite and Mammoth Lakes, p. 124. Kids will love staying in these covered wagons and tiny old-West-style cabins near Bodie State Historic Park.

Yosemite Lakes, Yosemite and Mammoth Lakes, p. 130. These cabins and yurts along the South Fork Tuolumne River attract families who want to swim and fish.

MOST UNUSUAL

Mono Hot Springs Resort, Sequoia and Kings Canyon, p. 195. These cabins are way out there in the middle of nowhere, existing only for the hedonistic pleasure of bathing in soothing hot springs.

Oak Flat Lookout Tower, Sequoia and Kings Canyon, p. 232. Spend the weekend in a fire lookout tower perched 40 feet above the ground on a mountaintop near Bakersfield.

White Lotus Foundation, Santa Barbara and Vicinity, p. 21. Sleep in a yurt and be a yogi for a few days at this yoga retreat center in the mountains above Santa Barbara.

Castlewood Theme Cottages, Los Angeles and Vicinity, p. 59. Spend the night in one of 10 theme cabins in Big Bear and live out your *Anthony and Cleopatra* or *Gone with the Wind* fantasies.

BEST IN THE DESERT

La Casa del Zorro Desert Resort, San Diego and Vicinity, p. 91. These luxurious cottages are just steps from the trailheads at Anza-Borrego Desert State Park.

Mojave Rock Ranch, Death Valley and the Deserts, p. 244. The secluded cabins at this resort near Joshua Tree National Park are creative desert masterpieces.

29 Palms Inn, Death Valley and the Deserts, p. 245. Located just outside the entrance to Joshua Tree National Park, many of these adobe bungalow and wood-frame cabins were built in 1928.

Two Bunch Palms, Death Valley and the Deserts, p. 248. Leave the real world behind at this luxurious hot springs oasis in Desert Hot Springs.

BEST VALUE

Virginia Creek Settlement, Yosemite and Mammoth Lakes, p. 124. A mere 20 bucks buys you a night for two in these tiny, old West cabins.

KOA Yosemite-Mariposa, Yosemite and Mammoth Lakes, p. 149. Where can you stay near Yosemite for 50 bucks a night? Right here at the KOA log cabins.

Topanga Ranch Motel, Los Angeles and Vicinity, p. 40. This is the only place in pricey Malibu that has cottages for less than $100 a night.

Green Valley Lake Cozy Cabins, Los Angeles and Vicinity, p. 52. A week at this pretty fishing and swimming lake in the San Bernardino Mountains will cost you less than $500 for 4–6 people.

Grant Grove Lodge, Sequoia and Kings Canyon, p. 206. Stay inside the border of Kings Canyon National Park for less than $90 for a cabin for two.

Catalina Cabins at Two Harbors, Los Angeles and Vicinity, p. 66. Available in the off-season from October to April only, these mobile home–style cabins on Catalina Island are offered for $25 to $40 a night.

Cuyamaca Rancho State Park Cabins, San Diego and Vicinity, p. 97. Leave your tent at home. For $15 to $22 a night, you can have a roof over your head in the midst of this beautiful state park campground.

MOST LUXURIOUS

Double Eagle Resort, Yosemite and Mammoth Lakes, p. 145. For a mountain resort, this place has plenty of "city" amenities, like a health spa and a gourmet restaurant.

Two Bunch Palms, Death Valley and the Deserts, p. 248. Getting past the guards at the entrance gate is a challenge, but once you're in, you will be pampered.

San Ysidro Ranch, Santa Barbara and Vicinity, p. 26. Your name is branded in block letters on a wooden plaque outside your cottage at this exclusive resort.

Santa Barbara Biltmore, Santa Barbara and Vicinity, p. 28. Situated right on Butterfly Beach, the Biltmore is the grand old dame of Santa Barbara.

Simpson House Inn, Santa Barbara and Vicinity, p. 24. Victorian elegance is the order of the day at Simpson House Inn.

Chateau Marmont, Los Angeles and Vicinity, p. 41. Bette Davis and Greta Garbo slept in these cottages; you can, too.

BEST FOR BEACH ACTIVITIES

Cayucos Vacation Rentals, Santa Barbara and Vicinity, p. 11. The little town of Cayucos is the quintessential beach town, where all recreation centers around the coast.

Santa Barbara Biltmore, Santa Barbara and Vicinity, p. 28. Butterfly Beach is only a few steps from your cottage at the Biltmore.

The Tides Motel, Santa Barbara and Vicinity, p. 15. Only 90 steps separate your cottage from the sands of Pismo Beach.

Crystal Pier Hotel, San Diego and Vicinity, p. 101. Located in Pacific Beach, these cottages on the historic Crystal Pier don't just overlook the ocean, they sit on top of it.

Topanga Ranch Motel, Los Angeles and Vicinity, p. 40. These rustic cabins in Malibu are right across the Pacific Coast Highway from the ocean.

Manzanita Cottages, Los Angeles and Vicinity, p. 73. You can walk to the lovely white sands of Laguna Beach from these cottages.

La Paloma Cottages, Los Angeles and Vicinity, p. 67. Located in Avalon on Catalina Island, these cottages offer access to every imaginable ocean and beach activity.

The Beach Cottages, San Diego and Vicinity, p, 102. These 17 cottages are located inches from the sand in Pacific Beach, San Diego's beach party town.

MOST SECLUDED

Muir Trail Ranch, Sequoia and Kings Canyon, p. 199. Because you rented the whole ranch and had to hike five miles to reach it, you probably won't have a lot of neighbors.

Paradise Canyon Cabins, Sequoia and Kings Canyon, p. 220. Located behind a locked gate on the lonely, winding road to Mineral King, the two cabins at Paradise Canyon are a hidden paradise.

Mojave Rock Ranch, Death Valley and the Deserts, p. 244. You won't hear anything at Mojave Rock Ranch's four cabins except the occasional howl of a coyote.

Seven Oaks Mountain Cabins, Los Angeles and Vicinity, p. 62. Located three miles off the main highway and with only six cabins, Seven Oaks will keep you sequestered from the crowds—even this close to Los Angeles.

OUR COMMITMENT

We are committed to making *Foghorn Outdoors: Southern California Cabins & Cottages* the most accurate, thorough, and enjoyable guide to cabin and cottage rentals in Southern California. Each ranch, campground, inn, and resort featured in this book has been carefully reviewed and accompanied by the most up-to-date information available. Be aware, however, that with the passing of time, some of the rates listed herein may have changed, facilities may have been upgraded (or downgraded), and changes in weather may close cabins or the roads leading to them. With these possibilities in mind, or if you have a specific need or concern, it's best to call the location ahead of time.

If you would like to comment on the book, whether it's to suggest a cabin or cottage we overlooked or to let us know about any noteworthy experience—good or bad—that occurred while using *Foghorn Outdoors: Southern California Cabins & Cottages* as your guide, we would appreciate hearing from you. Please address correspondence to:

> *Foghorn Outdoors:*
> *Southern California Cabins & Cottages,*
>   First Edition
> Avalon Travel Publishing
> 5855 Beaudry Street
> Emeryville, CA 94608
> U.S.A
>
> email: atpfeedback@avalonpub.com

If you send us an email, please put "Southern California Cabins & Cottages" in the subject line. Thanks.

CHAPTER 1

Santa Barbara and Vicinity

*T*he Santa Barbara region, which extends 200 miles from the artsy town of Cambria and the terraced vineyards of Paso Robles to the white sands of Ventura, encompasses what many consider to be Southern California's finest stretch of coast. The Santa Barbara county shoreline, curving upcoast from Carpinteria to Point Conception, has a southern, not western, exposure, which results in exceptionally mild weather. To the south, Ventura County's coast offers 40 miles of fine sandy beaches.

Lest you think the Santa Barbara region is all sun and sand, note that it also contains more than a million acres of national forest land in the Santa Barbara and Ojai backcountry—the southern section of Los Padres National Forest. This landscape is a conglomeration of pine-clad high mountain peaks, river-cut canyons, and chaparral-covered hillsides, which offer myriad hiking and mountain biking opportunities. The Santa Ynez Mountains, a centerpiece of southern Los Padres National Forest, are part of the unique Transverse Range, a system of mountains that defies the rules of California geography: It runs from east to west, rather than north to south.

Several recreation lakes and horse ranches are found in or near the mountains and foothills, with rental cabins and cottages available for visitors. Lake San Antonio and Lake Nacimiento near Paso Robles are both large bodies of water for waterskiing, bass fishing, swimming, and kayaking. If you're spending more than a few days at the lakes, you'll probably want to take a road trip to go wine tasting in the burgeoning Paso Robles wine country.

The Alisal, Circle Bar B, and Rancho Oso guest ranches all provide opportunities for horseback riding within steps of their cabins and cottages. Each ranch has its own flavor, from the luxurious Alisal to one-step-above-camping Rancho Oso.

The Santa Barbara region also contains its share of oddities and wonders, including the architecturally marvelous Hearst Castle, the Danish town of Solvang, and the rugged and remote islands of Channel Islands National Park. Hearst Castle can be visited with a stay at one of several cottage resorts in Cambria, Cayucos, or Paso Robles. Solvang can be explored from the enchanting Chimney Sweep Inn downtown. However, no accommodations are found on the Channel Islands—only campgrounds. A stay at a cottage resort in Ventura or Santa Barbara gives visitors the opportunity to visit two of the nearest islands, Anacapa and Santa Cruz, on day trips.

When most people think of Santa Barbara proper, they think of whitewashed, Spanish-style buildings, palm trees, and luxury resorts. And that image is largely accurate, as reflected in the cottages at the Santa Barbara Biltmore, El Encanto Hotel, and San Ysidro Ranch. It takes some serious money to spend a night at one of these places, but few would say it's not worth it. In the same class, but a different genre, are the quaint bed-and-breakfast cottages in downtown Santa Barbara, such as the Simpson House Inn and Cheshire Cat Inn.

Whereas the coast around Santa Barbara proper has been densely developed, many miles of sand to the north, from Goleta to Cayucos, retain a remote feel or small-town beach atmosphere. The quiet coastal towns of Cambria, San Simeon, and Cayucos are a foreshadowing of the remote Big Sur Coast to the north. Several cottage resorts and vacation rentals in the area provide the ideal setting for a small-town vacation at the coast.

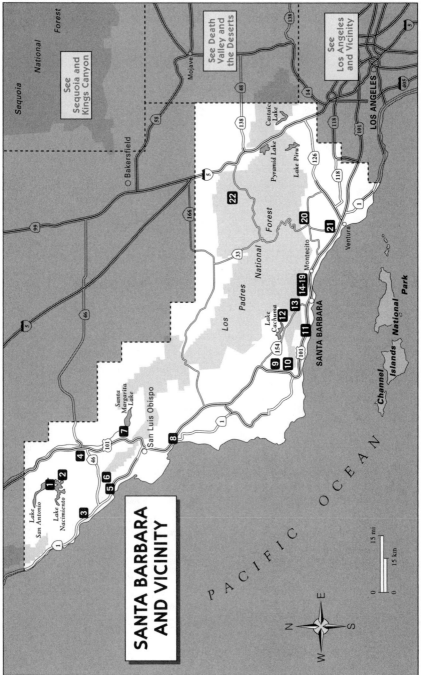

SANTA BARBARA
AND VICINITY

© AVALON TRAVEL PUBLISHING, INC.

CHAPTER 1
SANTA BARBARA AND VICINITY

1. LAKE SAN ANTONIO SOUTH SHORE RESORT

It's rare that a Southern California reservoir offers more than just waterskiing, bass fishing, and power boating, but Lake San Antonio does. Located in the Central Coast grasslands east of San Simeon and west of U.S. 101, Lake San Antonio has 5,700 surface acres of water—enough to keep boaters and anglers busy all summer long. But the lake is also a major habitat area for eagles, both bald and golden. Eagle Watch boat tours are an excellent reason to come to Lake San Antonio in winter.

Off U.S. 101 near Paso Robles

Luxury rating: 3

Recreation rating: 4

THIS CABIN RANKS . . .
*Best for Boating &
Water Sports*
Best for Fishing

Whatever the season, start your trip by booking a cabin at the lake's South Shore Resort—a busy place with a restaurant, grocery store, gas station, and marina. The resort rents one-, two-, and three-bedroom cabins with fully stocked kitchens and nice views of the lake. Don't expect cute log cabins; these are more in the order of mobile homes. They won't make the cover of *Architectural Digest,* but they serve their purpose.

Water sports are plentiful at Lake San Antonio, including all boating activities and fishing for striped bass, catfish, crappie, largemouth bass, and bluegill. The largemouth bass fishing can be exceptional, with catches of up to 100 per day not uncommon. Simultaneously, Lake San Antonio is far and away the most popular water-skiing lake on the Central Coast. You don't have your own boat? No problem: You can rent boats, motors, personal watercrafts, water-skiing equipment, and fishing tackle at the South Shore Marina. You can even rent a kayak or paddleboat and just paddle around in the lake's quiet coves.

If eagle-watching strikes your fancy, plan your stay for a weekend in late December to early March. On Friday, Saturday, and Sunday, the Monterey County Parks Department offers Eagle Watch Tours aboard *Eagle One,* a 56-foot tour boat. On Sunday, you can pay a few bucks extra and have brunch aboard the boat while you scan the skies for big birds.

Mountain biking and hiking are also possible activities, but save these for winter and spring, when the temperatures are cooler. Summertime bakes out here in the foothills, although nobody cruising around the lake seems to care.

Facilities: There are 17 cabins ranging in size from one to three bedrooms; each can accommodate 6 to 10 people. All cabins have fully equipped kitchens. A store and café are on-site.

Bedding: Linens and towels are provided.

Reservations and rates: Reservations are recommended. Fees range from $130 to $225 per night; weekly rentals are discounted. Fees are reduced from October to March. Pets are not permitted.

Directions: From U.S. 101 in Paso Robles, take the Highway 46 East exit (24th Street or G-14 West). Drive west on G-14 for approximately 14 miles, then turn right on Lake Nacimiento Road. Cross the dam at Lake Nacimiento, then turn left on Interlake Road. Drive seven miles to Lake San Antonio Road and turn right. Drive three miles to the South Shore entrance to the lake.

Contact: Lake San Antonio South Shore Resort, Star Route, Box 2620, Bradley, CA 93426; 805/472-2313 or 800/310-2313; website: www.tcsn.net/lsar.

Lake San Antonio South Shore Resort

2. LAKE NACIMIENTO RESORT

Lake Nacimiento and Lake San Antonio are practically side-by-side water bodies in the grassy foothills west of Paso Robles. Both are about the same size (5,000-plus acres), but whereas San Antonio is a long, narrow lake, Nacimiento has a large number of coves and arms that give it a more complex shape. The lake's varied outline allows plenty of room for water-skiers, anglers, swimmers, and kayakers to share the water without getting in each other's way.

Off U.S. 101 near Paso Robles

Luxury rating: 4

Recreation rating: 4

The lake is quite busy on summer weekends. The air temperature is usually hot and the water temperature is about 70 degrees. As a result, the majority of people put on their bathing suits as soon as they get out of bed and don't wear anything else all day.

Fishing is for bass, primarily, although sunfish, crappie, and catfish are sometimes caught. Nacimiento's big catch is white bass; it's the only lake in California that is stocked with these feisty little fish. In fact, the lake has so many white bass that there is no limit on how many you can catch. Largemouth bass are also stocked. The best action is usually in late spring and early summer.

Lake Nacimiento Resort is the only commercial facility on the lake, and in addition to its boat rentals, marina, and the Lakeshore Cafe restaurant, the resort rents cabins on a hill overlooking the lake. Technically, the cabins are called "lodges." They are modern, fancy affairs that look like townhouses. A dozen are clustered together and surrounded by a perfectly tended lawn, which seems otherworldly in these dry foothills.

The lodges come in three configurations: large units that sleep 10, small units that sleep four, and combination units that sleep 14. The combo units, as you probably guessed, are a large and small unit with the doors open in between. All units come with everything you need for daily living, with one exception: The kitchens have a range and microwave, but no oven. (Most people barbecue on the outside deck anyway.) Some units have a dishwasher, fireplace, and private deck, so make sure you request the features you want. The views are so lovely from the cabins' high vantage point that you shouldn't miss getting a lakeview deck.

If you need more choices, mobile homes and 30-foot camp trailers are also available for rent.

Facilities: There are 19 cabins that can be configured for 4, 10, or 14 people, plus mobile home and trailer rentals. All cabins have fully equipped kitchens. A store and restaurant are on-site.

Bedding: Linens and towels are provided.

Reservations and rates: Reservations are recommended. Fees range from $175 to $385 per night. Weekly rentals are discounted. Fees are reduced from November to February. Pets are not permitted.

Directions: From U.S. 101 in Paso Robles, take the Highway 46 East exit (24th Street or G-14 West). Drive west on G-14 for approximately 14 miles (it becomes Lake Nacimiento Road). Just before reaching the dam at Lake Nacimiento, turn left to reach the resort.

Contact: Lake Nacimiento Resort, Box 2770, 10625 Nacimiento Lake Drive, Bradley, CA 93426; 805/238-3256 or 800/323-3839; website: www.nacimientoresort.com.

Lake Nacimiento Resort

3. CAMBRIA PINES LODGE

Cambria Pines Lodge is a large resort and conference center in the artsy, coastside town of Cambria, not far from Hearst Castle and San Simeon. Most people know Cambria for its shopping and art galleries, or as a place to have lunch after touring William Randolph Hearst's mega-mansion. But outdoor lovers will also find plenty to do in Cambria.

For starters, there's San Simeon State Beach, accessible via a five-minute drive from Cambria Pines. Beachcombing and whale-watching are common activities. The gray whales are spotted most often from late November to January, when they migrate south. (On their springtime return, they are farther offshore and harder to see.) Poking around tidepools can be excellent at the state beach, especially during winter minus tides. The easiest beach access from Cambria Pines Lodge is at Leffingwell Landing on Moonstone Beach Drive, where blufftop nature trails head both north and south.

San Simeon State Beach is also a fine place to try your hand at surf fishing. Barred surf perch can be caught in December and January, and walleye

Off Highway 1 in Cambria

Luxury rating: 4

Recreation rating: 3

surf perch are available in any season. For larger fish, head out on a commercial boat to catch kelp bass, Pacific mackerel, and California halibut. Pier fishing is also possible off Hearst Memorial State Beach.

Cambria Pines' beautifully decorated cottages have king-size beds and fireplaces, and are located a few steps away from an enclosed indoor pool. Only one unit is freestanding, the Honeymoon Suite. The rest are duplexes, but still very quiet and private. The lodge is set in 25 acres of Monterey pines, with lovely gardens and landscaping. A walking path runs through the property and to the beach; the trailhead is located alongside unit number 810. A long set of stairs raises your heart rate on the first stretch, then you turn right on Burton Drive, left on Main Street, and cross Highway 1 to the beach. It's a nice way to explore Cambria Village and gain access to the ocean at the same time.

The cottages lack kitchen facilities, but it's not the end of the world. Breakfast is included in the room rate—a huge restaurant buffet with pancakes, eggs, potatoes, granola, orange juice, and coffee. For other meals, you can choose from a wide variety of restaurants in the town of Cambria, or eat at the lodge's restaurant.

Facilities: There are 16 one-bedroom cottages, plus numerous townhouse-style accommodations and motel rooms. The cottages do not have kitchens. Breakfast is included and a restaurant is on-site. There is an indoor pool.

Bedding: Linens and towels are provided.

Reservations and rates: Reservations are recommended. Fees range from $109 to $139 per night, which includes breakfast. The Honeymoon Suite is $200 to $300 per night. Pets are not permitted.

Directions: From San Luis Obispo at U.S. 101, take the Highway 1 exit and drive north through Morro Bay for 33 miles to Cambria. Just north of the downtown Cambria exit, take the Burton Drive exit east. Drive a quarter mile and Cambria Pines Lodge is on your left.

Contact: Cambria Pines Lodge, 2905 Burton Drive, Cambria, CA 93428; 805/927-4200 or 800/445-6868; website: www.cambriapineslodge.com.

OTHER CABINS AND COTTAGES NEARBY

- Cambria Vacation Rentals, 784 Main Street, Suite A, Cambria, CA 93428; 805/927-8200.

Cambria Pines Lodge

4. ORCHARD HILL FARM

Orchard Hill Farm is set on 36 acres in the rolling hills of Paso Robles. Surrounded by ancient oaks, grassy hillsides, and miles of vineyards, the bed-and-breakfast offers the utmost in privacy. Only one guest house is available for rent, and guests take over the whole building. They are then free to enjoy the pastoral scenery of this country ranch, the joie de vivre of neighboring wineries, and numerous recreational opportunities.

© ANN MARIE BROWN

Off Highway 46 in Paso Robles

Luxury rating: 4

Recreation rating: 3

The guest house, or "carriage house" as the owners call it, is a lovely Tudor-style building about 150 feet from the main house. It is beautifully appointed with leather armchairs, colorful fabrics, and tasteful antiques. Its two bedrooms each have their own full bath. A kitchen, dining area, and living room with fireplace separate the bedrooms. The house's best feature is its large deck, on which you can sit and look out over the countryside from your hilltop location.

The owners are willing to rent each of the house's bedrooms separately, but then you'd be sharing the kitchen and living area with strangers. It only makes sense to gather four people together—two couples or a family—and take over the entire house. Because the farm is located in the center of Paso Robles' burgeoning wine country, the guest house is frequently rented by two couples or a group of friends, who spend their days driving or cycling from winery to winery, tasting as they go. More than 50 wineries and over 200 vineyards around Paso Robles grow premium wine grapes.

Other area attractions are the lovely drive out Highway 46 to the beaches at Cambria, or the architecturally marvelous Hearst Castle at San Simeon. A day of boating and fishing can be had at nearby lakes Nacimiento and San Antonio.

Facilities: There is one two-bedroom guest house with a fully equipped kitchen, plus a dining room, living area, and fireplace.

Bedding: Linens and towels are provided.

Reservations and rates: Reservations are required. Fees are $250 to $300 per night. Pets are not permitted.

Directions: From U.S. 101 in Paso Robles, take the Highway 46 West exit and drive west for five miles. Turn right on Vineyard Drive and drive about 2.5 miles to Orchard Hill Farm on the left.

OTHER CABINS AND COTTAGES NEARBY
* Country House Inn, 91 Main Street, Templeton, CA 93465;
805/434-1598.

Orchard Hill Farm

5. CAYUCOS VACATION RENTALS

The little town of Cayucos is quintessential Central California coast, and that's why it's so likable. Located 13 miles south of Cambria and 10 miles north of Morro Bay, Cayucos is a seaside hamlet that hasn't been overdeveloped like most other coastal towns. All recreation revolves around the ocean—surfing, beachcombing, windsurfing, swimming, kayaking, and fishing—which is exactly the way it should be.

Off Highway 1 near Morro Bay

Luxury rating: 4

Recreation rating: 4

THIS CABIN RANKS . . .
Best for Beach Activities

More than 50 private homes in Cayucos are for rent through Cayucos Vacation Rentals, including many that are oceanfront or oceanview, or within walking distance of the beach. All rentals are fully furnished, including linens, so you only need to pack your clothes. Grocery stores, shops, and restaurants are available in town.

Most visitors rent a place in Cayucos for a few days; rates are discounted according to the number of nights you reserve. In summer, most places have a week-long minimum stay; they are typically rented out to families on a week's vacation.

Note that if you sign up for an oceanview house, your view could be from the east side of Highway 1. It's wise to pay more for a house on the west side, so you have beach access without crossing the highway. What the heck, if you're going on a beach vacation, you might as well be on oceanfront property. "Near-oceanfront" just isn't the same thing.

Cayucos's two state beaches—Cayucos State Beach and Morro Strand State Beach—provide long stretches of sand for all beach activities. Cayucos's other big attraction is its historic pier, which was built in 1875. Anglers can fish without a license from the pier; it is lit up for night fishing. Many people just stroll along it, enjoying the views and the seagulls.

If you feel like taking a side trip, Morro Bay State Park is only a short drive away. Visit its great blue heron rookery in spring, or hike on one of the nine dome-shaped, volcanic hills or "morros" in the area (but not Morro Rock itself). You can even rent a kayak and paddle around Morro Bay, or take a harbor cruise. Bike trails are plentiful, from level cruises to challenging hill climbs.

If you've never been there, another great side trip is a tour of Hearst Castle, only 20 miles to the north. Whatever else you want to say about it, it's a fascinating place—the opulent estate of newspaper magnate William Randolph Hearst, with 165 palatial rooms containing an outrageous display of art and artifacts.

Facilities: There are 52 private homes for rent, ranging in size from one to four bedrooms, all with fully equipped kitchens.

Bedding: Linens and towels are provided.

Reservations and rates: Reservations are required. Fees range from $75 to $300 per night. In summer, a week-long minimum stay is required. In winter, there is a two-night minimum. Pets are permitted in some rentals with prior approval.

Directions: From San Luis Obispo at U.S. 101, take the Highway 1 exit and drive north through Morro Bay for 18 miles to Cayucos. Stop at the rental office for Cayucos Vacation Rentals; they will give you a key and directions to your vacation rental.

Contact: Cayucos Vacation Rentals, 177 North Ocean Avenue, Cayucos, CA 93430; 805/995-2322 or 800/995-2322; website: www.cayucosvacationrentals.com.

Cayucos Vacation Rentals

6. COTTONTAIL CREEK RANCH

There aren't too many places around like Cottontail Creek Ranch. It's an 850-acre ranch in the coastal hills above Cayucos, with panoramic views of the Pacific coast from its ridgetops, trails for hiking and wildlife viewing, seasonal creeks, and fish ponds. You and a bunch of your best friends can rent it for a few days or a week.

Off Highway 1 in Cayucos

Luxury rating: 4

Recreation rating: 3

You won't be staying in the horse corral, either. The ranch house at Cottontail Creek is a 4,200-square-foot, five-bedroom, four-bath house. Yes, you read that right. It features a massive stone fireplace in the living room, open beam ceilings, gourmet kitchen, and three lofts, one of which houses a library.

Cottontail Creek Ranch's owners, the Lyon family, live on another part of the working ranch. In addition to raising cattle, they grow oranges, avocados, and kiwis. They'll gladly take you on a tour of the groves.

The ranch is most frequently rented by families holding reunions or celebrating special occasions, but a group of friends could use it as well, for no other reason than to have a good time. A week's stay doesn't come cheap; it costs $3,300 in summer, but that buys you a special kind of experience you won't get anywhere else. And for 10 people, the weekly fee works out to less than 50 bucks a night per person. Summer rentals are by the week only; the rest of the year there is a three-night minimum.

You want something to do at the ranch besides admire the place and wish you owned it? A large pond is available for catch-and-release fishing and kayaking. Horse owners can bring their own horses and ride around the 850 acres. Bikers and hikers can wander as they wish, or head over to Montana de Oro State Park.

If you want to spend a day swimming in the ocean or soaking up rays on white sand, you can do so with just a 10-minute drive to Cayucos. Hearst Castle is a half-hour away, and the charming waterfront of Morro Bay, with its harbor cruises and bike trails, is 15 minutes away.

Facilities: There is one ranch house with five bedrooms and four bathrooms that can accommodate up to 12 people. It has a fireplace and fully equipped kitchen.

Bedding: Linens and towels are provided.

Reservations and rates: Reservations are required. Fees are $3,300 per week from June to September, and $490 per night the rest of the year (with a three-night minimum). Pets are not permitted.

Directions: From U.S. 101 in San Luis Obispo, take the Morro Bay/Highway 1 exit and drive 18 miles to Old Creek Road. Turn right and drive 3.1 miles, past Whale Rock Reservoir, to Cottontail Creek Road. Turn left and drive 3.4 miles (road turns to gravel) to Cottontail Creek Ranch's gate. Continue another quarter mile to the house on your left.

Contact: Cottontail Creek Ranch, 1885 Cottontail Creek Road, Cayucos, CA 93430; 805/995-1787; website: www.cottontailcreek.com.

Cottontail Creek Ranch

7. KOA SANTA MARGARITA LAKE

The first time I stayed in a KOA cabin, I felt a little funny. The cute little log cabins with their front-porch swings looked a lot like children's playhouses, and there I was, trying to act like a serious guidebook writer.

But two nights in a cabin at KOA Santa Margarita Lake turned me into a believer. After a day of exploring around Santa Margarita Lake and the Santa Lucia Wilderness, I returned to my cabin for a hot shower, clean clothes, and a barbecue dinner outside on the porch. It rained later that night, but I was warm and dry in my cabin with electric heat and lights. It sure beat the heck out of eating freeze-dried lasagna, wearing dirty socks, and fussing with the zipper on my flimsy tent.

KOA Santa Margarita Lake is located only one mile from the lake, where you can rent boats, fish, and hike. In fact, you can do anything at

Off Highway 58 near San Luis Obispo

Luxury rating: 2

Recreation rating: 3

the lake except touch the water, which means no swimming, windsurfing, or waterskiing. Most people don't complain about the rules, however, because they come here to fish. Rainbow trout are stocked in winter and spring, and bass fishing is good in the summer. The lake is fair-sized—nearly 800 acres—and more scenic than you'd expect in this low-elevation foothill country. Tall, rocky crags form the backdrop behind the lake.

The KOA has 10 cabins, all partially shaded by canyon oaks. Each one has its own barbecue grill and picnic table out front. The camp has a small store where you can buy basic groceries and supplies. The Rinconada Store is a mile down the road, where you can buy tackle and bait.

If hiking is your bag, an overnight at the KOA puts you in a good position for exploring. Take a drive down U.S. 101 to Arroyo Grande and then head east to Lopez Lake, where you can access the trails at Lopez Lake Recreation Area. The best of these are the Duna Vista and Two Waters trails (check out the spring wildflowers). Or drive past Lopez Lake and into the backcountry to reach the Santa Lucia Wilderness trailheads along Lopez Creek, including those leading to popular Big Falls and Little Falls. The Santa Lucia Ranger District in Santa Maria can provide you with trail information and maps.

Facilities: There are 10 cabins that can accommodate up to five people, plus 54 campsites for tents or RVs. The cabins do not have kitchens. Restrooms and showers are located nearby.

Bedding: Linens and towels are not provided; bring your own.

Reservations and rates: Reservations are recommended. Cabin fees are $34 to $42 per night. Pets are permitted.

Directions: From San Luis Obispo, drive eight miles north on U.S. 101 to the Highway 58/Santa Margarita exit. Drive through the town of Santa Margarita on Highway 58. Turn right and follow the signs for Santa Margarita Lake. In eight miles, you will reach the KOA on the right, one mile before the lake.

Contact: KOA Santa Margarita Lake, 4765 Santa Margarita Lake Road, Santa Margarita, CA 93453; 805/438-5618 or 800/562-5619.

KOA Santa Margarita Lake

8. THE TIDES MOTEL

There are a few places left on the California coast that haven't been turned into condominiums or chain hotels, and The Tides Motel is one of them. Located in the Central Coast town of Pismo Beach, The Tides is the ideal place to wake up to the sound of the ocean, play at the beach all day, then return home to a clean, comfortable cottage.

© ANN MARIE BROWN

Off U.S. 101 in Pismo Beach

Luxury rating: 3

Recreation rating: 4

THIS CABIN RANKS . . .
Best for Beach Activities

Most of The Tides' cottages come with a serviceable kitchen, including the basic dishes and utensils you'll need for cooking. A few cottages are duplexes; make sure you request a single unit if you want one. The rooms come equipped with televisions, which you can ignore. The only telephone is the pay phone at the motel office.

Many visitors to The Tides do nothing but hang out on the beach all day. It's easily accessible from your cottage, as long as you don't mind walking the 90 steps down to the sand, and 90 steps back up.

The watery adventures possible in Pismo Beach are unlimited, including fishing, swimming, surfing, and exploring its 23 miles of coastline. Although the town has suffered from recent urbanization, there's still some of the old Pismo left, including a long fishing pier and wide, sandy beaches. Bustling seafood restaurants and coffee shops neighbor the surf shops and tackle stores, but they don't outnumber them.

Even if you don't fish, be sure to walk along the 1,250-foot Pismo Pier. If you are lucky enough to time your visit for an evening with a full moon and clear skies, you'll witness one of the world's greatest sights—moonlight on ocean waves. I suppose it doesn't look like this every night in Pismo Beach, but it made my trip unforgettable.

Although clamming at Pismo Beach isn't what it was in the late 1800s, when clams were so abundant that local farmers used them for animal feed and harvested them by plowing the sand, you can still dig for the tasty bivalves. The 1990s saw a resurgence in the clam population along the area's beaches; hopefully, the 21st century will see a complete comeback. To go clamming, you'll need a special shovel (available for rent at the hardware store in town) and your California fishing license.

If you need something else to do, surfboards, wet suits, boogie boards, and bicycles are for rent in town. That should be enough to keep you busy.

Facilities: There are five cottages that can accommodate two to eight people, plus 16 motel rooms. Most cottages have fully equipped kitchens.

Bedding: Linens and towels are provided.

Reservations and rates: Reservations are recommended. Fees range from $110 to $240 per night in summer; winter rates are discounted. Pets are not permitted.

Directions: From U.S. 101 in Santa Maria, drive north for 17 miles to Pismo Beach. Take the Price Street exit and drive west to The Tides Motel.

Contact: The Tides Motel, 2121 Price Street, Pismo Beach, CA 93449; 805/773-2493 or 888/234-2892.

OTHER CABINS AND COTTAGES NEARBY

• Beachfront Vacation Rentals, P.O. Box 27, Pismo Beach, CA 93448; 805/773-4771 or 800/732-3766.

The Tides Motel

9. CHIMNEY SWEEP INN

For the uninitiated, some background: Solvang is a popular tourist town northwest of Santa Barbara and south of Santa Maria. Its appeal is its Danish heritage; Danish architecture and culture preside throughout the town, including dozens of Danish bakeries. While most visitors find Solvang charming and picturesque, its detractors accuse it of being too Disneyland.

© ANN MARIE BROWN

Off Highway 246 in Solvang

Luxury rating: 5

Recreation rating: 3

No matter how you view it, Solvang is perfectly situated for an outdoor vacation in the Santa Ynez Mountains. Within a few miles are several state and county parks, plus Los Padres National Forest. If you want to explore, a cottage at Solvang's Chimney Sweep Inn is the perfect base camp.

But a "camp" this is not. The Chimney Sweep Inn has six cottages, all beautifully appointed, plus a manicured garden with a tiny stream, goldfish, and footbridges. I stayed in Dawn Treader, a two-story cottage with a large bedroom upstairs and a living room, dining area, and small kitchen downstairs. It has two fireplaces—one in the bedroom and one in the living room, two bathrooms with unusual antique fixtures, and French doors that open to a small patio and private hot tub.

But these are just the bold strokes. The real beauty of the place lies in the details, such as the hand-painted tile work, wide-plank pine floors, and ambient lighting. What impressed me the most was the automatic drapes in the bedroom. With a push of a button over the bed, the drapes open or close.

The six cottages are modeled after C.S. Lewis's books *The Chronicles of Narnia*. All of the cottages have king beds, fireplaces, and private patios, most with spas.

If you can bring yourself to leave this whimsical inn, go south on U.S. 101 to hike to the 80-foot waterfall at Nojoqui Falls County Park or the hot springs at Gaviota State Park. Or head west on Highway 246 to La Purisima Mission State Historic Park, where you can visit the historic mission and then hike around its lovely grounds. The 2.5-mile Las Zanjas and El Camino Loop is a good introductory walk. Take the short, steep side trail to Vista de la Cruz, where a cross on a hillside overlooks a sweeping view of the Pacific.

Facilities: There are six one- and two-bedroom cottages, plus eight lodge rooms and suites. All cottages have fully equipped kitchens, fireplaces, and private patios; some have whirlpool hot tubs.

Bedding: Linens and towels are provided.

Reservations and rates: Reservations are recommended. Fees range from $189 to $299 per night for cottages. A continental breakfast is included. Pets are not permitted.

Directions: From Santa Barbara, drive north on U.S. 101 for 40 miles to the Buellton/Highway 246 exit. Drive east on Highway 246 for three miles to Solvang, then turn right on 5th Street. In one block, turn left on Copenhagen Drive, and drive .2 mile to Chimney Sweep Inn on the right.

Contact: Chimney Sweep Inn, 1564 Copenhagen Drive, Solvang, CA 93463; 805/688-2111 or 800/824-6444; website: www.chimneysweepinn.com.

OTHER CABINS AND COTTAGES NEARBY

• Three Crowns Inn & Scandinavian Cottages, 1518 Mission Drive, Solvang, CA 93463; 805/688-4702 or 800/848-8484.

Chimney Sweep Inn

10. THE ALISAL GUEST RANCH & RESORT

No one will complain that there's nothing to do when they visit The Alisal Guest Ranch & Resort. The main attraction is horseback riding, but if you tire of it (or if your butt gets too sore), you can go hiking, mountain biking, fishing, windsurfing, or swimming. Or you can play golf or tennis, visit the historic Santa Ynez Mission, or even take your kids to The Alisal's petting zoo.

The 10,000-acre ranch and resort is a family vacation center in the Santa Ynez Valley. This lovely winery-filled valley, northwest of Santa Barbara near the Danish tourist town of Solvang, is home to a few wealthy folks like Michael Jackson and Jane Fonda. As you might expect, The Alisal caters to a big-budget crowd.

However, there are ways to make it more affordable. First, rent a cottage at the resort and bring your family with you. The nightly fee is a bit hefty for two adults, but you can add on your children or an additional adult for very little. Plus, the resort offers a ton of kids' activities, from horseback riding and fishing to art and outdoor games.

Off Highway 246 near Solvang

Luxury rating: 5

Recreation rating: 4

Or second, show up on weekdays from mid-September to early June, or any day except holidays from November through March, and take advantage of The Alisal's off-season rate package. The fee is almost half of the summer rate, and it includes horseback riding, fishing, tennis, and golf for two people, plus all meals and accommodations.

The Alisal's cottages look like ranch houses with covered porches on the outside. Each has one or two large rooms, with high-beamed ceilings, a wood-burning fireplace, refrigerator, and coffeemaker. The cottages don't have kitchens; the resort operates on a Modified American Plan—breakfast and dinner are included in your room rate. Typical of a guest ranch, meals are a big deal here, with plentiful portions and a wide menu. And get this: Men wear jackets to dinner.

The Alisal runs a fly-fishing school at its spring-fed 100-acre lake, which is also used for windsurfing and canoeing. Both beginning and experienced fly-fishing enthusiasts are welcome; you'll learn fly techniques, knots, tackle, and fly-casting skills.

If you run out of things to do at The Alisal, you can always head for Lake Cachuma, a 20-minute drive away, where 150,000 rainbow trout are planted each year. Bass, catfish, crappie, and perch are also plentiful. From November through February, you can take a two-hour eagle cruise on the lake with a park naturalist. With any luck, you'll see an American bald eagle, but if not, you'll definitely see some of Lake Cachuma's more than 200 species of resident and migratory birds.

Facilities: There are 73 one- and two-bedroom cottages at The Alisal Guest Ranch; none have kitchen facilities. Breakfast and dinner are served at the ranch dining room and included in the fee. Tennis courts and a golf course are on-site.

Bedding: Linens and towels are provided.

Reservations and rates: Reservations are required. Fees range from $385 to $475 per night for two people, which includes breakfast and dinner each day; each additional person is $75 per night ($45 for children under six). There is a two-night minimum stay. Reduced fees are available on the "round-up vacation package" from September through May. Pets are not permitted.

Directions: From Santa Barbara, drive north on U.S. 101 for 40 miles to Buellton and take the Solvang/Highway 246 exit. Drive east on Highway 246 for four miles through Solvang, then turn right on Alisal Road. Drive 3.5 miles on Alisal Road, past the golf course, to the Alisal Guest Ranch on the left.

Contact: The Alisal Guest Ranch & Resort, 1054 Alisal Road, Solvang, CA 93463; 805/688-6411 or 800/425-4725; website: www.alisal.com.

OTHER CABINS AND COTTAGES NEARBY
• Zaca Lake Resort, P.O. Box 187, Los Olivos, CA 93441; 805/688-5699.

The Alisal Guest Ranch & Resort

11. CIRCLE BAR B GUEST RANCH

Circle Bar B Guest Ranch is a study in contrasts—part horse ranch, part upscale hotel, part outdoor resort, and part dinner theater. Can any place be all those things and do them all well? Circle Bar B does.

Off U.S. 101 near Santa Barbara

Luxury rating: 4

Recreation rating: 4

THIS CABIN RANKS . . .
Best for Horseback Riding

The drive in tells you a lot about the place. As soon as you pull off Highway 101 on to Refugio Road, you know you're heading for something good. The road narrows and snakes its way through a lush canyon, crossing Refugio Creek a half dozen times on its 3.5-mile route to the ranch. In winter, the canyon is so lush and green you might think you're in the tropics.

As you near the ranch, you start seeing horses—lots of them—across the creek, grazing in the pasture, and hanging out in their stalls. At the ranch sign, you enter what looks like a small, western village. Alongside an office and large swimming pool are several cottages, horse corrals, and even a brightly painted, false-front building with a sign reading Blacksmith Shop. Behind the ranch is a deeply carved, curving canyon, bordered by tall, chaparral-covered hillsides, and crisscrossed by the ranch's horseback riding trails.

The cabins at Circle Bar B Guest Ranch are modern and beautifully decorated in western style. Two sizes are offered: large studios or two-bedroom suites with fireplaces and king or queen beds. Some have private decks or wet bars. None of the units come with kitchens, but the fee for a night's stay at Circle Bar B includes three hearty meals.

Most people ride horses while staying at the ranch; guided rides are offered every morning and afternoon. Each day's destination is a little different, but most likely you'll be treated to ridgetop views of the ocean and Channel Islands. If horses don't interest you, you can hike on the ranch's property, or drive four miles to Refugio State Beach, where you can swim, surf, or fish from the shore.

Most surprising of the ranch's offerings is its comedy theater performances on Friday and Saturday evenings in summer. Guests come from all over Santa Barbara County to enjoy an outdoor tri-tip barbecue, then when the theater bell rings, they head to the barn to watch the evening's play.

Facilities: There are seven one- and two-bedroom cabins, plus seven ranch rooms. None of the cabins have kitchens; meals are included in the price of your stay.

Bedding: Linens and towels are provided.

Reservations and rates: Reservations are required. Fees range from $225 to $285 per night for two people, including meals. Pets are not permitted.

Directions: From Santa Barbara, drive north on U.S. 101 for 18 miles and take the Refugio State Beach exit. Turn right (north) and drive 3.5 miles on Refugio Road to the Circle Bar B Ranch.

Contact: Circle Bar B Guest Ranch, 1800 Refugio Road, Goleta, CA 93117; 805/968-1113; website: www.circlebarb.com.

Circle Bar B Guest Ranch

12. RANCHO OSO GUEST RANCH

Did you ever want to spend the night the way the western pioneers did, in a group of covered wagons drawn into a safe, tight circle? Well, call out "Westward ho!" because here's your chance.

Off Highway 154 near Santa Barbara

Luxury rating: 2

Recreation rating: 3

THIS CABIN RANKS . . .

Best for Families

At Rancho Oso Guest Ranch in Santa Barbara's Santa Ynez Recreation Area, you can live out your pioneer fantasy in a rented covered wagon (minus the oxen), or stay in one of five Western-style bunkhouse cabins. Although Rancho Oso is one of the Thousand Trails chain of membership-style campgrounds, their cabins and covered wagons are open to nonmembers for rental.

The covered wagons look much like the real thing, except that their interiors contain only four simple cots, not an entire pioneer family's belongings. The five cute cabins are lined up in a row to look like the main street of an Old West town, complete with false fronts and clapboard siding. Each has a hitching post out front and a name plate; guests vie for the one marked Saloon.

As a rule, children tend to prefer camping in the covered wagons, whereas adults usually prefer the electric heat and privacy of the little cabins. Note that the cabins are very small; although they are supposed to accommodate five people, more than two will be a crowd. The cabins contain a full-size bed, plus a bunk bed with a twin upper bunk and a full-size lower bunk. Showers and restrooms are located a few steps away.

Although all of the units have electricity, none have kitchens, so your cooking must be done on the outdoor barbecue grills. Meals are available at Rancho Oso's café on weekends and holidays only.

Rancho Oso is a private land holding in Los Padres National Forest. The Santa Ynez River runs along one side of the ranch and is accessible for fishing and swimming. Most people rent horses and go for guided rides when they visit Rancho Oso (or they bring their own horse and ride solo). You can also venture off on your own two feet, hiking the many trails of the Santa Ynez Recreation Area. A favorite is the hilly Aliso Canyon Loop Trail, which begins at nearby Sage Hill Campground. Check out the spring wildflowers from February to May.

One more option: If you like to fish or water-ski, you'll want to spend at least one day on a boat at Lake Cachuma, only 12 miles away.

Facilities: There are five one-room cabins at Rancho Oso, plus 10 covered wagons. None have kitchen facilities. A general store and café are on-site.

Bedding: Linens and towels are not provided; bring your own.

Reservations and rates: Reservations are required. Fees are $45 per night for covered wagons and $69 per night for cabins. Covered wagons accommodate four people and cabins accommodate five. Pets are permitted in the covered wagons, but not in the cabins.

Directions: From U.S. 101 in Santa Barbara, take Highway 154 north for 11 miles to the Paradise Road turnoff on the right. Turn right on Paradise Road and drive 5.5 miles to the sign for Rancho Oso on the right. Turn right and drive 1.5 miles to the entrance kiosk; the cabins and covered wagons are located a quarter mile beyond the kiosk.

Contact: Rancho Oso Guest Ranch, 3750 Paradise Road, Santa Barbara, CA 93105; 805/683-5686; website: www.rancho-oso.com.

Rancho Oso Guest Ranch

13. WHITE LOTUS FOUNDATION

White Lotus Foundation is a nonprofit, spiritual foundation in the mountains above Santa Barbara that functions as a yoga retreat for teachers and students alike. If you are a yoga person, or even moderately curious about yoga, you'll enjoy a stay at White Lotus.

Although the foundation is often booked by large groups holding yoga classes or teacher workshops, White Lotus offers personal retreats for the general public. In their words: "Slip away from the city to our mountain oasis and enjoy a quiet, relaxing retreat."

Guests can sign up for a stay in one of White Lotus's six yurts—or domed tent structures—and then design their own restorative getaway. They can participate in Hatha yoga classes if they wish, or hike and swim on their own. (Small waterfalls and swimming holes in San Jose Creek are on the

© JULIE SHEER

Off Highway 154 near Santa Barbara

Luxury rating: 2

Recreation rating: 3

THIS CABIN RANKS . . .
Most Unusual

property.) What a pleasant way to leave the everyday world behind.

White Lotus's yurts provide minimalist accommodations in a beautiful canyon setting. If you've stayed in a tent cabin, this is one step up on the luxury scale. Set in a grove of canyon oaks, the yurts have wood floors and canvas sides, with doors and windows of heavy plastic. Inside, each has pillows, futons, and mats, plus a reading lamp and water dispenser. You must walk to the restroom, but it's a winner: A beautiful bamboo building serves as the outhouse, and the outdoor sink is made of stone and wood with a metal frog sculpture on the faucet. Showers are located in a separate building. The yurts are a steep five-minute walk from where you leave your car.

For meals, you can cook in the communal kitchen, but don't think about grilling a juicy steak. Anything nonvegetarian would be a huge faux pas. If you don't want to cook, a dining room serves gourmet vegetarian meals.

It's so peaceful here that it may be difficult to drag yourself out of the lotus position, but if you get inspired, there is much to see in neighboring Los Padres National Forest. Start with the Painted Cave of the Chumash Indians, or the short hike to the ruins of Knapp's Castle, or the swimming holes along Oso Creek, accessible via the Santa Cruz Trail out of Upper Oso Campground.

Facilities: There are six yurts that can accommodate up to four people. A communal kitchen is available for vegetarian cooking only; a dining room serves vegetarian meals. Restrooms are a short walk from the yurts.

Bedding: Linens and towels are not provided; bring your own.

Reservations and rates: Reservations are required. Fees are $65 per night. Pets are not permitted.

Directions: From U.S. 101 in Santa Barbara, take Highway 154 north for 5.8 miles. Shortly beyond Painted Cave Road, turn left into White Lotus Foundation's driveway.

Contact: White Lotus Foundation, 2500 San Marcos Pass, Santa Barbara, CA 93105; 805/964-1944; website: www.whitelotus.org.

White Lotus Foundation

14. EL ENCANTO HOTEL & GARDEN VILLAS

El Encanto Hotel is a historic and psychological landmark in Santa Barbara. Built in 1915, it's what the Ahwahnee Hotel is to Yosemite Valley—a statement of elegance and refinement, a place that stays the same while everything around it changes. From its hilltop location, the famous restaurant at El Encanto provides an unparalleled vista of Santa Barbara and the coast, and that view alone brings many guests back year after year.

Off U.S. 101 in Santa Barbara

Luxury rating: 4

Recreation rating: 3

The resort has only four free-standing cottages; the others are duplexes, triplexes, or suites. You can choose from two types of architecture: Spanish colonial (stucco and red tile roofs) or Craftsman style (lots of wood). A few units, in the $500-and-up category, have kitchens or kitchenettes, but for that price you might as well hire a personal chef, too.

The cottages are luxurious but not opulent; the decor is even a bit understated compared to other luxury resorts in Santa Barbara. Perhaps that's because at El Encanto, the grounds are the thing. With 10 landscaped acres of tropical gardens surrounding the buildings, it's more fun to walk the brick pathways, cross the miniature bridges, and sit on the well-placed benches *outside* the cottages than it is being *inside* the cottages. The landscaping is a mix of sunny lawn areas and lush gardens of palm and magnolia trees and hibiscus and rose bushes. A swimming-pool-sized lily pond lined with red bricks and bounded by a brick and wood arbor brings to mind the gardens of an English estate. Tennis courts and a lap pool are also found on the grounds.

El Encanto holds a prestigious spot on a hillside above the Santa Barbara Mission, which puts guests about a mile away from the trailhead for Tunnel and Jesusita trails, two of Santa Barbara's most popular local pathways. You can follow them three miles round-trip to Mission Creek's swimming holes and waterfalls, or five miles round-trip to 1,750-foot Inspiration Point, with its inspiring view of the coast. Beautiful Rattlesnake Canyon is also nearby for more hiking options.

Facilities: There are three one-bedroom cottages plus 12 cottage suites (duplex or triplex style). Some cottages have kitchens or kitchenettes. A restaurant, pool, and tennis courts are on-site.

Bedding: Linens and towels are provided.

Reservations and rates: Reservations are required. Fees are $239 to $629 per night. Pets are not permitted.

Directions: From U.S. 101 in Santa Barbara, take the Mission Street exit and drive north for 1.2 miles. Turn left on Laguna Street and drive to the Santa Barbara Mission, then turn right on Los Olivos Street. Drive a short distance and turn right on Alameda Padre Serra, continue uphill to Lasuen Road, turn left on Alvarado Place, then turn right into the guest entrance for El Encanto.

Contact: El Encanto Hotel & Garden Villas, 1900 Lasuen Road, Santa Barbara, CA 93103; 805/687-5000 or 800/346-7039.

El Encanto Hotel & Garden Villas

15. SIMPSON HOUSE INN

Downtown Santa Barbara is filled with bed-and-breakfast inns, including several with cottages, yet only one has been rated Five Diamond and proclaimed one of America's "Ten Most Romantic Inns." In every respect, the Simpson House is a notch above other inns in its class.

© SIMPSON HOUSE INN

Off U.S. 101 in Santa Barbara

Luxury rating: 5

Recreation rating: 3

THIS CABIN RANKS . . .
Most Luxurious

Secluded among an acre of immaculate English gardens, Simpson House has four garden cottages in addition to its guest room accommodations. Breakfast is served each morning in the main house, and tea, wine, and hors d'oeuvres are served each afternoon. (If you are staying in the cottages, you can have breakfast brought to your doorstep.) Although the main house is quite formal—filled with finely polished furniture, Victorian lamps, Oriental rugs, English antiques, and bustling servers in uniforms—the cottages have a more relaxed feel.

Pendle cottage has a full kitchen, skylights, woodburning fireplace, lace coverlet on the brass king bed, and white wood beamed ceilings. Plumstead cottage has a two-person whirlpool hot tub in the living room (it's the first thing you see as you walk in the door!), wet bar, woodburning fireplace, and upstairs bedroom. Greenwich and Abbeywood are duplex cottages and mirror images of each other. They both have hot tubs and fireplaces. Each of the cottages is very cozy and beautifully furnished. Each has a small, secluded patio area with a table and chairs.

The inn rents bicycles and provides guests with handouts on suggested walks, things to do, and restaurants. Myriad recreation options exist in or near downtown Santa Barbara, from the beaches and harbor (for swimming, surfing, whale-watching, sport fishing) to the forested canyons of Los Padres National Forest (for hiking and mountain biking). An excellent visitor information center is located near the Simpson House Inn at the corner of Cabrillo Boulevard and Santa Barbara Street.

For people who want to stay in a nice neighborhood away from the bustle of downtown Santa Barbara, yet still close enough to walk there, the Simpson House works. But keep in mind this isn't the kind of place where you put your muddy boots up on the couch.

Facilities: There are four one-bedroom cottages, plus six guest rooms in the main house. One cottage has a fully equipped kitchen.

Bedding: Linens and towels are provided.

Reservations and rates: Reservations are required. Fees are $535 to $550 per night for cottages, less for rooms. Pets are not permitted.

Directions: From U.S. 101 heading south in Santa Barbara, take the Mission Street exit and turn left. Drive east six blocks to Anacapa Street. Turn right on Anacapa, drive four blocks, then turn left on Arrellaga Street. Simpson House is on the left.

Contact: Simpson House Inn, 121 East Arrellaga Street, Santa Barbara, CA 93101; 805/963-7067 or 800/676-1280; website: www.simpsonhouseinn.com.

OTHER CABINS AND COTTAGES NEARBY

• Secret Garden Inn & Cottages, 1908 Bath Street, Santa Barbara, CA 93101; 805/687-2300; website: www.secretgarden.com.

• Glenborough Inn Bed and Breakfast, 1327 Bath Street, Santa Barbara, CA 93101; 805/966-0589 or 888/966-0589; website: www.glenboroughinn.com.

Simpson House Inn

16. CHESHIRE CAT INN & COTTAGES

The Cheshire Cat Inn is a charming and creative bed-and-breakfast in downtown Santa Barbara. It is comprised of a collection of buildings: two stately Queen Anne Victorians filled with a dozen guest rooms, a carriage house, and three cottages located across the street.

The two-bedroom cottages have everything you need for a comfortable, extended stay: full kitchens, fireplaces, television, a private deck or patio with outdoor hot tub, plus oak floors, "homey" pine furniture, and down comforters. You won't need to flip pancakes in your kitchen in the morning, because a gourmet breakfast is served on Wedgewood china in the main house. Wine and hors d'oeuvres are available in the afternoon.

The set-up is ideal for families or two couples. The cottages are furnished

Off U.S. 101 in Santa Barbara

Luxury rating: 4

Recreation rating: 3

in a comfortably elegant style; even small children couldn't get into too much trouble here. The maximum number of people in the cottages is four.

Once you're settled into your cottage, the inn's management basically leaves you alone to do your own thing, which is a bonus for people who enjoy privacy. And there is plenty to do in downtown Santa Barbara, from visits to the city's historic mission and Stearn's Wharf to shopping on State Street. The beach, and all beach activities, are the main draw on sunny summer days. If you seek some adventure, you can get on a dive boat, sportfishing boat, or whale-watching cruise. You can rent bikes (or bring your own) and cycle Santa Barbara's lengthy paved bike path, or you could board a Channel Islands ferry for day hiking and exploring on Anacapa or Santa Cruz Islands.

Facilities: There are three two-bedroom cottages that can accommodate up to four people. All have fully equipped kitchens.

Bedding: Linens and towels are provided.

Reservations and rates: Reservations are required. Fees are $325 to $375 per night for cottages, and $150 to $240 per night for rooms. Pets are not permitted.

Directions: From U.S. 101 in Santa Barbara, take the Arrellaga Street exit. Drive four blocks to Chapala Street and turn left. Drive one block to Valerio Street. The Cheshire Cat Inn is at the corner of Valerio and Chapala.

Contact: Cheshire Cat Inn & Cottages, 36 West Valerio, Santa Barbara, CA 93101; 805/569-1610; website: www.cheshirecat.com.

OTHER CABINS AND COTTAGES NEARBY

• Cabrillo Inn Spanish Vacation Cottages, 931 East Cabrillo Boulevard, Santa Barbara, CA 93101; 805/963-6774 or 800/648-6708; website: www.cabrillo-inn.com/rental.

Cheshire Cat Inn & Cottages

17. SAN YSIDRO RANCH

Lottery winnings burning a hole in your pocket? Lucky you, you can book a stay at San Ysidro Ranch.

A night at the Ranch is prohibitively expensive (try $1,850 a night for the Kennedy Suite, where JFK and Jackie honeymooned), so most people save it for very special occasions. San Ysidro's management understands this. When guests check in, they are asked if they are celebrating an anniversary or birthday. If they say yes, the front desk sends a cake, or strawberries and champagne, to their room.

© JULIE SHEER

Off U.S. 101 in Montecito

Luxury rating: 5

Recreation rating: 3

THIS CABIN RANKS . . .
Most Luxurious

San Ysidro Ranch is all about this kind of service. Another example: If you bring your dog with you (yes, they're allowed in the cottages), a dog bed and bottled water will be delivered to your room. Of course, you pay $100 extra for pets, so you might want to reconsider how badly Fido needs a vacation.

Your favorite newspaper is delivered to your cottage each day, tied in a red ribbon. Your name is branded in block letters on a wooden plaque outside your cottage, so you will feel like it's your very own home. Each cottage has a king bed, private deck, and fireplace or woodburning stove, and firewood is delivered daily. Except for these commonalities, each is unique in its room layout and furnishings, so there is nothing about staying here that reminds you of being in an impersonal hotel.

San Ysidro Ranch covers a whopping 500-plus acres, and only five of those are developed. Hiking trails crisscross the property, so you can wander as you wish. A horse stable, pool, fitness center, massage services, and two tennis courts are available. From the stable, you can access the San Ysidro Trail along San Ysidro Creek, a year-round stream with several lovely waterfalls. If you really want some exercise, hike to its terminus on East Camino Cielo; it's an eight-mile round-trip with a 2,800-foot elevation gain.

If you really want to stay here but are wondering if you can part with the money, know that San Ysidro Ranch is worth every penny. This is a place where every guest is treated like royalty. At the end of your stay, you'll feel like you've had a true taste of the good life.

Facilities: There are 12 cottages with deck and fireplace or woodburning stove, plus 26 rooms and suites. None have kitchens. Two restaurants are on-site, plus a pool, fitness center, and tennis courts.

Bedding: Linens and towels are provided.

Reservations and rates: Reservations are required. Fees are $595 to $895 per night for one-bedroom cottages, and $1,350 to $3,950 for larger cottages. Pets are permitted with a $100 fee.

Directions: From U.S. 101 in Montecito, take the San Ysidro Road exit and drive north for about one mile. Turn right on San Ysidro Lane and drive to the resort.

Contact: San Ysidro Ranch, 900 San Ysidro Lane, Santa Barbara, CA 93108; 805/969-5046 or 800/368-6788; website: www.sanysidroranch.com.

San Ysidro Ranch

18. SANTA BARBARA BILTMORE

If I could afford it, I'd stay at the Biltmore every time I visited Santa Barbara. Heck, if I could afford it, I'd live there.

Off U.S. 101 in Santa Barbara

Luxury rating: 5

Recreation rating: 4

THIS CABIN RANKS . . .
Most Luxurious
Best for Beach Activities

Even though it's a ritzy resort, the Biltmore is gracious and comfortable. Because it is situated on gorgeous Butterfly Beach, sandy feet and beachwear are typical attire around the property. And the Biltmore is one of the few luxury resorts in Southern California that allows dogs without any deposit or fee. You must not leave Fido unattended, however, so plan on ordering room service for your meals.

For the sake of full disclosure, you should know that not one of the Biltmore's cottages is a stand-alone building; each of their 12 cottages is split into as many as five suites. While that might disqualify another resort from this book, it doesn't rule out the Biltmore. Its oceanside location is perfect for beach lovers, and its grand style and service are without reproach, so it's easy to forgive the multiplex cottages.

The cottages are not on the ocean side of the resort; they're located in the back of the main building in a beautiful garden, nestled among palm trees and trumpet vines. The lush landscaping keeps the individual cottage suites very secluded. For the $500-and-up price tag, you can expect a fireplace, refrigerator, private patio, and a lot of expensive upholstery.

The Biltmore is the kind of place where you will probably not leave the property once you arrive. It has pretty much everything you could need or want, including two restaurants, a spa, a beauty salon, tennis courts, a putting green, an art gallery, a gift shop, croquet, shuffleboard, a swimming pool, and a fitness center. The beach, of course, is the main draw, so make sure you bring a suitcase full of swimwear.

Facilities: There are 12 cottages that are divided into 58 suites. None have kitchens. Stores, tennis courts, putting green, swimming pool, and restaurants are on-site.

Bedding: Linens and towels are provided.

Reservations and rates: Reservations are recommended. Fees are $495 to $2,200 per night (slightly less Sunday through Thursday). Pets are permitted in cottages.

Directions: From U.S. 101 in Montecito, take the Olive Mill Road exit west. Turn right on Channel Drive and enter the resort.

Contact: Santa Barbara Biltmore, 1260 Channel Drive, Santa Barbara, CA 93108; 805/969-2261 or 800/332-3442.

Santa Barbara Biltmore

19. THE MIRAMAR HOTEL & RESORT

Anyone who has ever driven south of Santa Barbara on U.S. 101 knows the cheerful blue-and-white buildings of the Miramar Hotel, a Montecito area fixture since the turn of the century. But big changes are in the works for the Miramar. Purchased in 1998 by Ian Schrager Hotels—the same company that owns the Empire Hotel in New York City and the Mondrian in Los Angeles—the Miramar is undergoing a massive $25 million facelift and has been closed for most of 2001. It is expected to reopen, transformed, in 2002.

© ANN MARIE BROWN

Off U.S. 101 in Montecito

Luxury rating: 4

Recreation rating: 4

Unlike the nearby Montecito resorts, such as the Biltmore Hotel and San Ysidro Ranch, the Miramar has always been relatively affordable and comfortably casual. In part, that's because of its drawbacks: It's situated too close to the freeway, and the Southern Pacific railway runs right through the middle of its grounds. (When the railway was completed in 1901, the Miramar was used as a passenger stop.) It will be interesting to see how the new owners compensate for these factors, and how that affects room and cottage prices.

According to renovation plans, the new resort's accommodations will vary widely. Several cottages will be located in the center of the 15-acre complex, without ocean views but with easy access to the beach. At the ocean's edge will be townhouse-style accommodations. These units will have the best views, but they won't be separate units—you'll share exterior walls with your neighbors.

The primary reason the Miramar has remained so popular for more than a century is its beach. The coastline in Santa Barbara County is considered by many to be the finest in all of California. The geography of the land faces south, not west as in most of the state; this creates a microclimate of exceptionally mild weather similar to that of the French Riviera. The Miramar's beach is ideal for surfing, swimming, and surf fishing, as well as traipsing along the sand, especially when the tide is low and beachcombing is good. You can walk to the west for about a mile to the Biltmore Hotel, passing Hammonds Beach, a famous surfing spot. Or walk to the east for a couple of miles to Lookout County Park.

Facilities: There are one- and two-bedroom cottages, plus oceanfront suites and hotel rooms. A restaurant is on-site.

Bedding: Linens and towels are provided.

Reservations and rates: Reservations are recommended. Fees range from $395 to $1,400 per night. Pets are not permitted.

Directions: From U.S. 101 at Montecito, take the San Ysidro Road exit south; the Miramar is alongside the highway on the south side.

Contact: Miramar Hotel & Resort, 1555 South Jameson Lane, Montecito, CA 93108; 805/969-2203; website: www.ianschragerhotels.com.

Miramar Hotel & Resort

20. EMERALD IGUANA COTTAGES

The Emerald Iguana Cottages are quintessential Ojai, which means they are artsy, eclectic, rustic, and even classy. Owned and operated by the same folks who run the nearby Blue Iguana Inn, Emerald Iguana's nine cottages are as individual as their whimsical names: Treehouse, Frog, Cricket, Lilypad, Toad, and so on.

© JULIE SHEER

Off Highway 33 in Ojai

Luxury rating: 4

Recreation rating: 3

Toad Cottage is the largest of the bunch. It's a lovely stone structure with three bedrooms, each with its own bath (one with a clawfoot tub, one with a whirlpool bath), plus a shady front porch. Two of the bedrooms have fireplaces. A particularly romantic unit is Treehouse Cottage, which has two levels. The upstairs bedroom is surrounded by uniquely shaped windows providing treetop views. The downstairs living room is decorated with exotic rugs and velvet drapes.

Each of the cottages is furnished with accessories from the owners' travels throughout the world. In Toad Cottage, these include an Indonesian headboard on the bed and Oriental rugs.

A pool and hot tub are located among the cottages, which are connected by stone walkways. Oaks, willows, and palms shade the grounds. A fountain made of green mosaic tiles, in the shape of an iguana, greets guests at the cottages' entrances. It is obvious that, from the furnishing of the cottages to the landscaping of the grounds, attention was paid to every detail. The entire resort is loaded with character; this, combined with its quiet location at the end of a side street, make Emerald Iguana a truly unique vacation spot.

While in Ojai, you have a long list of recreation options. The paved Ojai Valley bicycle trail runs alongside Highway 33. Lake Casitas, 15 minutes away, beckons swimmers, anglers, and boaters. And the hiking trails of Los Padres National Forest are within easy reach. The Ojai Ranger District office is right in town on Ojai Avenue; it can provide maps and trail information.

Facilities: There are nine cottages ranging in size from one to three bedrooms, all with fully equipped kitchens.

Bedding: Linens and towels are provided.

Reservations and rates: Reservations are recommended. Fees are $199 to $449 per night, less on weeknights. Weekly stays are discounted. Pets are not permitted.

Directions: From U.S. 101 in Ventura, take Highway 33 east to Ojai. When you pass the traffic light with a sign for Lake Casitas and Santa Barbara, continue on Highway 33 for a half mile more. Blue Iguana Inn is on the right at the corner of Highway 33 and Loma Drive; check in there for Emerald Iguana Cottages.

Contact: Blue Iguana Inn & Emerald Iguana Cottages, 11794 North Ventura Avenue, Ojai, CA 93023; 805/646-5277; website: www.blueiguanainn.com or www.emeraldiguana.com.

OTHER CABINS AND COTTAGES NEARBY

• Theodore Woolsey House, 1484 East Ojai Avenue, Ojai, CA 93023; 805/646-9779; website: www.theodorewoolseyhouse.com.

Emerald Iguana Cottages

21. THE PIERPONT INN

The Pierpont Inn has two secluded garden cottages in addition to its 62 rooms, nine suites, award-winning restaurant, and tennis and fitness club. With all cottage and room rates less than $300 per night, it's Ventura's more affordable answer to the big resorts in nearby Montecito and Santa Barbara.

And like those resorts to the north, the Pierpont overlooks the magnificent Pacific coastline. Getting to the beach is easy, as is accessing the 13-mile-long bike path that winds along the coast from San Buenaventura Beach to Emma Wood Beach. Perhaps best of all is the Pierpont's

© JULIE SHEER

Off U.S. 101 in Ventura

Luxury rating: 4

Recreation rating: 4

proximity to Channel Islands Harbor, where you can get on a boat for a day trip to Anacapa or Santa Cruz Islands, then spend the day hiking or kayaking.

There's also plenty to do on the resort property. Tennis and racquetball courts are plentiful. A fitness club offers aerobics classes and exercise equipment. A spa provides facials, body scrubs, massages, and other treatments.

The resort's two Tudor-style cottages are Gardenia and Rose Garden. Gardenia is the smaller of the two and has a canopy bed, English cottage–type furnishings, a breakfast nook, gas fireplace, and patio garden area. Rose Garden has two rooms, a massive brick fireplace, and roses that surround the cottage and creep over its roof. Both cottages were built in the 1930s and have a charming, old-style feel. Because they are located in the back of the resort, they have garden views and are much quieter than most of Pierpont's accommodations, which suffer from highway noise from U.S. 101.

Although there are many restaurants to choose from in Ventura, don't miss having a sunset dinner at Pierpont's restaurant, which offers lovely views of the Ventura coastline.

Facilities: There are two one-bedroom cottages without kitchens but with fireplaces. A restaurant, tennis and racquetball courts, fitness club, and spa are on-site.

Bedding: Linens and towels are provided.

Reservations and rates: Reservations are recommended. Fees are $165 to $275 per night for the cottages, including breakfast. Rooms are $110 to $195 per night. Pets are not permitted.

Directions: From U.S. 101 heading north in Ventura, take the Sanjon Road/Vista del Mar exit. Turn left to go under the overpass to Harbor Boulevard, then turn right on Harbor and immediately right again on Sanjon Road. The Pierpont Inn is on the right.

From Santa Barbara, drive south on U.S. 101, take the Seaward exit, and turn right on Harbor Boulevard, then right on Sanjon Road.

Contact: The Pierpont Inn, 550 Sanjon Road, Ventura, CA 93001; 805/643-6144 or 800/285-4667; website: www.pierpontinn.com.

The Pierpont Inn

22. MOUNTAIN PROPERTIES VACATION RENTALS

Are there any surprises left in the Southern California great outdoors? Yes, there's seldom-visited Mount Pinos. Never heard of it, right? At 8,831 feet, Mount Pinos is the tallest mountain in Los Padres National Forest. It's a beautiful peak covered with pine forest that gets a fair share of snowfall every winter.

Los Padres National Forest, off I-5 near Mount Pinos

Luxury rating: 4

Recreation rating: 4

Mount Pinos is accessed from the unlikely town of Frazier Park on I-5, just south of Grapevine. Go twelve miles westward; a right turn on Mil Potrero Highway takes you through Los Padres National Forest to the small town of Pine Mountain Club, where numerous cabin rentals are available.

Each cabin is someone's private vacation home, which comes with a fully equipped kitchen, linens, television, and all modern conveniences. The majority of homes have fireplaces or wood stoves, and firewood is often provided by the owner. Some cabins have views, some allow smoking, some have hot tubs, and so on, so make sure you request exactly what you want.

After you get settled in your cabin, head back to the main road to drive the remaining few miles to the top of Mount Pinos, where you'll find an awesome vista extending all the way to the San Joaquin Valley and the peaks of the Sierra Nevada. While you look around, watch for giant condors soaring in the sky; they are often seen here on the edge of the Chumash Wilderness.

If snow has fallen, many areas of the mountain will be open for cross-country skiing and snowshoeing (a national forest adventure pass is required; see pages xiii–xiv). If the snow has vanished, numerous hiking trails are available, including the beautiful Vincent Tumamait Trail from Mount Pinos's summit. Or try Cedar Creek Trail, which leads from Thorn Meadows Campground in nearby Lake of the Woods. The drive to the trailhead will take a little less than an hour; get an early start so you have plenty of time to hike the nine-mile round-trip to the Fishbowls along Piru Creek. In summer, the sandstone pools are popular swimming holes.

Several local hikes are possible right in Pine Mountain Club, including a short waterfall trail beginning on Woodland Drive. The nice folks at Mountain Properties Vacation Rentals can supply you with a street map and a list of trails and trailheads.

Facilities: There are 16 private vacation homes that can accommodate up to 12 people. All have fully equipped kitchens and modern conveniences, and some have fireplaces.

Bedding: Linens and towels are provided.

Reservations and rates: Reservations are required. Fees range from $80 to $165 per night. Weekly rentals are discounted. Pets are not permitted.

Directions: From Los Angeles, drive north on I-5 through the San Fernando Valley to Gorman. Just beyond Gorman, take the Frazier Park/Mount Pinos exit and turn west. Drive 12 miles on Frazier Mountain Park Road, which will become Cuddy Valley Road. At 12 miles, turn right on Mil Potrero Highway and drive six miles to Pine Mountain Club. Turn left at the gas station in town, across from the golf course, and enter the shopping center. Drive 50 yards on Pine Circle. Mountain Properties is located in the shopping center at the intersection of Pine Circle and Pine Valley Lane.

Contact: Mountain Properties Vacation Rentals, 16229 Pine Valley Lane, P.O. Box 6675, Pine Mountain Club, CA 93222; 661/242-2517; website: www.mtprop.com.

Mountain Properties Vacation Rentals

CHAPTER 2

Los Angeles and Vicinity

I slands, mountains, beaches, lakes, snowfall, surfing, skiing . . . the Los Angeles region offers all this diversity and more. The region is so large, and so varied, that it's impossible to make a blanket statement about it without dividing it into smaller pieces.

Two large national forests hold most of the high-country land in the region—Angeles and San Bernardino. The 700,000-acre Angeles National Forest contains the San Gabriel Mountains, which form a high, impenetrable shield that prevents Los Angeles's smog from dissipating. The mountains, which geologists claim are the most fractured and unstable in California (rock slides are an everyday occurrence), feature a wonderful network of more than 500 miles of maintained trails for hiking and biking, plus two small ski resorts at Mount Baldy and Big Pines.

You'll find a number of authentic mountain lodges in the San Gabriels, with cabins for rent in the summer sun or winter snow, including Mount Baldy Lodge and Snowcrest Lodge on Mount Baldy, and the Mountain View Motel near Wrightwood.

A few miles to the east, the San Bernardino Mountains in San Bernardino National Forest form one of the highest mountain ranges in California, with peaks that rise to more than 11,000 feet in elevation. The San Bernardinos also contain Southern California's three major recreation lakes: Big Bear, Arrowhead, and Silverwood, plus smaller lakes Gregory and Green Valley. Whether you water-ski, fish, windsurf, sail, canoe, or ride personal watercrafts, recreation opportunities abound on these lakes. In addition, Southern California's best skiing and snowboarding are found at two resorts at Big Bear (Snow Summit and Bear Mountain) and one at Running Springs (Snow Valley). With a base elevation of 6,800 feet and extensive snowmaking systems, these resorts provide consistent skiing typically from Thanksgiving through Easter.

Cabin resorts near the lakes and ski resorts in the San Bernardino Mountains are too numerous to count; some of the best are featured in the pages that follow.

Yet another mountain range is found in San Bernardino National Forest: the San Jacintos, topped by Mount San Jacinto at 10,804 feet, which towers over the low desert at Palm Springs. The San Jacinto mountains rise abruptly from the desert floor, and are completely separated from the other high-elevation ranges of Southern California by low passes and valleys. John Muir called the view from the summit of Mount San Jacinto "one of the most sublime spectacles seen anywhere on Earth."

To explore the dense cedar and pine forests of the San Jacinto Mountains, reserve a stay at one of the cabin resorts in the village of Idyllwild, a hiker-friendly town with easy access to numerous trailheads and mountain streams for fishing.

Combined, these three mountain ranges—San Gabriel, San Bernardino, and San Jacinto—contain Southern California's great triumvirate of hikeable peaks: Mount San Gorgonio at 11,490 feet, Mount San Jacinto at 10,804 feet, and Mount Baldy at 10,064 feet. Every Los Angeles–area hiker worth his or her salt will "bag" all three summits at some point in his or her career.

But if surf and sand appeal to you more than mountains and lakes, the Los Angeles region will not disappoint. In this chapter, you'll find cottage resorts within steps of the beaches at Malibu and Laguna, and one in the town of Avalon on Catalina Island. If you want to sleep even closer to the water, this chapter includes two boat-and-breakfasts, one in Newport and one in Long Beach, where you can spend the night on a yacht in a calm harbor.

And last but not least, even glittering Hollywood has a cottage resort where you can sleep like a movie star: the venerable Chateau Marmont. Its cottages and bungalows have served as home to the likes of Greta Garbo and Bette Davis. Will you be next?

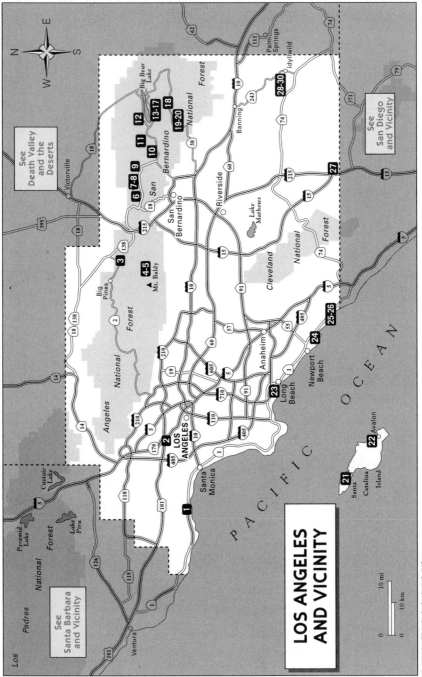

LOS ANGELES AND VICINITY

See Death Valley and the Deserts

See San Diego and Vicinity

See Santa Barbara and Vicinity

PACIFIC OCEAN

© AVALON TRAVEL PUBLISHING, INC.

CHAPTER 2
LOS ANGELES AND VICINITY

1. TOPANGA RANCH MOTEL

Let's just say right away that the cabins at Topanga Ranch Motel are nothing fancy. After all, what can you expect for less than 100 bucks a night in pricey Malibu? Not a heck of a lot. However, if you want to take advantage of all the great outdoor adventures of the Malibu coast and the Santa Monica Mountains, a stay at Topanga Ranch's cabins will allow you to do so and still go home with some change in your pocket.

© ANN MARIE BROWN

Off Highway 1 in Malibu

Luxury rating: 2

Recreation rating: 4

THIS CABIN RANKS . . .
Best Value
Best for Beach Activities

The cabins were built in the 1920s and are showing their age, but have been painted a cheerful red and white on the outside. They are spacious enough for a couple or a small family, and their fully equipped kitchens give you the option to cook your meals at home. Although the furniture is not exactly fashionable, remember: You're saving money.

The cabins are arranged motel-style, lined up in a row in the parking lot, with the busy Pacific Coast Highway not far away. The good news about the highway's proximity is that on its far side is the ocean, which means you are walking distance from the beach. Just throw your surfboard or your beach towel over your shoulder and look both ways before you cross.

If hiking interests you, the Santa Monica Mountains National Recreation Area awaits, as well as more than a dozen state and county parks in the immediate area. Take your pick from the trails at Point Mugu State Park, Leo Carrillo State Beach, Charmlee Natural Area, Malibu Creek State Park, Solstice Canyon Park, and Topanga State Park. Enough parks and paths exist within a half-hour drive of Malibu to keep you busy for a whole summer.

Facilities: There are 14 cabins ranging in size from one to two bedrooms, some with kitchens.

Bedding: Linens and towels are provided.

Reservations and rates: Reservations are recommended. Fees range from $75 to $100 per night. Small pets are permitted.

Directions: From Santa Monica, drive north on Highway 1 for six miles to Malibu. Look for the Topanga Ranch Motel on the east side of the road, just north of the junction with Topanga Canyon Boulevard.

Contact: Topanga Ranch Motel, 18711 Pacific Coast Highway, Malibu, CA 90265; 310/456-5486 or 800/200-0019; website: www.topangaranchmotel.com.

Topanga Ranch Motel

2. CHATEAU MARMONT

Chateau Marmont is legendary. Bette Davis and Greta Garbo slept here. Howard Hughes kept his harem here. Grace Kelly had affairs here. John Belushi died here. You get the picture.

Off U.S. 101 in Hollywood

Luxury rating: 5

Recreation rating: 3

THIS CABIN RANKS . . .

Most Luxurious

Built like a Gothic citadel, a Mediterranean castle, or something with spare parts from both, Chateau Marmont has nine garden cottages, two hillside bungalows, and two poolside bungalows, in addition to its 50 rooms. If you want to get a peek at a celebrity, or just feel like one yourself, Chateau Marmont is the place.

Originally an apartment building, the Chateau was transformed into a hotel in the late 1920s and has been a movie industry hangout ever since. Hotelier Andre Balazs purchased it in 1990 and completely renovated it in a mixed 1930s, '40s, and '50s style.

Each cottage, bungalow, and room has its own character. The bungalows are huge (1,500 to 2,500 feet and two or three bedrooms) and offer the utmost in privacy. Each has its own kitchen, fireplace, and secluded patio or yard. They have the ambience of a very nice home, not a hotel. That has been their appeal to celebrities for decades.

The garden cottages are smaller and more quaint (Arts and Crafts and mission-style furnishings). Each has a bedroom, living room, and kitchen. They are grouped around a landscaped courtyard and accessed by a separate street entrance from the main hotel. The cottage and bungalow grounds are lush and manicured, with plenty of bougainvillea, trumpet vines, and palms. Brick walkways lead from the buildings to the inviting pool and lounge area.

In addition to hanging out by the pool, most guests take advantage of the proximity of the Sunset Strip. The Chateau is set just above Sunset Boulevard, with its multitude of nightclubs, restaurants, record stores, and the like.

But to complete your Hollywood experience, you must head for Griffith Park and hike to the top of Mount Hollywood, elevation 1,625 feet. First-timers need to know that this is not the peak that bears the famous Hollywood sign (that's Mount Lee), although you can see that sign from this peak, which is the highest point in Hollywood. The round-trip is five miles from the trailhead near the Ferndell Nature Museum. Another option is to leave the hustle and bustle of Hollywood behind and explore the peaceful trails in nearby Franklin Canyon.

Facilities: There are nine garden cottages, two hillside bungalows, and two poolside bungalows, plus 50 rooms, suites, and penthouses. All cottages have fully equipped kitchens.

Bedding: Linens and towels are provided. Pets are not permitted.

Reservations and rates: Reservations are required. Rates are $400 per night for garden cottages, $875 per night for hillside bungalows, and $675 and $975 per night for poolside bungalows.

Directions: From U.S. 101 in Hollywood, take the Sunset Boulevard exit west and drive approximately four miles. Watch for Crescent Heights Boulevard; two blocks beyond it, turn right on Marmont Lane (easy to miss). The hotel is on the right.

Contact: Chateau Marmont, 8221 Sunset Boulevard, Hollywood, CA 90046; 323/656-1010 or 800/242-8328; website: www.chateaumarmont.com.

Chateau Marmont

3. MOUNTAIN VIEW MOTEL

It's December in Los Angeles, and you just can't conjure up the feeling of Christmas amid the crowded malls, Santa Claus bikinis, and palm trees swaddled in twinkling lights. So book yourself a cabin at Mountain View Motel and take the one-hour drive to Wrightwood, a snowy mountain town that knows how to do winter right.

© ANN MARIE BROWN

Off Highway 2 in Wrightwood

Luxury rating: 3

Recreation rating: 4

Mountain View Motel has cabins with and without whirpool hot tubs, fireplaces, wood-burning stoves, and kitchens, so be sure to get one that is right for you. Make sure you've brought your warm clothes, because the elevation is 6,000 feet and it gets mighty chilly up here. After a good night's sleep, take your pick from the ski resorts in nearby Big Pines—Ski Sunrise or Mountain High—and make a few runs down the mountain.

If wintertime isn't your cup of tea, the other seasons are also fine at Mountain View Motel. In spring, summer, or fall, the big attraction around Wrightwood is hiking in the San Gabriel Mountains, with dozens of trailheads located within a 30-minute drive of your cabin. The elevation is high enough so that the temperature is rarely too hot, and the air is always fresh and clean—free of the valley smog. If you want an easy stroll, three nature trails are just five minutes away in Big Pines, near the Forest Service Visitor Center. If you seek more of an adventure, try the classic climb to the peak of Mount Baden-Powell, starting from either the Vincent Gap or Dawson Saddle trailheads on Highway 2.

You can even do some fishing in the Big Pines area, at little Jackson Lake along the Big Pines Highway (Road N4). The Department of Fish and Game keeps the lake stocked with trout all summer; just drive up to the picnic area and fish from shore. If you've always wanted to try your hand at gold prospecting, Big Rock Creek is the place, just a few miles down Highway 2.

Facilities: There are 10 duplex-style cabins ranging in size from one to three bedrooms. Some have fully equipped kitchens, fireplaces, and hot tubs.

Bedding: Linens and towels are provided.

Reservations and rates: Reservations are recommended. Rates range from $69 to $149 per night. Pets are not permitted.

Directions: From I-10 at Ontario, drive east for seven miles and take I-15 north. Drive north on I-15 for 22 miles to Highway 138, then go west on Highway 138 for nine miles to the Highway 2 cutoff. Go west on Highway 2 for five miles to Wrightwood; Mountain View Motel is on the right as you drive through town.

Contact: Mountain View Motel, P.O. Box 458, 1054 State Highway 2, Wrightwood, CA 92397; 760/249-3553.

OTHER CABINS AND COTTAGES NEARBY

• Oriole Lodge & Cottage, 663 Oriole Road, P.O. Box 1959, Wrightwood, CA 92397; 760/249-3873; website: www.oriolelodge.com.

Mountain View Motel

4. MOUNT BALDY LODGE

© ANN MARIE BROWN

Off I-10 on Mount Baldy

Luxury rating: 3

Recreation rating: 4

Twenty years ago, when I was a college student in Claremont, my classmates and I would head to Mount Baldy at the first sign of snow in November. We'd stop our cars as soon as we drove into the white stuff for the sheer joy of throwing snowballs at each other. Other times, and in other seasons, we'd drive to our favorite trailhead at Ice House Canyon, and hike in the conifers amid cool, clean mountain air. It was a sweet, revitalizing shock to our smog-ridden lungs.

Years later, I finally stayed overnight at Mount Baldy Lodge. I found myself wondering how I could have spent so much time on the mountain without staying at these wonderful cabins. I rented cabin number 8, which has a huge stone fireplace. The bed was placed in a tiny alcove, separate from the main living area, which made it especially cozy.

All the cabins are old and rustic, with fine woodworking and details, but with modern conveniences like electric heaters. Although some are right next to the lodge restaurant and Mount Baldy Road, there is surprisingly little noise. The exception is when a band plays at the lodge; then you'll have to wait for them to quit before you can sleep. On the other hand, you could always dance till you drop, then retire to your cozy cabin.

On the down side, there are no kitchens in the cabins, but you can get your meals at the lodge restaurant or at nearby Buckhorn Lodge. On the up side, you wake up in a mountain wonderland, just a half-hour from sprawling suburbs and smog, but so far away. In winter, you can drive up the hill to the Mount Baldy ski lift. If the mountain is snow-free, you can head for hiking adventures at nearby trailheads. An easy hike is the 1.7 miles (one-way) on Bear Canyon Trail from Mount Baldy Village to Bear Flats. A longer, more challenging trip is Icehouse Canyon Trail to Three T's Trail, where you can pay a visit to three peaks: Thunder, Timber, and Telegraph.

Facilities: There are six studio and one-bedroom cabins with no kitchen facilities. A restaurant is on-site.

Bedding: Linens and towels are provided.

Reservations and rates: Reservations are recommended. Fees range from $69 to $119 per night. Pets are not permitted.

Directions: From I-10 at Ontario, exit on Mountain Avenue and drive north for six miles until Mountain Avenue joins Shinn Road. Bear left on Shinn Road and continue to Mount Baldy Road. Bear right and drive 5.5 miles north on Mount Baldy Road to Mount Baldy Village. Mount Baldy Lodge is on the right side of the road.

Contact: Mount Baldy Lodge, P.O. Box 699, Mount Baldy, CA 91759; 909/982-1115; website: www.baldylodge.com.

Mount Baldy Lodge

5. SNOWCREST LODGE

Snowcrest Lodge is an authentic mountain lodge, with a café and bar that look exactly like a café and bar in the mountains should look. Various stuffed animal heads hang from the walls, including that of a very impressive moose. The stone fireplace is large enough to pitch a tent in. The dining room is immense, with an assortment of mismatched furniture. It's the kind of place where you would feel embarrassed wearing a suit and tie.

There are six cabins at Snowcrest, and the best ones are the larger cabins that come with kitchens. (Bring your own utensils, pots, and pans—none are provided.) If you're on a budget, the smaller cabins are cheaper, but you won't be able to cook. The large cabins are built of stone and are as cute as can be, while the small ones are duplexes, and a bit shabby. All of the cabins have big stone fireplaces, heaters, bathrooms, and comfortable beds.

The main reason people come to Snowcrest Lodge is because it's only a half mile from the Mount Baldy Ski Lift. You wake up in the morning, have some breakfast at the restaurant or make your own in your cabin, and then a few minutes later you're on the chairlift. Sound easy? It is.

Off I-10 on Mount Baldy

Luxury rating: 3

Recreation rating: 4

THIS CABIN RANKS . . .
Best for Winter Sports

Another great activity for late winter and spring is hiking to San Antonio Falls, an 80-foot waterfall that drops in three tiers. The trailhead is only a quarter mile up the road from Snowcrest Lodge, so you can easily walk to it. The hike follows the ski lift maintenance road gently uphill for three-quarters of a mile to a sharp curve in the road, where the big waterfall pours. The best time to see the fall is when the snow starts melting, usually in February or March.

Very fit hikers can continue past the waterfall for another six miles to the peak of Mount Baldy at 10,064 feet. This is one of the greatest hikes in all of Southern California, a 13-mile epic trip. If you go too early in the season, you'll need to carry ice axes and crampons; it's easier to wait until the snow is gone. Then the only requirements are full water bottles, some snacks, and plenty of energy. Views from the peak of Mount Baldy are extraordinary—a panorama of desert, city, ocean, and even the southern Sierra Nevada.

More tame activities abound on Mount Baldy. Kids love to visit the town's trout pools, where you pay a couple of bucks to toss a line in the water. No fishing license is required. Snowcrest Lodge has its own Olympic-sized swimming pool, great for lounging in the sun or playing in the water. In winter, some folks bring their trash can lids or boogie boards up to the mountain and spend all day sledding down the hillsides.

Facilities: There are six cabins ranging in size from one to two bedrooms, some with kitchens, and all with fireplaces, heat, and bathrooms. Cooking and eating utensils are not provided. A restaurant and pool are on-site.

Bedding: Linens and towels are provided.

Reservations and rates: Reservations are recommended. Fees range from $75 to $95 per night. Pets are permitted with a $20 refundable deposit.

Directions: From I-10 at Ontario, exit on Mountain Avenue and drive north for six miles until Mountain Avenue joins Shinn Road. Bear left on Shinn Road and continue to Mount Baldy Road. Bear right and drive nine miles north on Mount Baldy Road, past Mount Baldy Village, to Snowcrest Lodge on the left side of the road.

Contact: Snowcrest Lodge, P.O. Box 383, Mount Baldy, CA 91759; 909/985-3012; website: www.snowcrestlodge.com.

Snowcrest Lodge

6. SLEEPY HOLLOW CABINS

Sleepy Hollow Cabins are right in the middle of the main drag of Lake Gregory, next door to the bowling alley. Does this sound like a peaceful mountain retreat? Of course not. But Sleepy Hollow's affordable cabins are within a couple blocks of the lake's popular swimming beach, which makes it ideal for families who want to while away their days at Lake Gregory.

Off Highway 18 in Crestline

Luxury rating: 3

Recreation rating: 3

If you've never ridden a water slide in your life, Lake Gregory is the place to do it. The lake is run by San Bernardino County and is much like a giant public pool. The water slide is scarier than it looks—go feet-first the first time, not head-first. The lake's swimming beach has lifeguards on duty, who make sure that everyone is out of the water at 5 P.M. each day. It seems too early in summer, but that's closing time at the lake.

You can fish at Lake Gregory, too. Rowboats are for rent, but most people fish from shore for brown trout in the winter and rainbow trout in the summer.

The cabins at Sleepy Hollow are basic but serviceable. All have full kitchens and microwaves; all except one have woodburning fireplaces. They are clustered around the resort's heated, 20-foot by 40-foot pool. A communal picnic area with gas barbecues is also available. There isn't much about the cabins' concrete setting that seems like nature, but most guests don't seem to mind.

If you crave a little nature, it isn't hard to find. Take a drive west out to Highway 138, then head north to the small town of Valley of Enchantment. Just beyond it, turn left at the sign for Camp Seeley. A short and easy hike on the Seeley Creek Trail leads past giant conifers to beautiful Heart Rock Falls, where Mother Nature has carved a perfect heart-shaped bowl out of granite. The waterfall drops about 25 feet in springtime.

While you're in the neighborhood, you might want to drive up to Silverwood Lake, a huge water-skiing lake that makes Lake Gregory look like a tiny puddle. The lake covers more than 1,000 acres with 13 miles of shoreline, and it's popular with anglers as well as boaters.

Facilities: There are six one- and two-bedroom cabins that can accommodate up to six people, plus two suites and several motel rooms. All cabins have fully equipped kitchens. A pool and communal picnic area with gas barbecues are on-site.

Bedding: Linens and towels are provided.

Reservations and rates: Reservations are recommended. Fees are $85 to $130 per night, or $530 to $700 per week. Pets are not permitted.

Directions: From I-10 near San Bernardino, take I-215 North five miles to Highway 30 East. Drive two miles east on Highway 30 and exit on Highway 18/Waterman Avenue. Drive north on Highway 18 for about 20 miles to the Lake Gregory/Twin Peaks turnoff (by the Cliffhanger Restaurant). Turn left on Lake Gregory Drive, then drive two miles to Lake Drive. Turn left; Sleepy Hollow Cabins is on the left.

Contact: Sleepy Hollow Cabins, P.O. Box 632, 24033 Lake Drive, Crestline, CA 92325; 909/338-2718 or 800/909-2718; website: www.mountaininfo.com /cabins4u.

OTHER CABINS AND COTTAGES NEARBY

• Crest Lodge, 23508 Lake Drive, P.O. Box 4944, Crestline, CA 92325; 909/338-7766.

Sleepy Hollow Cabins

7. ARROWHEAD PINE ROSE CABINS

There are folks who are in the cabin business, and there are folks who are in the cabin business and know how to do it right. The folks who run Arrowhead Pine Rose Cabins fall into the latter category.

© ANN MARIE BROWN

Off Highway 189 in Twin Peaks

Luxury rating: 4

Recreation rating: 3

First, they have a great location: near lakes Gregory, Silverwood, and Arrowhead in the San Bernardino Mountains. Next, they do everything they can to make your stay extraordinary. Instead of just basic, cookie-cutter cabins and cottages, the owners have made Arrowhead Pine Rose Cabins into individual handcrafted masterpieces. Each one is different, although they all have kitchens and most have fireplaces.

I stayed in Rustic Romance, which has an open-beamed ceiling, beautiful stone fireplace, and perfectly coordinated linens, rugs, lamp shades, and hand-painted detailing on the walls. The centerpiece of the room is a whirlpool hot tub with a natural stone waterfall. If this sounds a bit too Las Vegas for you, let me emphasize that the overall effect is tasteful, subtle, and even rustic—not splashy.

On the porches outside the cabins are big willow chairs, where you can while away the hours watching the birds or reading a book. If you want more activity, you can swim in the heated outdoor pool or soak in the hot tub, which is shaped like an arrowhead!

If you can tear yourself away from Arrowhead Pine Rose Cabins, you'll want to take advantage of all the outdoor recreation in the area. In the winter, skiing at Snow Valley is a major draw. Ice-skating on the year-round rink in nearby Blue Jay is also popular. (The rink suffered terrible damage in a February 2001 snowstorm, but is scheduled to reopen in fall 2002.)

Summer is the season for waterskiing, boating, and fishing on the area's lakes. Although many visitors are disappointed by the lack of public access to Lake Arrowhead, there are two good alternatives: big Lake Silverwood or little Lake Gregory. Silverwood is a huge reservoir that is popular for water-skiing, and Lake Gregory is a family-oriented place with swimming beaches, a water slide, and rental boats. Trout fishing is good in both lakes.

Facilities: There are 17 cabins ranging in size from studios to seven bedrooms. All have fully equipped kitchens, most have a fireplace. There are a pool and hot tub on-site.

Bedding: Linens and towels are provided.

Reservations and rates: Reservations are recommended. Fees range from $50 to $325 per night, with a two-night minimum stay on weekends. Pets are permitted in some cabins with prior approval.

Directions: From I-10 near San Bernardino, take I-215 North five miles to Highway 30 East. Drive two miles east on Highway 30 and exit on Highway 18/Waterman Avenue. Drive north on Highway 18 for about 20 miles to the Lake Gregory/Twin Peaks turnoff (by the Cliffhanger Restaurant). Turn left, then turn right almost immediately on Highway 189. Take Highway 189 East for two miles to Twin Peaks. Arrowhead Pine Rose Cabins is on the left side of the road.

Contact: Arrowhead Pine Rose Cabins, 25994 Highway 189, P.O. Box 31, Twin Peaks, CA 92391; 909/337-2341 or 800/429-7463; website: www.lakearrowheadcabins.com.

OTHER CABINS AND COTTAGES NEARBY
• The Antlers Inn and Cabins, P.O. Box 310, 26125 Highway 189, Twin Peaks, CA 92391; 909/337-4020.

Arrowhead Pine Rose Cabins

8. BRACKEN FERN MANOR

Bracken Fern Manor was built in 1929 as a private gambling club for movie stars and mobsters in the Prohibition years. The boys who ran the place, including tough guy Bugsy Siegel, would lure aspiring movie actresses to staff the upstairs brothel, where the young women would have a chance to meet movie industry heavies. No one is sure whether any of these women ever made it to the screen, but some of their letters were discovered when the inn was restored.

*Off Highway 18 near
Lake Arrowhead*

Luxury rating: 4

Recreation rating: 3

This fascinating historical landmark in Lake Arrowhead has one two-room cottage and 10 guest rooms. The cottage is located alongside the manor, but has its own separate parking and entrance. It has a fully equipped kitchen, fireplace, whirlpool hot tub, barbecue on the patio, and television and VCR. If you stay in the cottage, you won't be invited to breakfast with the other manor guests; be sure to bring groceries so you can make your own.

The cottage and manor are located only five minutes from Lake Arrowhead Village and all the services surrounding the lake, including boat cruises and fishing tours. Hikers will want to explore the trails of San Bernardino National Forest; the Heaps Peak Arboretum Trail is only a few minutes from Bracken Fern Manor on Highway 18. The three-quarter-mile interpretive trail features 24 points of interest about native plants and wildlife.

The best trail near Lake Arrowhead is the Pacific Crest Trail at Deep Creek. Another popular option is the short but steep hike to Deep Creek Hot Springs, where you can soak in one of several pools alongside the creek. The Arrowhead Ranger District of San Bernardino National Forest can provide you with maps and updated information.

Facilities: There is one two-room cottage that can accommodate up to four people, plus 10 guest rooms. The cottage has a fully equipped kitchen, plus fireplace, hot tub, and patio.

Bedding: Linens and towels are provided.

Reservations and rates: Reservations are required. The fee is $190 per night with a two-night minimum. Pets are not permitted.

Directions: From I-10 near San Bernardino, take I-215 North five miles to Highway 30 East. Drive two miles east on Highway 30 and exit on Highway 18/Waterman Avenue. Drive north on Highway 18 for about 25 miles to the Highway 173/Lake Arrowhead cutoff. Continue one mile beyond the Lake Arrowhead cutoff to Arrowhead Villas Road on the left. Turn left and drive two blocks to Bracken Fern Manor on the right.

Contact: Bracken Fern Manor, P.O. Box 1006, 815 Arrowhead Villas Road, Lake Arrowhead, CA 92352; 909/337-8557; website: www.brackenfernmanor.com.

Bracken Fern Manor

9. SADDLEBACK INN COTTAGES

Lake Arrowhead is a tough nut to crack. The mile-high lake is undoubtedly one of Southern California's most beautiful bodies of water, yet gaining access to it is darn near impossible. Almost every inch of its shoreline is private property, neatly lined with the vacation homes of the ultra-wealthy. Even though the lake is located in San Bernardino National Forest on public land, the public has never felt welcome there.

Off Highway 173 in Lake Arrowhead

Luxury rating: 4

Recreation rating: 4

That's why you should know about the cottages at Saddleback Inn. Located in the town of Lake Arrowhead, the Saddleback Inn's cottages are your chance to get close to Lake Arrowhead. Lakefront they are not, but around here, "lake-near" is as good as it gets.

When you drive up, Saddleback Inn looks like a nice, old-style hotel on a busy street. What isn't obvious is that behind the main building are nearly a dozen cottages, tucked into the conifers. They are mostly one-bedrooms; many have luxuries like whirlpool tubs and gas fireplaces. My favorites are numbers 24 and 36 (named Sooner and Maple Leaf); they are the most private. The Saddleback Inn also has two- and three-bedroom suites that sleep up to seven people.

How you spend your time at Lake Arrowhead depends on what season it is. In winter, the main attraction is downhill skiing and snowboarding at nearby Snow Valley Ski Resort in Running Springs. If Snow Valley's runs aren't treacherous enough for you, you can drive a few miles farther east to Big Bear Lake's two ski areas. The neighboring town of Blue Jay has a year-round ice-skating rink where hopeful Olympians and wobbly-ankled skaters glide away the hours. (The rink suffered damage in a winter 2001 snowstorm, but is scheduled to reopen in fall 2002.)

In summer, most vacationers want to get out on Lake Arrowhead. The only way to do so is on a commercial tour, unless you know somebody who lives on the lake. (No public boat launching is permitted.) Fishing and water-skiing tours are available. Or you can take a cruise on the *Arrowhead Queen*, a 60-seat paddlewheeler out of the shopping area known as Lake Arrowhead Village.

Facilities: There are eight one-bedroom cottages, plus 26 rooms and suites. None of the cottages have kitchens. Some have whirlpool tubs and fireplaces. A restaurant is on-site.

Bedding: Linens and towels are provided.

Reservations and rates: Reservations are recommended. Fees range from $103 to $169 per night on weekdays and $126 to $298 per night on weekends and holidays. Pets are not permitted.

Directions: From I-10 near San Bernardino, take I-215 North five miles to Highway 30 East. Drive two miles east on Highway 30 and exit on Highway 18/Waterman Avenue. Drive north on Highway 18 for about 25 miles to the Highway 173/Lake Arrowhead cutoff on the left. Drive two miles to Lake Arrowhead Village and Saddleback Inn on the right.

Contact: Saddleback Inn, P.O. Box 1890, 300 South State Highway 173, Lake Arrowhead, CA 92352; 909/336-3571 or 800/858-3334; website: www.saddlebackinn.com.

Saddleback Inn Cottages

10. GIANT OAKS LODGE

There is one primary reason that people come to stay at Giant Oaks Lodge, and that's to ski at Snow Valley Ski Resort. The ski area is a mere five miles from Giant Oaks, and Giant Oaks is a mere half-hour from San Bernardino. Add it up and you have an easy trip to the mountains for a weekend of fun in the snow.

© ANN MARIE BROWN

*Off Highway 330 in
Running Springs*

Luxury rating: 4

Recreation rating: 3

THIS CABIN RANKS . . .
Best for Winter Sports

With a base elevation of 6,800 feet, Snow Valley provides consistent white stuff from Thanksgiving through Easter for skiers and snowboarders. The emphasis is on families and beginners, with plenty of learn-to-ski packages. In summer, Snow Valley leads another life, when it transforms into a skateboard park with organized camps and classes for kids.

In any season, the cabins at Giant Oaks are a fine place to stay. All are beautifully decorated and many have mountain views. Surrounded by oaks, cedars, and pines, the cabins are mostly protected from road noise from nearby Highway 18. One "family-friendly cabin" has a full kitchen and stone fireplace; it's large enough for six people. Cabin 4 is the most romantic; it has a spa tub for two in a rock setting with a fireplace, plus a shower for two. Giant Oaks' smaller cabins do not have kitchens, but they do have fireplaces and spas. Each unit has a television (with HBO) and a telephone. An indoor heated pool and spa are available, and they are a welcome sight after a day on the slopes.

Facilities: There are six cabins that can accommodate up to six people, plus four rooms. One cabin has a fully equipped kitchen; the rest have microwaves, refrigerators, and coffeemakers. Some have fireplaces and hot tubs. A pool and spa are on-site.

Bedding: Linens and towels are provided.

Reservations and rates: Reservations are recommended. Fees are $129 to $199 per night for cabins, and $59 to $119 for rooms. Pets are not permitted.

Directions: From I-10 at Redlands, drive north on Highway 30 for five miles to the Highway 330 exit. Drive north on Highway 330 for 13 miles to Running Springs, at the junction with Highway 18. Giant Oaks Lodge is on the left.

Contact: Giant Oaks Lodge, 32180 Highway 18, Running Springs, CA 92382; 909/867-2231 or 800/786-1689; website: www.runningsprings.com.

OTHER CABINS AND COTTAGES NEARBY

• Rainbow View Lodge, 2726 View Drive, P.O. Box 1084, Running Springs, CA 92382; 909/867-1810; website: www.mountaininfo.com/rainbow.

Giant Oaks Lodge

11. GREEN VALLEY LAKE COZY CABINS

One of the best reasons to spend a cabin vacation at Green Valley Lake is because most other people will be somewhere else. Sure, the scenery is pretty, the lake has good fishing, and there are miles of trails to explore in San Bernardino National Forest. But that's true of many places in the nearby area, most notably Big Bear Lake and Arrowhead Lake. The difference is that the masses are assembled at those places; it's just you and a few others at Green Valley Lake.

The lake and the town are located at 7,200 feet, midway between Big Bear and Arrowhead in the San Bernardino Mountains. The important elements are in place: cool mountain air; big conifers; a pretty lake for fishing, swimming, and kayaking; and more than 50 rental cabins to choose from. The cabins are privately owned and Green Valley Lake Cozy Cabins manages them. Because they are private homes, they have many amenities: fully equipped kitchens, fireplaces or wood-burning stoves, televisions, stereos, microwaves, coffeemakers, and so on. Blankets and pillows are provided in each cabin, but bring your own sheets, pillowcases, and towels, and paper products like toilet paper and paper towels.

The cabins vary from one-bedroom bungalows in the forest to five-bedroom mini-mansions on the small lake. Most people stay for a week; the fee for seven nights is a real bargain at less than $500 for a cabin that sleeps four to six people.

*Off Highway 18 near
Green Valley Lake*

Luxury rating: 4

Recreation rating: 4

THIS CABIN RANKS . . .
Best Value

After you arrive at Green Valley Lake, take your pick from a huge selection of outdoor activities. In winter, the Green Valley Cross Country Ski Area is open down the road by Green Valley Campground. The most advanced trail leads 10 miles one-way to Fawnskin at Big Bear Lake. Also available is a small, family-run ski and snow play area just up the road from the lake.

In summer, anglers rent rowboats and row around the edges of Green Valley Lake, or fish with bait from the shoreline. Trout are planted regularly in spring and summer. No motorized boats are allowed on the small lake, so it is always quiet and serene. Plenty of swimmers access the lake as well.

Hikers can find a few short trails near Green Valley Campground, or they can drive down Camp Road and Meadow Lane to the Little Green Valley YMCA Camp. From there, hike the Little Green Valley Trail into Snow Valley. The trail is four miles one-way, nearly flat, and passes some large and glorious stands of big pines and cedars.

Facilities: There are 55 vacation rental cabins ranging in size from one to five bedrooms, all with fully equipped kitchens. All feature modern amenities.

Bedding: Linens and towels are not provided; bring your own.

Reservations and rates: Reservations are required. Fees range from $90 to $200 per night; a two-night minimum stay is required. Weekly rates are discounted. A $100 refundable cleaning deposit is required. Pets are permitted in some cabins with prior approval.

Directions: From I-10 at Redlands, drive north on Highway 30 for five miles to the Highway 330 exit. Drive north on Highway 330 for 13 miles to Running Springs. Turn east on Highway 18 and drive four miles to Green Valley Lake Road. Turn north on Green Valley Lake Road and drive three miles. The rental office is located at 33231 Green Valley Lake Road; check in there to get keys and directions to your cabin.

Contact: Green Valley Lake Cozy Cabins, 33231 Green Valley Lake Road, Green Valley Lake, CA 92341; 909/867-5335; website: www.mountaininfo.com/cozy.

Green Valley Lake Cozy Cabins

12. QUAIL COVE LODGE

Quail Cove Lodge has a lot going for it, but probably the best thing is its location: on the far edge of Big Bear Lake in the small town of Fawnskin, not the big town of Big Bear Lake. On weekends, it can be difficult to find a quiet spot in Big Bear Lake, but Fawnskin is always quiet. From your Quail Cove cabin, the only sound you'll hear is the lake lapping near your doorstep.

© ANN MARIE BROWN

Off Highway 38 in Big Bear

Luxury rating: 3

Recreation rating: 4

Two of the lodge's cabins are so close to the lake that you could cast a line out your bedroom window. If you really want a lakeside vacation, reserve cabin 1 or 2. Both are studios that sleep only two people, with full kitchen, fireplace, and queen bed. Cabin 2 has the prettiest view, both of the lake and the ski slopes. If you have a larger party, reserve cabin 6, which has three bedrooms, a fireplace, big dining room table, and a dishwasher. You can do all your own cooking in your fully equipped kitchen, or head for the multitude of restaurants in Big Bear.

Luckily for mountain bikers, Quail Cove is situated right across the highway from the Grout Bay Trailhead. The dirt roads leading to Butler Peak Lookout make a great 14-mile round-trip bike ride, with terrific views from the 8,400-foot peak. For hikers, Castle Rock Trail is close by, as is the uphill romp to Bertha Peak on the Cougar Crest Trail.

Anglers can fish right from the cabin property by casting or bait-dunking in the lake or the creek, or rent a motorboat at Gray's Landing, only a half mile away. In addition to fishing boats, you can also rent personal watercrafts, water-ski boats, and the like.

Facilities: There are six cabins ranging in size from studios to three bedrooms, all with fully equipped kitchens.

Bedding: Linens and towels are provided.

Reservations and rates: Reservations are recommended. Fees range from $89 to $239 per night. Pets are permitted with a $10 fee per night.

Directions: From I-10 at Redlands, drive north on Highway 30 for five miles to the Highway 330 exit. Drive north on Highway 330 for 13 miles to Running Springs. Turn east on Highway 18 and drive 14 miles to the Highway 38 fork at Big Bear Lake. Bear left on Highway 38 (Northshore Drive) and drive three miles to Quail Cove Lodge on the right side of the road.

Contact: Quail Cove Lodge, P.O. Box 117, 39117 North Shore Drive, Fawnskin, CA 92333; 800/595-2683; website: www.quailcove.com.

OTHER CABINS AND COTTAGES NEARBY

- Creek Runner's Lodge, 374 Georgia Street, P.O. Box 58, Big Bear Lake, CA 92315; 909/866-7473; website: www.pineknot .com/~creekrunner.
- Timberline Lodge, 39921 Big Bear Boulevard, P.O. Box 1955, Big Bear Lake, CA 92315; 909/866-4141 or 800/803-4111; website: www.thetimberlinelodge.com.
- Cienaga Creek Ranch, 43630 Rainbow Lane, Big Bear Lake, CA 92315; 888/336-2166.

Quail Cove Lodge

13. SHORE ACRES LODGE

There are so many lodging options at Big Bear Lake, including hundreds of cabins, that it's hard to know which is the best place to stay. One place I endorse wholeheartedly is Shore Acres Lodge, particularly for families visiting Big Bear Lake.

© ANN MARIE BROWN

Off Highway 18 in Big Bear

Luxury rating: 3

Recreation rating: 4

THIS CABIN RANKS . . .
Best for Boating & Water Sports

Shore Acres Lodge rents 11 cabins on its premises, but it also manages a huge list of private vacation homes in the nearby area. If you rent one of the latter, you still get full use of the resort's facilities, but you're away from the hubbub of the lodge. At Shore Acres, you get to choose the kind of vacation experience you want to have.

The 11 cabins on-site are cozy and comfortable. Although they are nestled in tall pine trees, many have lake views. A few are literally steps from the lake. All have fully equipped kitchens and barbecues on their decks, and most have fireplaces. A pool and spa are available, plus a children's playground and a private boat dock.

Fishing is excellent at Lagunita Point and Gibraltar Point, a few hundred yards from the lodge. Many people simply drop in a line from shore, but the best success is had by trolling. You can rent boats at nearby Holloway's Marina. A full list of water recreation activities are available on Big Bear Lake, from sailing to personal watercraft riding to swimming.

If you can leave your beach chair at the lake's edge for an afternoon, several excellent hiking trails are located nearby. On the north shore, one of the best trails starts a half mile west of the Big Bear Discovery Center on Highway 38. Cougar Crest Trail climbs two miles to a junction with the Pacific Crest Trail. Head east (right) for a half mile to the summit of Bertha Peak, elevation 8,502 feet. The peak is covered with transmitter towers, but these don't take away from the glorious view of Bear Valley, Holcomb Valley, and the Mojave Desert.

In the same neighborhood, the paved Alpine Pedal Path starts at the Big Bear Discovery Center, heads through a tunnel under Highway 38, and then follows the sparkling lakeshore for nearly three miles. This makes a perfect easy bike ride or hike for families.

Facilities: There are 11 cabins and dozens of private vacation rentals ranging in size from one to five bedrooms. All have fully equipped kitchens. The cabins have a deck with barbecue, and most have a fireplace. A pool, spa, children's playground, and private boat dock are available.

Bedding: Linens and towels are provided.

Reservations and rates: Reservations are recommended. Fees range from $90 to $210 per night. Pets are permitted with a $5 fee per night.

Directions: From I-10 at Redlands, drive north on Highway 30 for five miles to the Highway 330 exit. Drive north on Highway 330 for 13 miles to Running Springs. Turn east on Highway 18 and drive 14 miles to the Highway 38 fork at Big Bear Lake. Stay right on Highway 18 and continue 3.5 miles. Turn left on Lakeview Drive and drive three-quarters of a mile to Shore Acres Lodge.

Contact: Shore Acres Lodge, 40090 Lakeview Drive, P.O. Box 110410, Big Bear, CA 92315; 909/244-2327 or 800/524-6600; website: www.bigbearvacations.com.

OTHER CABINS AND COTTAGES NEARBY

- Pine Knot Guest Ranch, 908 Pine Knot Avenue, P.O. Box 3446, Big Bear Lake, CA 92315; 909/866-6500 or 800/866-3446; website: www.pineknotguestranch.com.
- Frontier Lodge, 40472 Big Bear Boulevard, Big Bear Lake, CA 92315; 800/457-6401; website: www.bigbearlake.net.

Shore Acres Lodge

14. WILDWOOD RESORT

The cabins at Wildwood Resort have something you rarely get in a rental cabin—space. I rented a studio cabin, but found it had more square footage than most one-bedrooms. The full kitchen had a large dining table, the bed was king-sized, and the big fireplace made the whole place warm and cozy. I was also surprised to find a coffeemaker, microwave, and toaster in addition to the usual pots, pans, and dishes in the kitchen.

The owners of Wildwood Resort run a tight and tidy ship. The outdoor

Off Highway 18 in Big Bear

Luxury rating: 3

Recreation rating: 4

pool and whirlpool hot tub are well cared for, and flowers are planted around the cabins in summer. Most people never see the blossoms, however, because most people come to Big Bear in the middle of winter. Skiing and snowboarding top the recreation list, with two large resorts just outside of town: Bear Mountain and Snow Summit. More atypical snow activities include the Alpine Slide at Magic Mountain, where you can go inner-tubing down a ski hill or try out the bobsled track. Cross-country skiing and snowshoeing are also popular.

Summer rates are much lower than winter rates at Wildwood, so don't neglect a warm-weather visit. In summer, Snow Summit ski resort turns into a mountain bike park. (You ride the ski lift uphill, then fly downhill like a maniac; it's fun.) Bike rentals are available. If you want to get out on the water, you can take a dinner or brunch cruise on Big Bear Lake aboard the *Big Bear Queen,* or rent your own boat at one of the lake's marinas. Fishing is excellent in Big Bear Lake; the best results come from trolling.

Miles of hiking trails exist in San Bernardino National Forest, some beginning right at the lake's edge. Waterskiing, personal watercraft riding, and windsurfing are all possible on the lake, with several marinas renting equipment and even providing lessons. Then there are the tamer pursuits, like golf and tennis, but who has time for the tamer pursuits?

Facilities: There are 32 cabins ranging in size from studios to two bedrooms, all with fully equipped kitchens. There are an outdoor pool and a hot tub.

Bedding: Linens and towels are provided.

Reservations and rates: Reservations are recommended. Fees range from $85 to $240 per night. Summer rates and weekdays are discounted. Pets are not permitted.

Directions: From I-10 at Redlands, drive north on Highway 30 for five miles to the Highway 330 exit. Drive north on Highway 330 for 13 miles to Running Springs. Turn east on Highway 18 and drive 14 miles to the Highway 38 fork at Big Bear Lake. Stay right on Highway 18/Big Bear Boulevard and continue three miles to the village of Big Bear Lake. Wildwood Resort is on the left side of the road.

Contact: Wildwood Resort, 40210 Big Bear Boulevard, P.O. Box 2885, Big Bear Lake, CA 92315; 909/878-2178 or 888/294-5396; website: www.wildwoodresort.com.

OTHER CABINS AND COTTAGES NEARBY

• Big Bear Mountain Resort Rentals, 40703 Lakeview Drive, Big Bear Lake, CA 92315; 909/878-2233.

- Boulder Creek Resort, P.O. Box 92, Big Bear Lake, CA 92315; 909/866-2665.
- Grey Squirrel Resort, 39372 Big Bear Boulevard, P.O. Box 1711, Big Bear Lake, CA 92315; 909/866-4335 or 800/381-5569; website: www.greysquirrel.com.

Wildwood Resort

15. BEAR MANOR CABINS AND LAKEVIEW LODGE

If you are new to Big Bear, you might feel a little put off when you see that almost everything in the town has the word "bear" worked into its title. The cabins at Bear Manor are no exception, but you'll quickly get over the annoying cuteness of their moniker when you see how nice your accommodations are, and how much fun awaits in Big Bear.

© ANN MARIE BROWN

Off Highway 18 in Big Bear

Luxury rating: 4

Recreation rating: 3

Bear Manor Cabins and Lakeview Lodge are run by the same folks. Both have one major element in common: hot tubs in every unit. Otherwise, they're different. Bear Manor Cabins are made for two people and are older in style with knotty pine interiors, fireplaces, and small kitchenettes (some have gas cooktops and convection ovens; all have microwaves, refrigerators, toasters, and coffee makers). If you're a larger group, you'll stay at Lakeview Lodge's cabins or townhouses, which can sleep 4 to 10 people. In addition to the ubiquitous hot tubs, Lakeview Lodge's units have full kitchens, fireplaces, and two or three bedrooms.

Big Bear is best known for skiing in winter and water sports in summer, but don't miss out on the excellent hiking trails that start at or near the lake. Off Mill Creek Road on the south shore, an easy half-mile trail leads to the Champion Lodgepole Pine, a 400-year-old tree with a circumference of 20 feet. It stands 112 feet tall, and because it's a lodgepole, it's the straightest 112 feet of lumber you'll ever see. If you show up in early summer, check out the wildflowers in the adjacent meadow.

From the same trailhead, the Siberia Creek Trail parallels trickling Siberia Creek for 1.5 miles until it reaches "the Gunsight," a granite rock formation that looks like its name. A more challenging trail leads to Castle Rock from a turn in the highway near the lake's Boulder Bay. A short but steep climb through granite boulders and ponderosa pines brings you to increasingly larger boulders, the largest of which is Castle Rock. As you climb, keep turning around to check out the views of Big Bear Lake. The view from the top is breathtaking.

Facilities: There are six cabins that can accommodate two people, plus eight larger cabins and townhouses that can accommodate up to 10 people. The two-person cabins have kitchenettes; the larger cabins have full kitchens.

Bedding: Linens and towels are provided.

Reservations and rates: Reservations are recommended. Fees are $79 to $249 per night; weekdays are discounted. Pets are not permitted.

Directions: From I-10 at Redlands, drive north on Highway 30 for five miles to the Highway 330 exit. Drive north on Highway 330 for 13 miles to Running Springs. Turn east on Highway 18 and drive 14 miles to the Highway 38 fork at Big Bear Lake. Stay right on Highway 18/Big Bear Boulevard and continue three miles to Bear Manor Cabins on the right.

Contact: Bear Manor Cabins and Lakeview Lodge, 40393 Big Bear Boulevard, P.O. Box 3874, Big Bear Lake, CA 92315; 909/866-6800 or 800/472-2327; website: www.bigbearlakecabins.com.

OTHER CABINS AND COTTAGES NEARBY

- Smoketree Resort, 40210 Big Bear Boulevard, Big Bear Lake, CA 92315; 909/866-2415 or 800/352-8581.
- Cal-Pine Chalets, 41545 Big Bear Boulevard, Big Bear Lake, CA 92315; 909/866-2574 or 800/965-7463; website: www.cal-pine.com.

Bear Manor Cabins and Lakeview Lodge

16. CASTLEWOOD THEME COTTAGES

Castlewood is far and away the most unique and creative place to stay in Big Bear. If you're the kind of person who enjoys a little whimsy, and who wants to stay somewhere that is the antithesis of an ordinary motel room or plain cabin, Castlewood will tickle your fancy.

Each of Castlewood's 10 cabins is elaborately decorated around a theme. What theme, you ask? Well, the King Arthur cabin looks like a chamber in a medieval castle, with fake stone, velvet drapes, stained glass, and a coat of arms over the fireplace. King Arthur and Guinevere costumes hang on the wall. The Gone With the Wind cabin is a miniature two-story Southern mansion, with Vivian Leigh's portrait over the mantle and two of Scarlett's dresses and Rhett's hat and cane hanging in the closet. The cabin has a massive television set with surround sound and a video of . . . well, you know.

Off Highway 18 in Big Bear

Luxury rating: 4

Recreation rating: 4

THIS CABIN RANKS . . .
Most Unusual

The Captain's Quarters cabin features a treasure chest spilling out gold and jewels. A hatch in the floor opens to display the skeleton of a pirate. You'll hear his voice calling "Yo ho ho." The Enchanted Forest cabin is one of the most elaborate: It's three levels with a canopy of trees and a grotto in the lower level with a waterfall hot tub. Forest sounds play from hidden speakers.

Then there are the Crystal Cave and Anthony and Cleopatra cabins. And yet another, my favorite, The Castle Garden, which includes a talking suit of armor (he tells dragon stories).

Perhaps the best thing about this quirky resort is that the exteriors of the small cabins belie their interiors. From the outside, they look like typical Big Bear Bavarian-style cabins, perhaps a little tidier and better painted than most. So, a wonderful surprise awaits when you step inside the door.

Whatever their theme, all of the cottages have whirlpool tubs and fireplaces, televisions and VCRs, coffeemakers, microwaves, and small refrigerators. And because they are located a few blocks off Big Bear Boulevard, Big Bear's full array of recreation options are within easy reach. But then again, it's quite possible that these cottages will keep you so entertained that you'll never step outside your door.

Facilities: There are 10 one-bedroom cottages that can accommodate two people. None of the cottages have kitchens, but they do have whirlpool tubs, fireplaces, televisions and VCRs, coffeemakers, microwaves, and small refrigerators.

Bedding: Linens and towels are provided.

Reservations and rates: Reservations are recommended. Fees are $119 to $299 per night; holiday rates are higher. A two-night minimum stay is required on weekends. Pets are not permitted.

Directions: From I-10 at Redlands, drive north on Highway 30 for five miles to the Highway 330 exit. Drive north on Highway 330 for 13 miles to Running Springs. Turn east on Highway 18 and drive 14 miles to the Highway 38 fork at Big Bear Lake. Stay right on Highway 18/Big Bear Boulevard and continue five miles, past the village of Big Bear Lake, to Main Street. Turn right and drive a quarter mile; Castlewood is on the left.

Contact: Castlewood Theme Cottages, 547 Main Street, P.O. Box 1756, Big Bear Lake, CA 92315; 909/866-2720; website: www.castlewoodcottages.com.

OTHER CABINS AND COTTAGES NEARBY

• Black Forest Lodge, 41121 Big Bear Boulevard, Big Bear Lake, CA 92315; 909/866-2166; website: www.blackforestlodge.com.

- Goldmine Resort, 42268 Moonridge Road, P.O. Box 198, Big Bear Lake, CA 92315; 800/641-2327; website: www.bigbear-goldmine-lodge.com.
- Log Cabin Resort Rentals, 39976 Big Bear Boulevard, Big Bear Lake, CA 92315; 909/866-8708 or 800/767-0205; website: www.logcabinresorts.com.

Castlewood Theme Cottages

17. OUR SECRET GARDEN MOUNTAIN RETREAT

Our Secret Garden is unlike any of the other cabin resorts in Big Bear. It's outside of town and away from the lake by about a mile. It's situated in a peaceful residential neighborhood, far from the weekend hustle and bustle of Big Bear. And its adorable white cabins are clustered around colorful summer gardens. Even their interiors reflect a garden theme—each one is focused around a different flower: roses, sunflowers, tulips, and lilacs.

Off Highway 18 in Big Bear

Luxury rating: 4

Recreation rating: 4

THIS CABIN RANKS . . .
Best for Winter Sports

The four cabins at Our Secret Garden are sized for two, with all of the standard amenities for romance: fireplaces, hot tubs, and comfortable robes. One cottage, Sunflower, has a fully equipped kitchen; the rest have refrigerators and microwaves.

Ski enthusiasts will enjoy the fact that Our Secret Garden is only minutes from the slopes of Snow Summit and Bear Mountain. With more than 120 inches of annual snowfall and extensive snowmaking systems, both ski resorts provide a multitude of skiing and snowboarding options. Combined, their two areas offer more than 20 chairlifts and 500 groomed acres. The owners of Our Secret Garden will show you their secret back way to get to the lifts.

Even though you are outside of town at Our Secret Garden, you are still close enough to walk to restaurants, shopping, and the lake. Pine Knot Landing is less than a half mile away, where you can rent boats and stock up on fishing supplies in summer. Big Bear is filled with trout, bass, and catfish, and anglers share the waters with sailboats, personal watercrafts, and water-skiers.

Facilities: There are four one-bedroom cabins that can accommodate two people. All have a fireplace and hot tub. One cabin has a fully equipped kitchen.

Bedding: Linens and towels are provided.

Reservations and rates: Reservations are recommended. Fees are $109 to $169 per night. Pets are not permitted.

Directions: From I-10 at Redlands, drive north on Highway 30 for five miles to the Highway 330 exit. Drive north on Highway 330 for 13 miles to Running Springs. Turn east on Highway 18 and drive 14 miles to the Highway 38 fork at Big Bear Lake. Stay right on Highway 18/Big Bear Boulevard and continue three miles to the village of Big Bear Lake. Bear right on Village Drive, then stay on Village Drive as it curves around and changes names to Pennsylvania Drive. Turn right on Marin Drive, then left on Berkley Lane.

Contact: Our Secret Garden Mountain Retreat, 784 Berkley Lane, Big Bear Lake, CA 92315; 909/866-0966; website: www.bigbearsecretgarden.com.

OTHER CABINS AND COTTAGES NEARBY

- Golden Bear Cottages, 39367 Big Bear Boulevard, Big Bear Lake, CA 92315; 909/866-2010 or 800/461-1023; website: www.goldenbear.net.

- Lakeview Forest Resort, 40715 Lakeview Drive, P.O. Box 1976, Big Bear Lake, CA 92315; 909/866-8686 or 800/211-1085; website: www.bigbearparadise.com.

Our Secret Garden Mountain Retreat

18. SEVEN OAKS MOUNTAIN CABINS

Everybody in Southern California knows about Big Bear Lake, and almost everybody in Southern California knows about the Falls Recreation Area, where Big Falls tumbles down the mountainside. But in between those two stellar destinations is a place that almost nobody knows about—Seven Oaks Mountain Cabins.

Seven Oaks Cabins are hidden, situated three miles off the main highway. You don't find them by accident. The resort has only six small, rustic cabins (you could barely squeeze in a family of five). They have fully equipped kitchens, but otherwise, they are bare bones: no phones or television sets, no fancy decor. There's nothing else on the stretch of road surrounding Seven Oaks, so if you want nightlife, you're going to have to make your own. Pack along the Yahtzee game.

Of course, who cares about nightlife when you have a complete array of national forest adventures to look forward to? The Santa Ana River runs right through Seven Oaks's grounds and provides excellent stream fishing prospects. The river is typically about 10 to 15 feet across and a foot deep—a perfect fishing creek. It is stocked with rainbow trout every other week in spring and summer. A few of the cabins overlook the river; make sure you request one of them.

*Off Highway 38 near
Angelus Oaks*

Luxury rating: 2

Recreation rating: 4

THIS CABIN RANKS . . .
Most Secluded

Those who love to fish can also head for little Jenks Lake, which is pretty year-round but especially scenic in early spring, when the surrounding mountains are snow-covered. The biggest peak you see is Mount San Gorgonio, the tallest mountain in Southern California at 11,490 feet. Jenks Lake isn't stocked until May each year, but it's worth visiting any time.

Be sure to check out the numerous hiking and mountain biking trails in the area. If you aren't up for the 14-mile round-trip to the top of Mount San Gorgonio on the Vivian Creek Trail, you can find plenty of shorter options nearby. Don't miss the Ponderosa Vista Nature Trail and the Whispering Pines Trail, which are conveniently located right across the highway from each other. You can walk both of them in just over an hour, while getting a good lesson in the natural and human history of the area.

If you're not feeling ambitious, you can always just hang out at the lodge at Seven Oaks. It's not the slightest bit fancy, but it's the kind of place where you can play pool or Ping Pong and exchange a few stories with the lodge owners, who are really nice people.

Facilities: There are six one-bedroom cabins, all with fully equipped kitchens.

Bedding: Linens and towels are provided.

Reservations and rates: Reservations are recommended. The fee is $70 per night for two people, plus $5 for each additional person (up to five). Pets are permitted with a $5 fee per night.

Directions: From I-10 just west of Redlands, take the Highway 38 exit. Drive 25 miles on Highway 38 to Angelus Oaks, then continue six more miles to Glass Road. Turn left and drive three miles (keep to the left at all junctions). Seven Oaks is on the right side of the road.

Contact: Seven Oaks Mountain Cabins, 40700 Seven Oaks Road, Angelus Oaks, CA 92305; 909/794-1277.

Seven Oaks Mountain Cabins

19. THE LODGE AT ANGELUS OAKS

The cabins at The Lodge at Angelus Oaks are the embodiment of rustic and cozy. This is the kind of vacation place that makes you want to say goodbye to civilized life forever. For starters, they have a first-rate location on the Rim of the World Highway, halfway between Big Bear Lake and the Falls Recreation Area. Two of San Bernardino National Forest's premier recreation spots are within a few minutes' drive of your cabin, but you're not stuck in the middle of town with a whole bunch of tourists.

Off Highway 38 in Angelus Oaks

Luxury rating: 2

Recreation rating: 4

The possibilities for outdoor adventures are endless and change with each passing season. In winter, the snow usually falls thick and fast for at least a few weeks, which opens up possibilities for snow play. In spring, summer, and fall, hiking is spectacular in the national forest and San Gorgonio Wilderness. Trails range from very easy ones for families—like the half-mile walk to Big Falls, Southern California's largest year-round waterfall—to very difficult ones, like the 14-mile round-trip ascent of Mount San Gorgonio, Southern California's tallest peak at 11,490 feet.

Families can enjoy a fishing trip to nearby Jenks Lake, where they can stand on the shoreline and cast for stocked trout. Experienced anglers can drive down the Middle Control Road from Angelus Oaks to Forest Service Road 1N09. From there, they can access Bear Creek, a wild trout area on a tributary stream to the Santa Ana River. The limit is two fish, with a minimum length of eight inches. Only artificial lures or flies with barbless hooks can be used in Bear Creek.

However you decide to spend your days, you'll end each one by returning home to your Angelus Oaks cabin. The cabins are minimalist and the paint's peeling, but hey, this is the mountains. You can make dinner in your cabin's kitchen, or barbecue outside, or head for the restaurant a mile down the road. Evenings can be spent in the main lodge, playing pool or listening to somebody play the lodge organ, or looking through the telescope at the stars. I found the main lodge to be so cozy—like an old Canadian hunting lodge right out of a movie set—that I spent almost every evening there, playing board games in front of the fire.

Facilities: There are eight cabins that can accommodate up to six people. All cabins have fully equipped kitchens. The lodge has a fireplace and a pool table.

Bedding: Linens and towels are provided.

Reservations and rates: Reservations are recommended. Fees range from $55 to $90 per night. Pets are permitted with prior approval and a $5 fee per night.

Directions: From I-10 just west of Redlands, take the Highway 38 exit. Drive 25 miles on Highway 38 to Angelus Oaks. The Lodge at Angelus Oaks is on the right side of the road.

Contact: The Lodge at Angelus Oaks, 37825 Highway 38, Angelus Oaks, CA 92305; 909/794-9523; website: www.angelusoakslodge.com.

The Lodge at Angelus Oaks

20. WHISPERING PINES

Whispering Pines is a set of cheerful red cabins located right off Highway 38, the Rim of the World Scenic Byway. It's in the town of Angelus Oaks at 6,000 feet in elevation—the first town you reach when driving into the mountains from the Los Angeles basin.

© ANN MARIE BROWN

Off Highway 38 in Angelus Oaks

Luxury rating: 3

Recreation rating: 4

The five cabins at Whispering Pines can be configured according to how large your party is. Four of them are duplexes with interior doors that open to become single units (the fifth unit is always a single.) If you are traveling with your family, you'll be all set here, and you'll be able to close the doors when your kids stay up giggling all night.

As this book goes to press, Whispering Pines is undergoing a management change. Claire Maxwell, a lovely woman who has run the resort single-handedly for many years, is retiring and moving back downhill to the lowlands. Claire will be sorely missed in the small town of Angelus Oaks, but it will be exciting to see what the new owners have in store for Whispering Pines.

Two things will certainly stay the same: The wonderful pine trees surrounding the cabins and the marauding bears, who patrol the area at night searching for untethered garbage cans. Another element that will not change is Whispering Pines's wonderful location, a few miles from the Big Falls Recreation Area and San Gorgonio Wilderness. Hikers have their pick of trails; first on my list is a visit to Big Falls, Southern California's largest year-round waterfall at more than 500 feet. (It's most impressive in springtime, shortly after a snowmelt.)

In winter, you can bring your sleds and snowman-making supplies to the snow-play areas around Angelus Oaks or Big Falls, then let loose. In mid-summer, the Big Falls area is excellent for blackberry picking. Fill up your berry baskets, and then go bake a pie in your Whispering Pines kitchen.

Right off Highway 38, the South Fork, Forsee Creek, and Aspen Grove trailheads (all near Jenks Lake) head into the San Gorgonio Wilderness. In summer or autumn, be sure to walk at least the first section of the Aspen Grove Trail, which leads to one of a very few aspen groves found this far south in California. The drive to the trailhead alone is worth the trip; it provides fabulous views of the surrounding mountains and valleys.

Facilities: There are five cabins that can accommodate up to six people. Some cabins have fully equipped kitchens.
Bedding: Linens and towels are provided.

Reservations and rates: Reservations are recommended. Fees range from $50 to $100 per night. Pets are not permitted.

Directions: From I-10 just west of Redlands, take the Highway 38 exit. Drive 25 miles on Highway 38 to Angelus Oaks. Turn right at the fire station sign; Whispering Pines is a few yards off Highway 38. If you reach the Lodge at Angelus Oaks, you've passed it.

Contact: Whispering Pines, P.O. Box 237, 5850 Manzanita Avenue, Highway 38, Angelus Oaks, CA 92305; 909/794-9644.

Whispering Pines

21. CATALINA CABINS AT TWO HARBORS

If you study the ways of Southern California vacationers, you find that in the winter months, most people head to the mountains to ski. The others stay home. This is a puzzling phenomenon, since the finest days at the Southern California coast often occur in winter, creating perfect vacation conditions. Nonetheless, from October to March, long stretches of Southern California sand do not have a single human footprint on them.

Two Harbors, Catalina Island

Luxury rating: 2

Recreation rating: 4

THIS CABIN RANKS . . .
Best Value

If the beaches seem empty along the mainland in winter, you should see what it's like at Two Harbors on Catalina Island. Although Catalina's big city of Avalon still attracts winter visitors, Two Harbors becomes ghostly quiet. It's so quiet that the mobile home–style cottages in town, which serve as summer housing for Two Harbors employees, are left vacant for the winter. The cottages are then made available for rent to anybody who wants an inexpensive vacation.

Inexpensive? How about 25 bucks per night for two people during the week, and 40 bucks per night on the weekends? Keep in mind that the cottages are only available from October to April. Also, don't come with high expectations. The "cottages" are trailer homes, stuck in the middle of town next to the tennis courts and children's playground.

Each cottage is just large enough for two people; you have your choice of bunk beds or a double bed. You will have a heater and refrigerator. Just outside the cottages is a communal kitchen area with picnic tables, barbecues, gas burners, and even a microwave. You can bring groceries from the mainland, then supplement your stock with supplies from the

Two Harbors General Store, located a short walk away. Make sure you bring your own cooking and eating utensils, as well as bedding and towels. None of these items are provided. You won't have your own bathroom, either, but restrooms, showers, and laundry facilities are located nearby.

You'll also be on your own for planning outdoor activities. The bike, kayak, and scuba rental concessionaires disappear for the winter, so you must bring your own equipment from the mainland.

Of course, many visitors need only their hiking boots, because excellent trails lead from Two Harbors. A terrific easy walk (only a half mile long) heads across the narrowest part of the island to Catalina Harbor. At the harbor's southwest edge, you'll spot a single bench on a hillside knoll that is perfectly placed for sunset-watching.

Longer hikes are possible along the island's dirt roads to Cherry Cove and Parson's Landing. If you are lucky enough to time your trip for late winter or early spring, you'll see Cherry Cove's native Catalina cherry trees blooming bright white, as well as acres of prickly pear cactus flowering across the island.

Facilities: There are 18 mobile home–style housekeeping cabins; each accommodates two people. Communal kitchen facilities are available outside the cabins; refrigerators are provided inside the cabins. Restrooms and showers are located nearby.

Bedding: Linens and towels are not provided; bring your own.

Reservations and rates: Reservations are required. Fees range from $25 per night on weekdays to $40 per night on weekends. Pets are not permitted.

Directions: Catalina Express provides year-round ferry transportation to Two Harbors from San Pedro. Advance reservations are recommended. Phone Catalina Express at 310/519-1212 or 800/618-5533.

Contact: Santa Catalina Island Company, P.O. Box 737, Avalon, CA 90704; 310/510-1550; website: www.scico.com.

Catalina Cabins at Two Harbors

22. LA PALOMA COTTAGES

The island of Catalina has two faces: the subdued, rustic profile of Two Harbors on the north side of the island, and the bustling, metropolitan profile of Avalon on the south side. If outdoor adventure is your thing, you'll find it in both places. But if you want your adventure combined with a few good restaurants and some nightlife, Avalon is the place to go.

Avalon is the city on Catalina that never sleeps. While Two Harbors has a busy season (summer) and a dead season (winter), Avalon stays busy year-round. Even on weekdays, it's surprising how many people are touring the streets, shops, and businesses in Avalon's downtown, and signing up for a whole variety of commercial tours and outdoor adventures. At Avalon, everything is for rent or for sale; you don't even need to bring gear with you. The long list of recreation possibilities includes snorkeling, scuba diving, sport fishing, kayaking, horseback riding, swimming, hiking, and ocean

© ANN MARIE BROWN

Avalon, Catalina Island

Luxury rating: 3

Recreation rating: 5

THIS CABIN RANKS . . .
Best for Beach Activities

rafting. All you have to do is get on a ferry in Los Angeles and show up at the Avalon pier.

La Paloma Cottages is one of the few establishments in Avalon that offers cottage-style accommodations. La Paloma is located on Sunny Lane, a side street a few blocks from the busy downtown area. Although it has lovely outdoor flower-box gardens, iron balconies, and brick walkways, the interiors of the cottages are unremarkable. But hey, they're clean and affordable, so who's complaining?

This is Avalon, so your accommodations are urban in style and ambience. The cottages are packed in, one right next to the other, much like motel rooms. They do not have ocean views, although some of La Paloma's apartment units do have views. All the basic necessities are provided in the cottages, and some have fully equipped kitchens. Best of all, La Paloma prides itself on being diver-friendly. Translation: They don't mind if you leave a trail of sand in your cottage.

Facilities: There are eight cottages and seven apartment-style units that can accommodate two to six people. Some have fully equipped kitchens.

Bedding: Linens and towels are provided.

Reservations and rates: Reservations are recommended. Fees range from $69 to $149 per night. Pets are not permitted.

Directions: Several companies provide ferry transportation to Avalon from San Pedro, Long Beach, Redondo Beach, and Newport Beach. Advance reservations are recommended. Phone Catalina Express at 310/519-1212 or 800/618-5533, Catalina Explorer at 877/432-6276, or Catalina Passenger Service at 949/673-5245 or 800/830-7744.

Contact: La Paloma Cottages, P.O. Box 1505, Avalon, CA 90704; 310/510-1505 or 800/310-1505; website: www.catalina.com/lapaloma.html.

OTHER CABINS AND COTTAGES NEARBY

• Catalina Cottages and Hermosa Hotel, P.O. Box 646, 131 Metropole Street, Avalon, CA 90704; 310/510-1010 or 877/453-1313; website: www.catalina.com/hermosa.

La Paloma Cottages

23. DOCKSIDE BOAT AND BED

You've stayed at bed-and-breakfasts; well, this is a boat-and-breakfast. For people who want to indulge in the fantasy of owning their own yacht, it doesn't get any better than this.

© JULIE SHEER

Off I-710 in Long Beach

Luxury rating: 3

Recreation rating: 3

Dockside Boat and Bed offers three boats for nightly rentals in Long Beach's Rainbow Harbor. Take your pick from a 53-foot authentic Chinese junk, a 44-foot Pacemaker motor yacht, or a 50-foot Hawaiian sailboat. Now don't get carried away: You don't get to sail any of them, you just get to sleep on them.

Mei Wen Ti, the Chinese junk, is Dockside's showpiece accommodation. It is the roomiest of the boats and loaded with character. Built in China in 1990 and displaying a hand-painted exterior, it is purported to be the only authentic Chinese junk on the West Coast. There's enough room on deck for eight people to hang around and eat egg rolls, or have drinks and watch the sun set. Down below is a cozy master stateroom (that's a bedroom for you landlubbers) with a queen bed. (Although the deck provides enough room for up to eight people, a maximum of four are permitted overnight.) The galley (right, that's the kitchen) seats four and has a refrigerator, microwave, coffeemaker, and toaster. The boat features Asian touches throughout.

Bit O' Whimsy, the motor yacht, features crisp navy and white lines and elegant wood detailing in its cabin. The first stateroom has two twin bunks and the master stateroom has a queen size bed.

Alihilani, the Hawaiian sailboat, is the most rustic of the three yachts. It looks like it has seen some weather at sea, but is still comfortable and cozy, with three tiny staterooms and two tiny bathrooms.

The boats are moored at Rainbow Harbor, which is next to the Aquarium of the Pacific and the shops of Shoreline Village. The *Queen Mary* is directly across the water. The most coveted rental nights at Dockside are summer Saturdays, when boat-and-bed guests have the best seat in the house for the weekly fireworks display alongside the *Queen Mary*. The Fourth of July show is supposed to be out of this world.

After smelling the salt air, listening to the gentle lapping of the waves, and being lulled to sleep by the rocking of your boat, what else do you do at Dockside Boat and Bed? There's always personal watercraft riding, sea kayaking, whale-watching trips, sport fishing, tours of the *Queen Mary* and the Aquarium of the Pacific, and miles of beachfront boardwalks and trails for walking, running, inline skating, and bicycling (bikes are available for rent). Pretty much anything you want to do is available at Rainbow Harbor; take your pick.

Facilities: There are three rental yachts that can accommodate up to four people. All have small galleys with a microwave, refrigerator, toaster, and coffeemaker.

Bedding: Linens and towels are provided.

Reservations and rates: Reservations are required. Fees are $175 to $240 per night for two people (including taxes). A continental breakfast is included. Pets are not permitted.

Directions: From Los Angeles, take I-710 south to where it ends at Shoreline Drive in Long Beach. Keep heading south on Shoreline Drive, then turn west (right) on Pine Avenue. Park at the turnaround parking circle by the pier (temporary parking) and walk to Dock 5, the first dock on the right. Dockside's office is on a houseboat.

Contact: Dockside Boat and Bed, Rainbow Harbor, Gate 5, (mail to 316 East Shoreline Drive) Long Beach, CA 90802; 562/436-3111; website: www.boatandbed.com.

OTHER CABINS AND COTTAGES NEARBY

- Seal Beach Inn and Gardens, 212 5th Street, Seal Beach, CA 90740-6115; 562/493-2416 or 800/HIDEAWAY; website: www.sealbeachinn.com.

- Lord Mayor's B&B Inn, 435 Cedar Avenue, Long Beach, CA 90802; 562/436-0324; website: www.lordmayors.com.

Dockside Boat and Bed

24. BOAT AND BREAKFAST NEWPORT

If you've ever dreamed of living on a boat and going to sleep to the music of tinkling halyards on metal masts, your ship just came in. Boat and Breakfast Newport can make your dreams come true.

Boat and Breakfast rents out private boats—yachts, actually—for overnight stays. Each yacht comes equipped with a private bath, TV and VCR, and all linens and towels.

The yachts run the gamut, from the 37-foot *Serenade* at only $220 per night to the 65-foot *Victoria* at $375 per night. *Serenade* is just right for a romantic night for two, with its V-berth beds. *Victoria* can sleep up to seven people, and it is Coast Guard–certified for cruising with up to 49 passengers. The yacht is often rented for an afternoon or evening wedding (a two-hour bay cruise costs $700). Afterwards, the bride and groom spend the night on the boat.

Each rental yacht offers excellent water views, but some are moored closer to the shops and restaurants, while others are farther out in the

© ANN MARIE BROWN

Off Highway 55 in Newport Beach

Luxury rating: 3

Recreation rating: 3

harbor. Make sure you ask about the location of the boat you rent; you want to be in a first-rate spot for sunsets.

You're allowed to cook on board on only some of the yachts—the ones with electric ranges. For safety reasons, renters aren't permitted to use propane-fueled stoves. No matter; a continental breakfast is brought to your boat each morning. In addition, a restaurant in the marina will bring you dinner, room-service style, for a fee. Many people just pack along their own take-out dinner, plus a bag of groceries for snacks. Evening cocktails on the aft deck usually hold an important place in the itinerary, so don't forget your supplies.

There isn't much incentive to leave your yacht and head for dry land, but after your stay is over, you might take a stroll on the lovely sands of Newport Beach.

Facilities: There are eight rental yachts that can accommodate up to seven people. Some have fully equipped galleys.

Bedding: Linens and towels are provided.

Reservations and rates: Reservations are required. Fees range from $220 to $375 per night for two people; each additional person is $50 per night. A continental breakfast is included. Pets are not permitted.

Directions: From I-5 at Santa Ana, take Highway 55 south to Costa Mesa. Highway 55 becomes Newport Boulevard; follow it for two miles until it crosses the Pacific Coast Highway. Just beyond the Pacific Coast Highway, turn left on Via Lido. Drive about 100 yards, then turn left on Via Oporto. Boat and Breakfast Newport is located in Lido Marina Village at 3400 Via Oporto.

Contact: Boat and Breakfast Newport, 3400 Via Oporto, Suite 103, Newport Beach, CA 92663; 949/723-5552 or 800/262-8233; website: www.boatbed.com.

Boat and Breakfast Newport

25. CASA LAGUNA INN

Casa Laguna Inn offers a classic Southern California experience: red-tile roofs and Spanish architecture, towering palm trees punctuating views of the Pacific, and lush, flower-filled gardens with trickling, musical fountains. It is truly a getaway spot in one of Orange County's most vacation-minded cities, Laguna Beach.

If you're unfamiliar with the area, there's much to do. The main part of town, about a mile from Casa Laguna, is filled with myriad art galleries, up-

Off Highway 1 in Laguna Beach

Luxury rating: 5

Recreation rating: 3

scale clothing stores, surf shops, antique stores, and restaurants. Hikers and bikers head for Crystal Cove State Park, where 2,000 acres of wooded canyons and coastal hills wait to be explored. Park rangers conduct guided nature hikes in the winter, but it's easy enough to wander on your own.

If you want to go stick your toes in the sand, two beautiful beaches are a short walk from the inn: Victoria Beach (soft white sand) and Moss Point (good tidepools and rock formations). Mid-December to April is prime time for whale-watching; you might get lucky from the coast, or you can increase your chances by taking a whale-watching tour out of Dana Point.

Casa Laguna has 19 rooms and suites, plus a spectacular cottage that is set on the hillside, overlooking the swimming pool. It's a one-bedroom bungalow with a full kitchen, sitting room with fireplace, and large living/dining room with ocean views. Unusual features include a piano, stained glass windows throughout, and beautiful Catalina tiles. The cottage's wraparound deck is its showpiece, offering expansive blue-water Pacific views. Not surprisingly, the cottage is often rented for honeymoons.

Casa Laguna's suites offer an alternative for families or groups of four, although they are not freestanding units, so they aren't quite as private as the cottage. They come with separate bedrooms and a sofa-sleeper in the living room. Some have kitchens, fireplaces, and ocean views.

It's hard to guess how many gardeners must be employed at Casa Laguna. The grounds are a wealth of bougainvillea, queen palms, banana trees, ferns, and impatiens. Many nooks and crannies on the property provide spots to find your own private sanctuary, including four blossom-filled patios, a gazebo and potting shed located behind the cottage, and a classic California bell tower, with its staircase leading to an observation deck. Framing wide ocean views, the bell tower has "sunset" written all over it.

Guests at Casa Laguna enjoy a buffet breakfast served in the main house each morning (juice, coffee, bagels, eggs, fruit), plus wine, cheese, and hors d'oeuvres each evening. The food is ample and elegantly served.

Only one downside is apparent at Casa Laguna, and that's the steady hum of traffic from the Pacific Coast Highway. But with all the visual stimulation at this lovely inn, you'll soon tune it out and focus on your scenic surroundings.

Facilities: There is one one-bedroom cottage, plus 19 rooms and suites. The cottage and two suites (units 1 and 2) have fully equipped kitchens.

Bedding: Linens and towels are provided.

Reservations and rates: Reservations are required. The cottage fee is $295 per night for two people, including breakfast. The suites are $195 to $295 per night. There is a two-night minimum stay on weekends. Pets are permitted with prior approval and a $5 fee per night.

Directions: From I-405 in Irvine, take the Highway 133/Laguna Canyon Road exit. Turn west and drive eight miles to Pacific Coast Highway. Turn south and drive 1.5 miles to the resort on the left (east) side.

Contact: Casa Laguna Inn, 2510 South Coast Highway, Laguna Beach, CA 92651; 949/494-2996 or 800/233-0449; website: www.casalaguna.com.

Casa Laguna Inn

26. MANZANITA COTTAGES

Manzanita Cottages is the place to indulge your Hansel and Gretel fantasies, if you have any. It's also the place to get away from the hustle and bustle of downtown Laguna Beach, which can be quite overwhelming on summer weekends, while still having access to all the town offerings.

© JULIE SHEER

Off Highway 1 in Laguna Beach

Luxury rating: 4

Recreation rating: 3

THIS CABIN RANKS . . .
Best for Beach Activities

Tucked away in a secluded garden compound in a residential neighborhood of Laguna Beach, Manzanita Cottages features four small cottages and one studio apartment. All have been quaintly restored with tons of Old World charm. Think Solvang and you've got the picture: shingled roofs, brightly painted front doors, open-beamed ceilings, fireplaces, hardwood floors, and hand-painted tiles.

The cottages have weathered a few lives before their present incarnation. They were built in 1927 by Harry Greene, a film producer, who wanted a secluded compound where he could invite his Hollywood friends for overnight getaways. Legend has it that Joan Crawford was a frequent guest.

Owners came and went over the years, and by the time present owners Debbie and Todd Herzer bought the property, the place was in disrepair. With a desire to create the ambience of a 1930s vacation retreat, but with the added benefits of modern amenities, the Herzers went to work on renovations and opened Manzanita Cottages to the public in late 1999.

Although only about 500 square feet in size, each of the cottages is completely self-contained and fully stocked for housekeeping. They are decorated with tasteful furnishings and artwork, but their best feature is that each has a private patio accessed by French doors in the bedroom. The surrounding grounds are beautifully landscaped with fragrant flowers and vines.

If you can bring yourself to leave your adorable cottage, it's only a 10-minute walk to the Laguna village area, with its many shops, restaurants, and diversions. It's a 10-minute drive to the Festival Center on Laguna Canyon Road, where two hugely popular festivals take place each summer: the Sawdust Art Festival and Pageant of the Masters. Crystal Cove State Park is a few miles to the north on Highway 1 for hiking and biking activities. For something really special, check out Laguna Coast Wilderness Park, a 5,000-acre wildlife sanctuary, where naturalists conduct guided hikes and mountain bike rides. Entry to the park is by reservation only, except for certain days and times; phone ahead at 949/494-9352.

And of course, Laguna is renowned for its miles of sandy beaches. Main Beach, considered to be the center of beach life in Laguna, is a brief walk from the cottages.

Facilities: There are four cottages that can accommodate up to four people, plus a studio apartment that can accommodate two people. Each has a fully equipped kitchen.

Bedding: Linens and towels are provided.

Reservations and rates: Reservations are required. Fees are $180 to $250 per night depending on the season and length of stay. Rates are discounted for weekly and monthly stays. There is a one-week minimum stay in summer and two-night minimum stay in spring and fall. Pets are not permitted.

Directions: From I-405 in Irvine, take the Highway 133/Laguna Canyon Road exit. Turn west and drive eight miles to Pacific Coast Highway. Turn south and drive to Legion Street (the fourth traffic light). Turn left and drive to where Legion Street ends at Park Avenue. Turn right and drive one short block to Manzanita Drive; turn left on Manzanita. The cottages are the third property on the left.

Contact: Manzanita Cottages, 732 to 738 Manzanita Drive, Laguna Beach, CA 92651; 949/661-2533; website: www.manzanitacottages.com.

Manzanita Cottages

27. ZOSA RANCH & GARDENS

Zosa Gardens is an avocado ranch transformed. Set in the warm, dry hills between Temecula and Escondido, this 22-acre Spanish hacienda is a place where a couple or family can go for a secluded weekend, or a larger group can hold a small wedding or family reunion.

The grounds and gardens are the star of the show. Citrus and exotic fruit trees, palms, and 150 avocado trees dot the property. Oleander and bougainvillea bloom with profusion amid an elegant gazebo, koi pond, courtyard fountains, tennis courts, and swimming pool.

There are two main units on the property: a two-bedroom cottage and one guest house with four suites. The guest house is often rented as one unit

Off I-15 in Temecula

Luxury rating: 3

Recreation rating: 3

for a large group. A highlight is the bathroom in the master suite, which has a black, two-person whirlpool and a window overlooking the surrounding hills. The house has a huge patio with a whirlpool and fire pit.

The two-bedroom cottage is a charming little blue house with white shutters, fronted by a trickling fountain surrounded by flowers. The interior decor is country floral, with lots of wicker and bamboo. It is large enough for a small family or two couples to be comfortable. It, too, has its own whirlpool on the patio.

You can do your own cooking in the cottage or guest house, but you won't need to bother with breakfast. A generous meal is served each morning in the main ranch house—fruit, omelets, eggs Benedict, fresh-squeezed orange juice from the ranch's trees, and the like.

Zosa Gardens is set in a rural area, so if you're someone who needs something to do right outside your door, you won't be happy here. However, if you're willing to drive a few minutes, you can head for Temecula, which is loaded with wineries and has an Old West–style main street featuring antique shops and restaurants. Or, in a half hour you can be at the coast at Oceanside, where sport fishing, boating, surfing, and pier fishing are available. The San Diego Wild Animal Park is also a half-hour drive away.

Cycling is possible on many of the rural roads surrounding Zosa Gardens. Hikers shouldn't miss the chance to explore nearby Palomar Mountain State Park. In the state park, try the Lower Doane Valley and Weir Trail Loop (big conifers and grassy meadows) or the trail to the 1880s Scott's Cabin. Or, in neighboring Cleveland National Forest, take the trail from Observatory Campground to Palomar Observatory, home of the 200-inch Hale telescope.

Facilities: There is one two-bedroom cottage that can accommodate four people and a guest house with four suites that can accommodate eight people, all with fully equipped kitchens.

Bedding: Linens and towels are provided.

Reservations and rates: Reservations are required. Fees are $250 per night for the cottage, and $190 to $250 for each individual suite or $700 per night for the entire guest house. Rates include breakfast. Pets are not permitted.

Directions: From I-15 in Temecula, drive south for 12 miles to Route 76 (Pala Road). Turn right (west) and drive a short distance to old Highway 395. Turn left (south) and drive to West Lilac Road. Turn left and drive 1.5 miles to Lilac Walk. Turn right and Zosa Gardens is on the left.

Contact: Zosa Ranch & Gardens, 9381 West Lilac Road, Valley Center, CA 92026; 760/723-9093 or 800/711-8361; website: www.zosagardens.com.

Zosa Ranch & Gardens

28. KNOTTY PINE CABINS

The derivation of the name Idyllwild is simple: First, "idyll," as in "idyllic," suggests peace or contentment in a picturesque or rustic setting. Then "wild," as in, you can still find some wilderness there. Hooray for that.

Off Highway 243 in Idyllwild

Luxury rating: 3

Recreation rating: 3

Idyllwild is located at 5,500 feet in elevation, roughly west of Palm Springs and south of Banning, on the border of the San Jacinto Wilderness. The town is in the midst of San Bernardino National Forest, near 10,160-foot Newton B. Drury Peak and 10,804-foot San Jacinto Peak. It has plenty of splendid scenery, particularly big conifers and granite walls.

Because the Idyllwild area was never developed for downhill skiing, it doesn't get anywhere near the amount of winter traffic as Big Bear to the north, but it does good business with summer hikers. In fact, on summer holiday weekends it can be difficult to get a wilderness permit for some of the best trails in the area, including the spectacular Devils Slide Trail to the top of 8,828-foot Tahquitz Peak.

Make your trip easier by visiting during non-holiday periods and by reserving a stay at Knotty Pine Cabins. Tucked among tall pines and oaks, Knotty Pine is close enough to downtown Idyllwild so you can walk to shops and restaurants if you like. All cabins have fireplaces and porches; all except one have a kitchen. Barbecue grills are available.

While you're in Idyllwild, be sure to hike the Devils Slide Trail. The route is 8.4 miles round-trip and offers incredible views from the fire lookout tower on top of Tahquitz Peak. A slightly easier hike is possible on Deer Springs Trail to the overlook at Suicide Rock, providing good views of Tahquitz Peak and Idyllwild. Easiest of all is the Ernie Maxwell Scenic Trail, a good family walk through the pines and cedars. All of these trailheads are within a 15-minute drive of Knotty Pine Cabins.

For picnicking or fishing, take a drive over to pretty little Lake Fulmor on Highway 243, where you and your kids can cast a line in the water from shore. Or stop at the picnic area across the highway from Lake Fulmor at Fuller Mill Creek, where you can fish for stocked trout in springtime. Another option is to seek out the pretty waterfall on Fuller Mill Creek, just a few hundred feet from the highway on the east side.

Facilities: There are eight cabins ranging in size from studios to three bedrooms. All except one have fully equipped kitchens.

Bedding: Linens and towels are provided.

Reservations and rates: Reservations are recommended. Fees range from $57 to $130 per night. There is a two-night minimum on weekends. Pets are permitted in some cabins for a $10 fee.

Directions: From I-10 at Banning, take Highway 243 south and drive 27 winding miles to Idyllwild. Just before you reach the village, look for a sign on the left for Knotty Pine Cabins. Turn left and drive up the driveway.

Contact: Knotty Pine Cabins, 54340 Pine Crest, P.O. Box 477, Idyllwild, CA 92549; 909/659-2933.

OTHER CABINS AND COTTAGES NEARBY

• Woodland Park Manor, 55350 South Circle Drive, P.O. Box 86, Idyllwild, CA 92549; 909/659-2657; website: www.wood landparkmanor.com.

Knotty Pine Cabins

29. FERN VALLEY INN

It's so quiet at Fern Valley Inn in Idyllwild that you can hear the squirrels chewing on pine cones. No kidding. The inn is located away from the downtown area of Idyllwild, only a half mile from Humber Park and its trailheads. Quite simply, it couldn't be better situated for people who like quiet, and for people who like to hike.

The 11 cabins at Fern Valley are on the small side, but the management accommodates larger groups in one of their many rental vacation homes. If the most you need is a two-bedroom cabin, you can stay right at Fern Valley. The cabins are grouped around a heated outdoor swimming pool. All have fireplaces and queen beds; some have full kitchens. They are decorated with antiques and handmade quilts, and each has a patio or deck where you can sit outside and listen to the birds (or the squirrels chewing on pine cones). Some cabins are duplexes, so make sure you request a single unit if you want one.

Off Highway 243 in Idyllwild

Luxury rating: 4

Recreation rating: 4

While you're vacationing at this 5,300-foot mountain paradise, you might want to do some exploring. Fishing enthusiasts can head to tiny Lake Fulmor for shoreline fishing, or to Fuller Mill Creek for creek fishing. Horseback riding is available at stables nearby. And best of all is the proximity of trailheads at Humber Park, including the spectacular Devils Slide Trail to Tahquitz Peak (8.4 miles round-trip, wilderness permit required), and the easy but scenic Ernie Maxwell Trail (5.2 miles round-trip). The former leads to an operating fire lookout with a panoramic view of the San Jacinto and Santa Rosa Mountains. The latter offers some good views of Tahquitz Peak, especially on the way back.

If you want to hike someplace where you're more likely to be alone, drive out to Idyllwild's Dark Canyon Campground and try the Seven Pines Trail, which meets up with the North Fork of the San Jacinto River. Hike out and back as far as you like; any distance on this trail is satisfying.

Facilities: There are 11 single and duplex cabins, ranging in size from studios to two bedrooms. All have decks or patios. Some cabins have fully equipped kitchens. There is a heated pool on-site. A wide range of vacation homes are also available for rent.

Bedding: Linens and towels are provided.

Reservations and rates: Reservations are recommended. Fees are $80 to $125 per night for two people, plus $10 for each additional person. Pets are not permitted.

Directions: From I-10 at Banning, take Highway 243 south and drive 27 winding miles to Idyllwild. Drive through town, following Village Center to its end. Turn left on South Circle Drive. Drive a half mile and turn right on Fern Valley Road. Fern Valley Inn is on the right.

Contact: Fern Valley Inn, 25240 Fern Valley Road, P.O. Box 116, Idyllwild, CA 92549; 909/659-2205 or 800/659-7775; website: www.fernvalleyinn.com.

OTHER CABINS AND COTTAGES NEARBY

• Strawberry Creek Inn, 26370 Highway 243, Idyllwild, CA 92549; 909/659-3202 or 800/262-8969; website: www.straw berrycreekinn.com.

Fern Valley Inn

30. WILDER CABINS

If you like your mountain cabins with a little history attached, you'll like Wilder Cabins. In 1932, Ida and Sylvester Wilder built a summer home in Idyllwild. Since then, four generations of Wilders and their friends have vacationed at their homestead, and you can, too.

Wilder Cabins offers three one-room cabins for rent, and each one is tucked into the forest alongside Strawberry Creek. Squirrel's Inn has a view of the creek and a queen bed. Cozy Rest is the largest cabin, with a queen and twin bed; it can sleep three. Journey's End is the most enchanting cabin. To reach it, you cross a wooden bridge and walkway over the creek. It has one queen bed and a private porch. All of the cabins have

Off Highway 243 in Idyllwild

Luxury rating: 3

Recreation rating: 3

kitchen facilities; buy your groceries in downtown Idyllwild a quarter mile away, and you're all set.

True to their history, the cabins are summer cabins, which means they don't have heat or fireplaces. They are available for rent only from May through September. The property surrounding them consists of a secluded cedar and pine grove with picnicking and reading areas. Even though there is so much hiking and fishing to do in the Idyllwild area, it's tempting to spend your days just hanging out on the Wilder property, pondering what life was like in Ida and Sylvester's time.

Facilities: There are three one-room cabins that can accommodate up to three people. All cabins have fully equipped kitchens.

Bedding: Linens and towels are provided.

Reservations and rates: Reservations are recommended. Fees are $65 per night for two people. The resort is open from May through September. Pets are permitted.

Directions: From I-10 at Banning, take Highway 243 south and drive 27 winding miles to Idyllwild. Drive through town, following Village Center to its end. Turn left on South Circle Drive; Wilder Cabins is the second driveway on the left.

Contact: Wilder Cabins, 54550 South Circle Drive, P.O. Box 31, Idyllwild, CA 92549; 909/659-2926; website: www.wildercabins.com.

OTHER CABINS AND COTTAGES NEARBY

• The Quiet Creek Inn, 26345 Delano Drive, P.O. Box 240, Idyllwild, CA 92549; 909/659-6110 or 800/450-6110.

Wilder Cabins

CHAPTER 3

San Diego
and Vicinity

*S*an Diego is a sun-drenched region with 76 miles of beaches, two distinct mountain ranges—the Palomar and Laguna-Cuyamaca Mountains—and one giant-sized desert, Anza-Borrego. Blessed with a nearly perfect year-round climate and stunning natural beauty, San Diego has long been a favorite destination of vacationers from California and worldwide.

The huge county's landscape is so varied that it is best described by splitting it into parts. In few other places of the world can you swim in the ocean, hike to a 6,500-foot mountain peak, and admire the stillness of a desert palm grove, all in the same day.

Let's begin with the desert. Anza-Borrego Desert State Park encompasses 600,000 acres of palm groves, year-round creeks, slot canyons, and badlands. It is California's largest state park and more than three times the size of Zion National Park. Desert flora runs the gamut from the expected, like barrel cactus and mesquite, to the rare: stands of jumping cholla cactus and aptly named elephant trees. Majestic and endangered bighorn sheep are commonly seen from park roads and trails. Two accommodations in this chapter, La Casa del Zorro Desert Resort and Stagecoach Trails Resort, provide you the opportunity to stay within a few miles of the park's borders.

The Cuyamaca Mountains are mostly contained within Cuyamaca Rancho State Park, where 110 miles of trails await hikers. The 4,000- to 6,500-foot elevations in the park host mixed forests of ponderosa and Jeffrey pine, fir, incense cedar, and live and black oak. Cuyamaca Peak, San Diego County's second highest peak at 6,512 feet, is found in this state park, plus seven rustic cabins in two of the park's campgrounds. Lake Cuyamaca, just outside of the park borders, is a popular spot for trout and bass fishing.

Alongside the Cuyamacas are the Lagunas, which are managed as part of Cleveland National Forest. With a dramatic setting that overlooks the desert thousands of feet below, the Lagunas are easily explored on foot, bike, or horseback. Several times each winter, they are covered in snow. Two mountain resorts, Blue Jay Lodge and Laguna Mountain Lodge, offer cabin rentals near the summit of Mount Laguna.

Near the Laguna-Cuyamaca Mountains lies one of San Diego County's most interesting country towns—Julian, the apple capital of Southern California. Each year in autumn, the town comes alive with apple festivals and events. Several local bakeries make pies year-round, as well as other apple delicacies. In addition to its gastronomic delights, the town of Julian is centrally located for exploring surrounding parklands, including William Heise County Park and Cleveland National Forest, whether by bike or on foot. A number of cabin accommodations are available in or near Julian.

The Palomar Mountains' most notable feature is the Palomar Observatory, home of the 200-inch Hale telescope, which for many years was the world's largest. The entire mountain range extends only 25 miles along the northern border of San Diego County, but what it lacks in size it makes up for in beauty. Its 6,000-foot elevation gives rise to dense stands of fir, cedar, spruce, and black oak. Most of the land in the Palomar Mountains is part of Palomar Mountain State Park or Cleveland National Forest. The easiest way to explore this area is by staying at Lake Henshaw Resort; in addition to its proximity to Palomar Mountain, the resort is right across the road from great fishing at Lake Henshaw.

Two excellent city parks are also located in San Diego: Balboa Park, with its museums, galleries, theaters, restaurants, and the world-famous San Diego Zoo; and 5,000-acre Mission Bay Park, with its labyrinth of bikeways, swimming beaches, lawns, and boating and fishing charters. Sailing, waterskiing, and windsurfing are popular, as well as visiting Sea World, one of the world's largest oceanariums. Several cottage resorts are located in or near downtown San Diego.

Last but never least are the 76 miles of San Diego beaches. They require no introduction, only a reminder to pack along your sunscreen and a few extra towels. The pages that follow contain several lodgings from which you can gaze at (or walk to) the ocean.

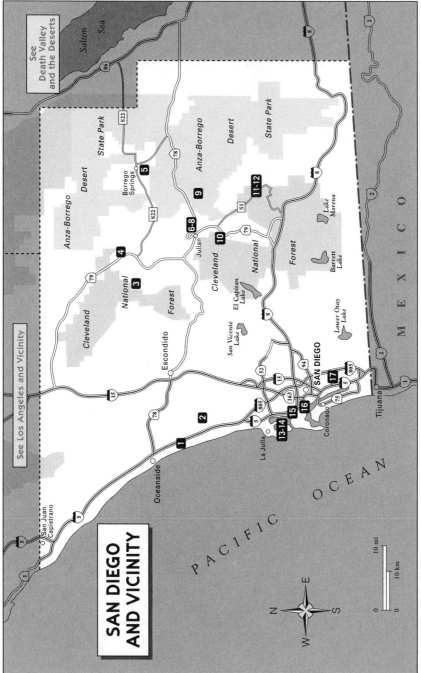

CHAPTER 3
SAN DIEGO AND VICINITY

1. ADVENTURE IN CAMPING TRAVEL TRAILERS

Have you ever camped in a tent on a cold, rainy night? You put up your rain fly, adjust your ground tarp, snuggle in with your mate, and hope it doesn't last long. Sleepless hours crawl by while you are possessed by the nagging fear that water is seeping in through the tent seams.

Off I-5 at San Diego Coast State Beaches

Luxury rating: 2

Recreation rating: 4

When the sun comes out in the morning, do you ever wonder if those people in RVs and travel trailers are just a hair smarter than you? Parked next door in the campground, they cheerfully cook breakfast over a hot fire while you yawn and dry out your socks.

Purchasing a travel trailer may seem too far-fetched or high-priced, but renting one for your next vacation isn't. A company called Adventure in Camping takes care of the details; you reserve your choice of trailer models, then decide where you want to camp along the San Diego coastline.

Your options include the following state beaches: South Carlsbad, Mission Bay, San Elijo, and San Onofre. Of these, South Carlsbad and San Elijo are the most popular. At both blufftop campgrounds, the beach is easily accessed by a series of wooden stairways. In addition to the usual activities like surf fishing, swimming, beach walking, and surfing, campers can go snorkeling or diving at an offshore reef.

Because the campgrounds are set on a bluff about 50 feet above the ocean, you won't have much trouble finding a good place to watch the sun set. Half the campsites overlook the water; don't even consider the rest, which face the road or train tracks.

Adventure in Camping delivers your trailer to your chosen campsite, levels the trailer, and sets it up for use. When you arrive, the kitchen appliances work, the water runs, and the toilets flush. At the end of your stay, you drive off in your own car, and Adventure in Camping picks up the trailer.

If you want serious luxury, you can rent a trailer with all the options, like a television and VCR, microwave oven, and generator. But even the basic model comes with a full bath and kitchen, including all cooking and eating utensils, plus battery-run lights, hot and cold running water, and forced air heat. The only thing that isn't provided is linens; bring your own towels and sleeping bags.

Facilities: The rental trailers range from 18 to 27 feet long, in a variety of floor plans that sleep three to seven people.

Bedding: Linens and towels are not provided; bring your own.

Reservations and rates: Reservations are required. Fees range from $190 to $227 for two nights. A $100 cleaning and damage deposit is required. Pets are permitted with a $10 fee.

Directions: For San Elijo State Beach: From San Diego, drive north on I-5 for 25 miles and take the Lomas Santa Fe exit. Turn west and follow Lomas Santa Fe until you reach the Pacific Coast Highway. Turn north on Pacific Coast Highway and drive 2.5 miles to San Elijo State Beach, near Chesterfield Drive.

For South Carlsbad State Beach: From San Diego, drive north on I-5 for 30 miles and take the Poinsettia exit. Turn west and follow Poinsettia to the park entrance.

Contact: Adventure in Camping, P.O. Box 100, PMB 311, Mammoth Lakes, CA 93546; 858/452-6594 or 800/417-7771; website: www.adventurein camping.com.

Adventure in Camping Travel Trailers

2. THE INN AT RANCHO SANTA FE

Built in 1923, The Inn at Rancho Santa Fe has been run by the same family for three generations. Although all of its low-slung, Spanish-style accommodations edged by wide green lawns are appealing, its freestanding

© ANN MARIE BROWN

Off Highway S-6 in Rancho Santa Fe

Luxury rating: 4

Recreation rating: 3

adobe cottages are something special. Each is beautifully decorated in a traditional, understated style and ideally suited for a relaxing getaway.

The inn is located in one of San Diego's wealthiest neighborhoods, and it attracts a fairly upscale crowd. Because the cottages are separate from the main inn, you can choose to socialize or not, depending on what you want out of your vacation. While many guests come here to play tennis or golf on the premises, others simply use Rancho Santa Fe as a base for exploring the area's attractions, including San Diego's marvelous Wild Animal Park, 20 miles east. Cyclists can take to the country roads around Rancho Santa Fe, and hikers and joggers will find more than 20 miles of trails strung throughout the area. Mountain bikers and hikers can also head for Los Penasquitos Canyon Preserve, 12 miles to the south.

If you want to spend some time at the ocean, the inn has a lovely beach cottage eight miles away in Del Mar. Day use of the cottage is included in your stay; it has easy access to the sand and surf, plus dressing rooms, showers, and a private patio.

The intimate one- and two-bedroom cottages at The Inn at Rancho Santa Fe have two baths, a living room with fireplace, a patio, and a full kitchen. The three-bedroom cottages have the same features, plus three full baths. If you don't want to cook on your vacation, the inn has two restaurants: The Library and the Garden Room.

Facilities: There are eight cottages ranging in size from one to three bedrooms. All have fully equipped kitchens. Guest rooms and suites are also available. Two restaurants, tennis courts, and a golf course are on-site.

Bedding: Linens and towels are provided.

Reservations and rates: Reservations are required. Fees are $340 to $660 per night. Pets are not permitted.

Directions: From San Diego, take I-5 north for 20 miles to the Lomas Santa Fe Drive (Highway S-8) exit. Turn east and drive 4.5 miles to the inn on the right.

Contact: The Inn at Rancho Santa Fe, P.O. Box 869, Rancho Santa Fe, CA 92067; 858/756-1131 or 800/843-4661.

The Inn at Rancho Santa Fe

3. LAKE HENSHAW RESORT

"Take a boy fishing. Take a girl fishing, too." That's what the sign says at Lake Henshaw Resort, and it sums up the spirit of the place. Lake Henshaw is no Lake Tahoe in terms of natural beauty, but it's a great place to catch catfish or bass, then cook them up for dinner in a comfortable hillside cabin.

Lake Henshaw is located near the charming country hamlet of Santa Ysabel, just a few miles from the border of Cleveland National Forest and Palomar Mountain State Park. At 2,727 feet in elevation, the lake looks much like a wide, shallow, flooded meadow, complete with cows lining the edges. It boasts nearly 25 miles of shoreline.

The cabins at Lake Henshaw Resort are across the road from the lake. They come in a variety of sizes and configurations and are spaced far enough apart to prevent you from breathing down your neighbor's neck. Be sure to ask for one of the upper hillside cabins, which are farthest from the road. Each cabin has a full kitchen, complete with cooking and eating utensils. A sign inside states: "Please do not clean fish or game in the cottage. Facilities for this are provided in the campground." Fair enough.

Because Henshaw is a private lake, a $5 per person lake-use fee is charged, whether you bring your own boat or rent one from the resort. (Children under 13 are free.) A five-mile-per-hour speed limit is enforced

© ANN MARIE BROWN

Off Highway 76 near Santa Ysabel

Luxury rating: 3

Recreation rating: 4

on the water, and no canoes, rafts, or boats less than 10 feet long are allowed. (Swimming is not permitted in Lake Henshaw.)

The resort's small store can keep you supplied with all the fishing advice and tackle you want, plus snacks and drinks. A café offers basic fare; a frequent dinner special is All You Can Eat Catfish. For more elaborate shopping or restaurants, the town of Santa Ysabel is a mere 10 miles away, and the larger town of Julian is another seven miles beyond that.

If the fish aren't biting, many other activities are possible near Lake Henshaw, including hiking on 6,140-foot Palomar Mountain. The conifers on the mountain are big and beautiful, reminiscent of the southern Sierra. Go see the famous Palomar Observatory and its Hale telescope, or the Santa Ysabel Mission. On warm days, pay a visit to the San Luis Rey River day-use area, a couple of miles down Highway 76, for swimming, inner tubing, and picnicking.

Facilities: There are 18 cabins ranging in size from studios to two bedrooms. All have fully equipped kitchens. A private campground with RV and tent sites is also available. A small grocery store and café are on-site.

Bedding: Linens and towels are provided.

Reservations and rates: Reservations are recommended. Fees range from $45 to $70 per night. Pets are permitted with prior approval.

Directions: From Escondido on I-15, take Highway 78 east for 32 miles to Santa Ysabel. Turn left (north) on Highway 79 and drive seven miles, then turn left on Highway 76 and drive four miles to Lake Henshaw Resort on the left.

Contact: Lake Henshaw Resort, 26439 Highway 76, Santa Ysabel, CA 92070; 760/782-3487 or 760/782-3501; website: www.lakehenshawca.com.

Lake Henshaw Resort

4. WARNER SPRINGS RANCH

Most San Diegans know Warner Springs Ranch as a private golf and tennis resort in the far north region of the county. The ranch is immense—2,500 acres—and filled with history: It was founded as a trading post in 1844 by John Warner, who recognized the benefits of its natural hot springs.

If you aren't a member of the private resort, the easiest way to take part in a vacation here is to sign up for a spa package. The package provides lodging in one of the ranch's bungalows, three meals a day, and a spa treatment, such as a one-hour massage. The rest of the ranch's amenities are then yours for the taking, although you must pay extra to play golf or go for a horseback ride.

Off Highway 79 in Warner Springs

Luxury rating: 4

Recreation rating: 4

Many guests simply hang around Warner Springs' three huge pools, which offer both hot mineral water and ordinary pool water. If you want to do something more active, horseback riding is as popular as golf and tennis; the ranch offers guided rides daily on its miles of trails. For guests with children, the list of activities is long: arts and crafts, pony rides, beginner horseback riding, junior tennis clinic, and so on.

However you arrange your vacation package, you'll stay in the resort's lovely bungalows, which are classic, old California–style with rustic pine interiors and red tile roofs. Many cottages have fireplaces; about half are air-conditioned. All are blissfully free of telephones and televisions.

If you want to ignore all the organized activities and go for a solitary hike, you're in the perfect spot for bagging the summit of Hot Springs Mountain, elevation 6,533 feet, the highest peak in San Diego County. For a much easier hike, the trail into Love Valley in Cleveland National Forest is a short drive away (three miles up Highway S-7 on the west side of Lake Henshaw). Additionally, the Pacific Crest Trail crosses through Warner Springs, and Anza-Borrego Desert State Park is only a half hour away.

Facilities: There are 240 cottages ranging in size from one to three bedrooms; none have kitchens. A general store and restaurant are on-site.

Bedding: Linens and towels are provided.

Reservations and rates: Reservations are recommended. Fees are $150 to $300 per night for two people. Package fees include three meals a day and spa services. Pets are not permitted.

Directions: From San Diego, drive north on I-15 for 15 miles and take the Scripps Poway Parkway exit. Turn east and drive 10 miles to Highway 67, then turn north (left). Follow Highway 67 through Ramona to Santa Ysabel, then turn north (left) on Highway 79. Drive 15 miles to Warner Springs Ranch.

Contact: Warner Springs Ranch, 31652 Highway 79, P.O. Box 399, Warner Springs, CA 92086; 760/782-4200 or 760/782-4255; website: www.ranchspa.com.

Warner Springs Ranch

5. LA CASA DEL ZORRO DESERT RESORT

La Casa del Zorro is the most luxurious place in or near Anza-Borrego Desert. It may seem extravagant to rent a cottage with terry bathrobes, two TV sets, a morning newspaper at the front door, and bath towels folded into fancy shapes like dinner napkins. But if you're going to spend some time adventuring in the desert, you might as well have a comfortable home base. Why rough it 24 hours a day?

Off Highway S-3 near Borrego Springs

Luxury rating: 5

Recreation rating: 3

THIS CABIN RANKS . . .
Best in the Desert

The cottages at La Casa del Zorro are the antithesis of roughing it. Each detached one- to four-bedroom casita comes with a long list of luxuries. Even the one-bedroom casita is generously oversized, with a large separate bedroom, a bathroom and dressing area, combination living/dining room, and a kitchenette tucked into a corner. The four-bedroom casitas have a sizable amount of property around them, plus their own swimming pools. All have kitchenettes (microwave oven, small refrigerator, coffeemaker, and a basic set of dishes and silverware). Some casitas have an outdoor spa; others have fireplaces for those chilly desert nights. The casitas are ideal for families with young children, since parents can keep an eye on their kids, but everybody has their own space.

If the kitchenettes don't match up to your culinary needs, you can rent a barbecue grill from the front desk and cook on your casita's patio, or have your meals in one of La Casa del Zorro's restaurants. The main restaurant is formal (jackets required), but the next-door lounge and pub serves a full menu of food in a casual atmosphere. (They didn't even blink at my dirty hiking boots and sweatshirt.) The food at both locations, best described as California cuisine, is first-rate. Try the kit fox salad with dates and butter lettuce or the lobster medallions.

Many guests at La Casa del Zorro never leave the resort grounds. After all, La Casa has three swimming pools and hot tubs, six lighted tennis courts, a fitness room, aerobics classes . . . you get the idea. But if "civilized" recreation doesn't interest you, head for nearby Anza-Borrego Desert State Park. Within a 20-minute drive, you can access several trailheads, including the one for Borrego Palm Canyon near the park's excellent visitor center. The trail leads to a grove of more than 800 native palm trees and a boulder-lined waterfall. Bighorn sheep are often spotted on the high canyon walls.

Facilities: There are 19 casitas ranging in size from one to four bedrooms, all with kitchenettes. Some include an outdoor pool or spa and fireplace. Resort rooms are also available. A restaurant, three swimming pools, hot tubs, tennis courts, and fitness center are on-site.

Bedding: Linens and towels are provided.

Reservations and rates: Reservations are recommended. Fees range from $175 to $1,025 per night, depending on season and size of accommodations. Pets are not permitted.

Directions: From Julian, drive east on Highway 78 for 19 miles to Highway S-3/ Yaqui Pass Road. Turn left (north) on Highway S-3 and drive six miles to La Casa del Zorro Desert Resort, on the right side of the road.

Contact: La Casa del Zorro Desert Resort, 3845 Yaqui Pass Road, Borrego Springs, CA 92004-5000; 760/767-5323 or 800/824-1884; website: www.lacasadelzorro.com.

La Casa del Zorro Desert Resort

6. JULIAN BED AND BREAKFAST GUILD

The biggest event in the charming mountain town of Julian is apple season from September to November, when the primary activity of locals and tourists alike is visiting bakeries and taste-testing apple pies. But if mountain biking, horseback riding, fishing, and hiking interest you as much as baked goods, you're in luck. Julian is the place for all these things.

© ANN MARIE BROWN

Off Highway 79 in Julian

Luxury rating: 4

Recreation rating: 4

Plan your trip with a phone call to the Julian Bed and Breakfast Guild, a group of individuals who are the keepers of 20 different cabins and country lodgings. (Make sure you state specifically that you want a cabin; other accommodations are also available.) The colorful names of the cabin offerings tell you how special they are: Lutz Castle, Little Nest, the Artist's Loft, Rocking Horse, Mountain High, and so on. All the cabins are different, but most are in a wooded or country setting and include a fireplace, fully equipped kitchen, television, and VCR. Many have whirlpool hot tubs or spas.

I stayed at Lutz Castle, a 50-year-old adobe cottage a few miles outside of town. The innkeepers were a lovely couple who did everything possible to make me feel at home, and to provide me with information on outdoor recreation around Julian. The choice of nearby parks is wider here than almost anywhere in Southern California—William Heise County Park, Cuyamaca Rancho State Park, Volcan Mountain Wilderness, Cleveland National Forest, and Anza-Borrego Desert State Park—and all are within a 30-minute drive. You can hike, mountain bike, or ride your horse on hundreds of miles of trails.

For tamer excursions, visit the area's wineries or the Santa Ysabel Mission. Or take an interesting tour of Eagle and High Peak Mines, Julian's hard rock gold mines that date back to 1870. Anglers should pay a visit to Lake Cuyamaca, only 12 miles away, for spring trout fishing and summer bass fishing.

Each of Julian's four seasons has its own charm: In spring, the plentiful lilac bushes and daffodils bloom; in summer, the mountain breezes keep the temperature comfortable; in fall, the area's black oaks do their color-changing trick and the apple harvest occurs; and in winter, you might get caught in a snowstorm. As the saying goes, it's all good.

Facilities: There are 20 lodgings ranging in size from one to two bedrooms. Some have fully equipped kitchens and a hot tub or spa.

Bedding: Linens and towels are provided.

Reservations and rates: Reservations are recommended. Fees range from $60 to $200 per night, depending on season and type of accommodations. Pets are permitted in some lodgings.

Directions: From San Diego, drive east on I-8 for 40 miles to the Highway 79 exit. Drive north on Highway 79 for 25 miles to Julian.

Contact: Julian Bed and Breakfast Guild, P.O. Box 1711, Julian, CA 92036; 760/765-1555; website: www.julianbnbguild.com. Lutz Castle, P.O. Box 1285, Julian, CA 92036; 760/765-0208; website: www.lutzcastle.com.

Julian Bed and Breakfast Guild

7. SHADOW MOUNTAIN RANCH

Shadow Mountain Ranch is a unique bed-and-breakfast in the Pine Hills area outside of Julian, San Diego's famous apple town. Situated on eight forested acres, the ranch has four theme cottages that are filled with whimsy and fantasy.

The Gnome Home is not only packed with gnome carvings, books, and figurines, it also resembles a gnome's home. The ranch owners describe the exterior as looking like a tree stump; I'd call it something closer to a mushroom. Regardless, the cabin has hand-carved doors and furniture, and a rock waterfall shower and sink.

The Tree House is nestled high in the branches of an ancient oak tree. A stairway leads up to it from the deck below. The Enchanted Cottage sits on a grassy knoll overlooking the pine trees. It has a cozy window seat, woodstove, and Bavarian-style exterior with an arched wooden doorway.

Manzanita Cottage is a two-bedroom unit that sits alongside a meadow. It is the only cottage with a kitchen, and is large enough for two couples.

There is much to do on the ranch property, including swimming in the lap pool, soaking in the hot tub, feeding the ranch animals, and participating in archery, badminton, croquet, and horseshoes. A hearty country breakfast is served each morning, plus tea in the afternoon, and a glass of sherry or warm vanilla milk in the evening. Shadow Mountain Ranch has no facilities for children; this is primarily an adult bed-and-breakfast.

Off Highway 79 in Julian

Luxury rating: 4

Recreation rating: 4

The ranch is perfectly situated for a visit to William Heise County Park, just two miles down the road. First-timers should hike the Desert View and Canyon Oak Loop to check out the high vista at Glen's View. Or drive to the nearby Cleveland National Forest trailheads off Eagle Peak Road. In winter or spring, don't miss a visit to Cedar Creek Falls, accessible via the California Riding and Hiking Trail. Anglers, don't forget fishing and boating on Lake Cuyamaca, only 12 miles away, which is the largest stocked trout fishery in San Diego County.

Facilities: There are four one- and two-bedroom cottages that can accommodate two to four people. One cottage has a fully equipped kitchen.

Bedding: Linens and towels are provided.

Reservations and rates: Reservations are recommended. Fees range from $120 to $240 per night, including breakfast. Pets are not permitted.

Directions: From San Diego, drive east on I-8 for 40 miles to the Highway 79 exit. Drive north on Highway 79 for 25 miles to Julian. Turn left on Highway 78, drive one mile past town, then turn left on Pine Hills Road. Drive three miles and turn left on Frisius Road; Shadow Mountain Ranch is on the right.

Contact: Shadow Mountain Ranch, P.O. Box 791, 2771 Frisius Road, Julian, CA 92036; 760/765-0323.

OTHER CABINS AND COTTAGES NEARBY

• Random Oaks Ranch, 3742 Pine Hills Road, Julian, CA 92036; 760/765-1094; website: www.randomoaks.com.

Shadow Mountain Ranch

8. PINE HILLS LODGE

The Pine Hills Lodge in Julian is part cabin resort, part historic lodge and Western pub, and part dinner theater. Built in 1912, the lobby has an open-beamed log ceiling, huge native-stone fireplace, and inviting willow chairs. The adjacent Pine Hills Pub is popular with Julian locals and visitors alike; it's the kind of place that fills up whenever a big football game is on television.

Off Highway 79 in Julian

Luxury rating: 3

Recreation rating: 3

The lodge's cabins look quite ordinary on the outside, but have been completely remodeled on the inside. They feature wrought iron and wood furniture, down comforters, and fireplaces or woodburning stoves. The best of the lot are North Star, a one-bedroom cabin with a screened porch, king-sized bed, and sitting room with wood-burning stove; and Blue Bird One, a two-bedroom cabin with a stone fireplace and antique claw-foot tub.

None of the cabins have kitchens; a continental breakfast is served in the dining room each day and the lodge restaurant is open most nights for dinner. The town of Julian is only five minutes away, with several casual but good restaurants. Try breakfast at the Julian Cafe (out-of-this-world apple oatmeal pancakes) or any meal at the Julian Grille or Rongbranch Cafe. In addition to good food, you'll find a warm Western ambience at all of Julian's establishments, a tribute to its rich history as a 19th-century gold mining town.

One of Pine Hills Lodge's highlights is its weekend dinner theater, with musicals and comedies performed following a country barbecue of baby-back ribs, baked chicken, and all the trimmings. Combined cabin and theater packages are available on Friday nights.

The surrounding area is filled with recreation opportunities, from hiking the trails of nearby William Heise County Park to exploring the more remote areas of Cleveland National Forest. Following the rainy season, a few surprisingly tall waterfalls are found in the canyons near Pine Hills Lodge; get a Forest Service map and find your way to Cedar Creek Falls or the Three Sisters. The rest of the year, mountain biking and hiking are possible on the California Riding and Hiking Trail, and road cycling opportunities are endless on the hilly country roads around Julian.

Facilities: There are 12 cabins ranging in size from one to two bedrooms. Some cabins are duplexes; none have kitchens. Lodge rooms are also available. A restaurant is on-site.

Bedding: Linens and towels are provided.

Reservations and rates: Reservations are recommended. Fees range from $92 to $175 per night. Pets are permitted.

Directions: From San Diego, drive east on I-8 for 40 miles to the Highway 79 exit. Drive north on Highway 79 for 25 miles to Julian. Turn left on Highway 78, drive one mile past town, then turn left on Pine Hills Road. Drive 2.5 miles and turn right at the sign for Pine Hills Lodge.

Contact: Pine Hills Lodge, 2960 La Posada Way, P.O. Box 2260, Julian, CA 92036; 760/765-1100; website: www.pinehillslodge.com.

OTHER CABINS AND COTTAGES NEARBY

• Julian Gold Rush Hotel, 2032 Main Street, P.O. Box 1856, Julian, CA 92036; website: www.julianhotel.com.

Pine Hills Lodge

9. STAGECOACH TRAILS RESORT

You won't rent a cabin or cottage at Stagecoach Trails Resort; instead, it will be a mobile home. But you can't be too picky when you're in the middle of 600,000-acre Anza-Borrego Desert State Park. In this southern stretch of the huge desert, your only other options are tent camping or sleeping in the shade of a mesquite tree. Suddenly, a trailer starts to look really good.

© ANN MARIE BROWN

Off Highway S-2 near Agua Caliente Hot Springs

Luxury rating: 2

Recreation rating: 3

Stagecoach Trails Resort is located in the desolate but beautiful Shelter Valley area of Anza-Borrego. Its convenient proximity to the park's trailheads at Blair Valley allow you to hike to see Native American pictographs and the remains of a 1930s desert homestead. It's also near Agua Caliente County Park, where you can soak away your cares in hot spring pools; the water temperature is 96°F year-round. Another few miles to the south is Mountain Palm Springs Campground at Anza-Borrego, where hiking trails lead to five different palm groves, including Pygmy Grove's 50 short palms, and spectacular Palm Bowl, ringed by more than 100 palms.

The trailer rentals include everything you need for your stay, including kitchen utensils and linens. If you don't want to cook inside your trailer, a fire ring and charcoal barbecue are outside. Two of the trailers have large decks where you can sit out and watch the desert days turn to desert nights.

The best season to visit Anza-Borrego is unquestionably early spring, when you can witness the spectacle of blooming desert wildflowers. Phone the park's wildflower hotline (760/767-4684) in season to find out the exact status of the bloom; it usually occurs between mid-February and mid-March. If you can't make it then, plan your trip for any time from November until May, when the desert has comfortable temperatures for hiking and exploring almost every day. Summer is too hot for anything but stargazing and sitting still.

Facilities: There are five rental trailers that can accommodate up to four people. A general store is on-site.

Bedding: Linens and towels are provided.

Reservations and rates: Reservations are recommended. Fees are $50 per night with a two-night minimum. Pets are permitted with a $5 fee per night.

Directions: From Julian, drive east on Highway 78 for 11 miles to Highway S-2. Turn right and drive four miles to the resort on the right.

Contact: Stagecoach Trails Resort, 7878 Great Southern Overland Stage Route of 1849, Julian, CA 92036; 760/765-2197 or 877/896-2267.

Stagecoach Trails Resort

10. CUYAMACA RANCHO STATE PARK CABINS

© ANN MARIE BROWN

Off Highway 79 near Julian

Luxury rating: 2

Recreation rating: 4

THIS CABIN RANKS . . .
Best for Value

Cuyamaca Rancho State Park is one of San Diego's biggest and loveliest parks, with a whopping 25,000 acres of deciduous forest, conifers, chaparral, meadows, and rocky peaks. Better still, with elevations ranging from 4,000 to 6,500 feet, it's one of the few places in San Diego where the air is cool and clear year-round.

Adding to the park's delights are more than 100 miles of hiking trails, including the easy four-mile round-trip to the top of Stonewall Peak, elevation 5,730 feet, and the harder 5.5-mile round-trip to the top of Cuyamaca Peak, elevation 6,512 feet. Both offer stunning 360-degree views; from Cuyamaca Peak, you can see all the way to Mexico and the Pacific Ocean. Mountain bikers and equestrians have miles of park trails open for their pleasure, and anglers will find excellent trout and bass fishing prospects at Lake Cuyamaca.

If you want to stay in the park but don't want to car camp, reserve one of Cuyamaca Rancho State Park's seven cabins. Six are scattered around Paso Picacho Campground, and one is located at nearby Los Caballos Camp.

All the cabins are identical, with one important exception: The Nature Den at Paso Picacho. Whereas the others are newly constructed pine cabins, The Nature Den is a charming old stone and wood building built in 1933 by the Civilian Conservation Corps. It offers a few luxuries, including cots with mattresses, electricity, a coffeemaker, microwave oven, and fireplace. As at the other cabins, you must take a short walk to use the campground restroom and shower facilities.

The remaining cabins are 12-foot by 12-foot one-room structures, with bunk beds that sleep four (there are no mattresses, so bring a sleeping bag and pad), deck, picnic table, fire ring, and barbecue. The park allows as many as eight people per cabin, but if your group is more than four, bring along a tent for the extras. The cabin named Cypress has the best location; it's in a secluded spot up on a hill.

You'll need to reserve your stay as much as six months in advance for the summer months; the rest of the year is easier. And if you're traveling with your diamond tiara, take note: None of the cabins have locks on their doors, but you may bring your own padlock if you wish.

Facilities: There are six cabins at Paso Picacho Campground and one at Los Caballos Horse Camp. Each cabin can accommodate four people. Water and restrooms are located nearby. One cabin (The Nature Den) has electricity, a microwave oven, and a coffeemaker.

Bedding: Linens and towels are not provided; bring your own.

Reservations and rates: Reservations are required; phone Reserve America at 800/444-7275 or visit their website: www.ReserveAmerica.com. Fees range from $15 to $22 per night. Pets are permitted.

Directions: From San Diego, drive east on I-8 for 40 miles to the Highway 79 exit. Drive north on Highway 79 for 11 miles, then turn left (west) into Paso Picacho Campground.

Contact: Cuyamaca Rancho State Park, 12551 Highway 79, Descanso, CA 91916; 760/765-0755 (see above for reservations phone number).

Cuyamaca Rancho State Park Cabins

11. BLUE JAY LODGE

The Laguna Mountain Recreation Area is a fun-filled land of outdoor adventure within an hour's drive of downtown San Diego. Favorite activities include hiking, horseback riding, mountain biking, and as unlikely as it sounds, frolicking in the snow. At just shy of 6,000 feet in elevation, the Laguna Mountains are San Diego's backyard snow play area, at least during the few weeks each year when the white stuff sticks to the ground.

In any season, there is so much fun outdoor recreation in the Lagunas that you should plan to stay for a few days. If you like your cabin vacation a little on the eccentric side, Blue Jay Lodge might be your place. Although

© ANN MARIE BROWN

Off Highway S-1 on Mount Laguna

Luxury rating: 3

Recreation rating: 4

it looks normal enough from the outside, inside the Blue Jay's restaurant and saloon is some funky decor: The barstools are bright red tractor seats; wagon wheels and antique farming tools hang from the ceiling and walls, interspersed with a few dozen trophy fish; the dining tables and benches are carved from giant Northwest pine trees; and two stuffed bears stand on their back paws, with teeth bared and tongues wagging.

The Blue Jay Lodge does not allow children nor pets; each of the cabins is for one or two adults only. All the log cabins have cozy fireplaces, but bring your own firewood. Also, make sure you pack along dishes, utensils, and cooking supplies, because the cabins have full kitchens, but not so much as a plastic spoon.

Although they are quaint one-room structures, built in the 1920s, the cabins are surprisingly large, with a separate sleeping area, kitchen/dining area, and living area. The cabin I visited had some rather whimsical furniture, including a bed made of logs. After a good night's rest on it, I sat outside on the deck in the morning and watched the acorn woodpeckers flitting in the oak trees. The cabins are spaced far enough apart for privacy and quiet.

Not-to-be-missed activities in the Laguna Mountain Recreation Area include a four-mile round-trip hike to Garnet Peak, for spectacular views of the Anza-Borrego Desert. Shorter walks can be taken on the Lightning Ridge Trail, Desert View Nature Trail, and the Wooded Hill Nature Trail. Hiking, mountain biking, and equestrian trails are also available in Cuyamaca Rancho State Park, a short drive away.

Facilities: There are four cabins that can accommodate two people each. All have kitchens, but none have cooking or eating utensils. An on-site restaurant is open Friday through Sunday only.

Bedding: Linens and towels are provided.

Reservations and rates: Reservations are recommended. Fees are $85 per night. Pets and children are not permitted.

Directions: From San Diego, drive east on I-8 for 47 miles to the Highway S-1/ Sunrise Scenic Byway turnoff. Drive north on Highway S-1 for 10 miles to the town of Mount Laguna. Blue Jay Lodge is on the east side of the road.

From Julian, drive south on Highway 79 for six miles, then turn left and continue south on Highway S-1 for 15 miles to the town of Mount Laguna. Blue Jay Lodge is on the east side of the road.

Contact: Blue Jay Lodge, P.O. Box 150, Mount Laguna, CA 91948; 619/473-8844.

Blue Jay Lodge

12. LAGUNA MOUNTAIN LODGE

Blue Jay Lodge and Laguna Mountain Lodge are located across the road from each other, near the summit of Mount Laguna in the Laguna Mountain Recreation Area. Both offer an authentic mountain cabin experience in all four seasons of the year, but Blue Jay Lodge's cabins are only large enough for two adults, and pets are not permitted. If you are traveling with kids or Fido, plan a stay at Laguna Mountain Lodge, which has cabins ranging in size from one to three bedrooms. Some have fireplaces and kitchens, so be sure to ask for exactly what you want.

Off Highway S-1 on Mount Laguna

Luxury rating: 3

Recreation rating: 4

Just like at Blue Jay Lodge, Laguna Mountain Lodge's cabin kitchens are not equipped with utensils, dishes, pots, or pans. If you plan to cook, come prepared. If you plan to eat out, understand that there are few services in the Lagunas. Unless you're willing to drive, you're confined to the restaurant at Blue Jay Lodge (open from Friday to Sunday only) and the small grocery store at Laguna Mountain Lodge.

Trails for hikers, mountain bikers, and equestrians are plentiful in the area, and road cyclists can ride the spectacular scenic byway. Laguna Mountain Lodge is located next to the Forest Service's Laguna Mountain Visitor Information Station, where you can pick up maps and get all the information you need. If you're lucky enough to time your visit for when snow is on the ground, you won't need any instructions. Just get out there and make some snow angels, or, for the more sophisticated, try sledding or cross-country skiing.

Facilities: There are 15 cabins ranging in size from one to three bedrooms, plus motel units. Most cabins have kitchens; none have cooking or eating utensils. A general store is on-site.

Bedding: Linens and towels are provided.

Reservations and rates: Reservations are recommended. Fees range from $65 to $110 per night. Pets are permitted in some cabins for a $7 fee.

Directions: From San Diego, drive east on I-8 for 47 miles to the Highway S-1/Sunrise Scenic Byway turnoff. Drive north on Highway S-1 for 10 miles to the town of Mount Laguna. Laguna Mountain Lodge is on the west side of the road.

From Julian, drive south on Highway 79 for six miles, then turn left and continue south on Highway S-1 for 15 miles to the town of Mount Laguna. Laguna Mountain Lodge is on the west side of the road.

Contact: Laguna Mountain Lodge, P.O. Box 146, 10678 Sunrise Highway, Mount Laguna, CA 91948; 619/445-2342 or 619/473-8533; website: www.lagunamountain.com.

Laguna Mountain Lodge

13. CRYSTAL PIER HOTEL

The Crystal Pier Hotel is not a hotel at all, but a series of side-by-side cottages perched on top of weather-beaten Crystal Pier in Pacific Beach. From your cottage, you overlook a large expanse of wide blue ocean, and simultaneously, you sit on top of it. The surf rumbles beneath you day and night; it's much like being on a boat at sea, but without needing the Dramamine.

© ANN MARIE BROWN

Off I-5 in Pacific Beach

Luxury rating: 4

Recreation rating: 4

THIS CABIN RANKS . . .
Best for Beach Activities

Twenty cottages were built on the pier in the 1930s. Six more were added in the 1990s, near the pier's end. The end units are more modern, with nicer amenities and a slightly higher price tag. These are by far the best choice; their views are exquisite and they offer the most privacy.

All 26 cottages are charming blue and white buildings, each with a design carved into its wooden shutters: starfish, dolphins, sailboats, even Mickey Mouse. Each has a full kitchen, allowing you to prepare your meals, then carry your food to your deck for an oceanside picnic. And each cottage comes with a precious privilege: one parking space on the pier and a key code for the driveway gate.

Although the Crystal Pier Hotel is wildly popular in summer, the best time to visit is in fall or winter. Not only do the hotel's rates drop after October 1, but also the beach crowds dissipate and the carnival atmosphere of Pacific Beach quiets down. If you surf, swim, beachcomb, or just like to walk on the sand and gaze at the waves, you'll be in heaven.

There's one more perquisite worth mentioning: because you're situated on a pier just above the ocean, you can go fishing right outside your door. The hotel rents equipment if you didn't bring your own.

Facilities: There are 26 one- and two-bedroom cottages, all with kitchenettes.

Bedding: Linens and towels are provided.

Reservations and rates: Reservations are recommended. Fees range from $175 to $240 per night. Pets are not permitted.

Directions: From I-5 in Pacific Beach, exit at Garnet Avenue and drive west to the ocean. Crystal Pier is located at the end of Garnet Avenue.

Contact: Crystal Pier Hotel, 4500 Ocean Boulevard, San Diego, CA 92109; 858/483-6983 or 800/748-5894; website: www.crystalpier.com.

Crystal Pier Hotel

14. THE BEACH COTTAGES

If you have a family or a group of friends that wants to play at the beach for a few days or a week, The Beach Cottages are the ideal vacation home base. Located inches from the sand in Pacific Beach, the cottages come fully equipped with towels, linens, dishes, and silverware, so all you need to pack are your bathing suits and surfboards.

Off I-5 in Pacific Beach

Luxury rating: 3

Recreation rating: 4

THIS CABIN RANKS . . .
Best for Beach Activities

Keep in mind that this won't be a peaceful, solitary getaway. Pacific Beach (or "PB," as the locals say) is a hopping party town, with a wide and varied selection of bars and late-night eateries. Its oceanfront biking-jogging-rollerblading trail runs between The Beach Cottages and the sand, and upon its level pavement rides, strides, and rolls a perpetual chain of beach people. Basically, you'll be living in a fishbowl. Also, the cottages are placed about a foot apart, so you'll certainly get to know your vacationing neighbors.

Nonetheless, you won't find a Southern California beach experience more authentic than this one. Volleyball, bikinis, ice cream, perfect San Diego weather . . . they have it all here. Pacific Beach is especially popular with surfers, so if you are one or enjoy watching them, you'll be happy here.

Kids will find much to amuse themselves: The beach is an obvious magnet, but when parents insist that it's time to get out of the water, they can play shuffleboard or ping-pong in the common area between the cottages. Those with bikes or rollerblades can join the throngs on the paved beach trail; it runs nearly two miles south to the Mission Bay breakwater.

If you decide you're ready for some peace and quiet, drive a few miles north to Torrey Pines State Reserve and walk a few of its short but sweet coastside trails. Be sure to check out the views of the dramatic coastal badlands from Razor Point Trail.

Facilities: There are 17 one- and two-bedroom cottages that can accommodate up to six people, all with fully equipped kitchens. Apartments and motel rooms are also available.

Bedding: Linens and towels are provided.

Reservations and rates: Reservations are recommended. Fees are $140 to $200 per night. Pets are not permitted.

Directions: From I-5 in Pacific Beach, exit at Garnet Avenue and drive west to Mission Boulevard. Turn left, drive four blocks, and turn right on Reed Avenue. The Beach Cottages are at Reed Avenue and Ocean Boulevard.

Contact: The Beach Cottages, 4255 Ocean Boulevard, San Diego, CA 92109; 858/483-7440; website: www.beachcottages.com.

The Beach Cottages

15. SAN DIEGO VACATION COTTAGES

San Diego Vacation Cottages is a company run by a couple of transplanted Australians who have the right idea about how to structure a fun, economical vacation. Their formula is simple: offer cottages and apartments for rent in appealing neighborhoods, where people can stay for a few days, a week, or longer and be surrounded by the comforts of home, not the impersonal amenities of a hotel.

© ANN MARIE BROWN

Off I-5 in Old Town and Ocean Beach

Luxury rating: 3

Recreation rating: 3

The company offers cottages in two locations within a short distance of each other: Old Town and Ocean Beach. The Old Town cottages are small garden bungalows that were completely remodeled in 2000. Despite their small size, they are bright and cheerful inside, with Mexican-style decor (Saltillo tile and colorful fabrics) and brand-new kitchens. Although the cottages share common walls, they are surprisingly quiet and private both inside and out. Each unit includes a flower-lined patio and barbecue. All of Old Town's shops and restaurants, plus Old Town State Historic Park, are within walking distance.

The Ocean Beach cottages were remodeled in 1999, and also feature new kitchens and furnishings. They are similar to the Old Town cottages, but with bright-colored beach decor instead of Mexican styling, and a choice of one, two, or three bedrooms. The beach is a one-block walk from the cottages. Because they are situated right next door to Mission Bay, guests can take advantage of personal watercraft riding, sailing, biking, and windsurfing at Mission Bay Park.

Both locations are only minutes from San Diego's popular attractions: Sea World, the Historic Gas Lamp District, and San Diego Zoo, plus many natural attractions, including the rare trees at Torrey Pines State Reserve and the tidepools at Cabrillo National Monument.

Facilities: There are 12 one-bedroom cottages in Old Town and 10 one-, two-, and three-bedroom cottages in Ocean Beach. All cottages have fully equipped kitchens.

Bedding: Linens and towels are provided.

Reservations and rates: Reservations are recommended. Fees are $89 to $219 per night. Pets are not permitted.

Directions: From I-5 in downtown San Diego, drive north for five miles to the Old Town exit. Turn east and drive two blocks to Congress Street; follow Congress Street until it becomes San Diego Avenue. The reservations office is at 2422 San Diego Avenue.

Contact: San Diego Vacation Cottages Booking Office, 2422 San Diego Avenue, San Diego, CA 92110; 619/291-9091; website: www.sandiegovacation apts.com.

San Diego Vacation Cottages

16. SAN DIEGO YACHT AND BREAKFAST

They don't call them cottages at San Diego Yacht and Breakfast, they call them "floating dockside villas." And if spending the night in a floating villa doesn't float your boat, you can choose between a few luxury yachts.

Off I-5 on Harbor Island

Luxury rating: 3

Recreation rating: 3

San Diego Yacht and Breakfast, located on Harbor Island, bills itself as the world's only "floating resort." What makes it unique from other boat-and-breakfast companies is that it is a full-service property with a heated pool, bicycle rentals, and on-site catering. You don't just have access to your rented boat or villa, you also have access to amenities that are usually associated with a hotel or motel.

The floating villas look a lot like tall, square mobile homes set in the shallow harbor water. Three are 700 square feet in size and fully equipped with washer and dryer, microwave, television, and VCR. They sleep four comfortably. One villa, the Capistrano, is a whopping 1,250 square feet spread out over two stories. It has three bedrooms and a great view of the marina from the upper level. If you want a more traditional boat to spend the night in, San Diego Yacht and Breakfast has a 41-foot luxury yacht with a mahogany-and-teak interior and two staterooms, plus three 55-foot Bluewater yachts.

You can prepare your own meals in all of the yachts and villas, but you won't need to worry about breakfast: Each guest receives a coupon for a full breakfast at a harbor café. No matter which accommodation you choose, understand that San Diego Yacht and Breakfast's location on Harbor Island puts it within a couple miles of San Diego airport. Although you won't hear much plane traffic at night, you will hear it during the day.

San Diego Yacht and Breakfast also offers charter services on its yachts and sailboats. For an extra fee, you can hire a captain (since you're not allowed to drive the yacht yourself) and go for a cruise around the bay before retiring for the night.

Facilities: There are four floating villas and four yachts for nightly rentals. They can accommodate four to six people. All boats have fully equipped galleys.

Bedding: Linens and towels are provided.

Reservations and rates: Reservations are recommended. Fees are $150 to $325 per night. Pets are not permitted.

Directions: From I-5 heading south in San Diego, take the Highway 209/Rosecrans Street exit. Drive south about three miles, then turn left on Nimitz Boulevard and drive to its end. Turn left on North Harbor Drive, drive two miles, then turn right on Harbor Island Drive. Turn right for Marina Cortez G-Dock.

Contact: San Diego Yacht and Breakfast, 1880 Harbor Island Drive, G-Dock, San Diego, CA 92101; 619/297-9484 or 800/922-4836; website: www.yachtdo.com.

San Diego Yacht and Breakfast

17. SAN DIEGO METRO KOA

The San Diego Metro KOA is one of the largest and busiest KOA campgrounds in California. It's no surprise, considering the popularity of San Diego as a vacation destination and the low cost of staying in a KOA cabin.

The KOA has 24 cabins, both the old-style one-room log cabins that sleep four and the newer two-room cabins that sleep six. The one-room cabins have twin bunk beds and a double bed (all with mattresses, but you must bring your own bedding). The two-room cabins have two sets of bunk beds in one room and a double bed in the second room.

Additionally, a KOA Kamper Kitchen is placed among the cluster of cabins. This is a gazebo-style kitchen (roof but no walls) which consists of sinks, stove tops, and a propane barbecue. It is shared among everyone in the campground, but is mostly used by cabin guests.

The campground is loaded with extra amenities, including a year-round

heated pool, playground, convenience store, and children's bike rentals. Everything is packed tightly into a fairly small space, but nobody seems to mind.

Most people use the KOA as a base for exploring San Diego and going to the beach. The campground is within minutes of Silver Strand State Beach and the attractions of Coronado Island. Sea World, Mission Bay Park, Balboa Park, and Birch Aquarium are a 20-minute drive to the north. Lovers of tidepools and history should head for Cabrillo National Monument, where they can visit the historic Point Loma Lighthouse, walk the Bayside Trail, and study the invertebrate life at Cabrillo's tidepools.

Off I-805 in Chula Vista

Luxury rating: 2

Recreation rating: 3

Facilities: There are 18 one-room cabins and six two-room cabins. A shared outdoor kitchen is available. Heated pool, playground, and small general store are on-site.

Bedding: Linens and towels are not provided; bring your own.

Reservations and rates: Reservations are recommended. Fees are $45 to $65 per night. Pets are not permitted.

Directions: From I-5 in Chula Vista, take the Bonita Road exit. Drive west for one mile to Second Avenue. Turn right and drive one mile to the KOA on the right.

Contact: San Diego Metro KOA, 111 North Second Avenue, Chula Vista, CA 91910; 800/562-9877; website: www.sandiegokoa.com.

San Diego Metro KOA

CHAPTER 4

Yosemite and Mammoth Lakes

*P*lunging waterfalls, stark granite, alpine lakes, pristine meadows, giant trees, snowbound slopes, and raging rivers—you'll find them all in this region, which encompasses not only world-famous Yosemite National Park but also the popular recreation areas of Mammoth Lakes and the eastern Sierra, and the central Sierra foothills and recreation lakes.

One of the most plentiful areas for outdoor recreation, the Yosemite region offers something for everybody—hikers, anglers, boaters, skiers, rock climbers, bikers, equestrians, and those who simply want to breathe the mountain air. Along with limitless recreation opportunities come an abundance of interesting places to stay—ski chalets, cozy bed-and-breakfast cottages, fishing camp–style rustic cabins, and hike-in tent cabins.

The centerpiece of this region, of course, is Yosemite National Park, a must-see on every traveler's itinerary. Because it receives more than four million visitors each year, you'd expect the park to be constantly overrun. But vacation-wise visitors understand that the best way to see the famous park is to show up in the off-season (October to April), or keep to weekday trips in summer.

The off-season happens to be prime time in Yosemite, anyway. Spring is the optimal season to view Yosemite Valley's famous waterfalls, three of which are among the tallest in the world. Autumn is the best time to admire the towering granite of El Capitan, Half Dome, and Sentinel Rock, as the Valley's many deciduous trees turn colors, then drop their leaves. Winter brings the chance to downhill ski and snowboard at Badger Pass, or cross-country ski and snowshoe on Glacier Point and among the Giant Sequoias.

Whereas the park accommodations described in this chapter may be difficult or impossible to obtain on Memorial Day or Fourth of July weekends, many lodgings are hungry for guests in the off-season, or even on Tuesday nights in summer. Your chances for a roof over your head in the busy season are greater if you consider staying at one of several lodgings just outside the park boundary. Most are still within a 45-minute drive of Yosemite Valley, and many are even closer to Yosemite's high country on Tioga Road and Glacier Point Road. Keep in mind there are many ways to make a Yosemite vacation work—even in the peak months, and even without having reservations months in advance.

Nearly as popular as the national park itself are the resort towns just to the east, particularly Mammoth Lakes and June Lake on the U.S. 395 corridor. With easy access from Los Angeles and San Diego (a straight shot up U.S. 395), the eastern Sierra has long been a favorite destination for Southern Californians.

Heavily visited for skiing and snowboarding in winter, the eastern Sierra is also ideal for fishing, hiking, and biking in the warmer seasons. Expect a more rugged, dramatic landscape than what you'll find in the western Sierra; the east side boasts higher peaks and a steeper escarpment than the gentler west side. This means a longer, and more deeply snow-bound, winter. It also means strenuous hiking and biking in summer (most trails include a steep climb!) and sometimes highly technical fishing (bring your float tube and fly fishing gear).

Resorts in the eastern Sierra are frequently full-service enterprises, and may include cabins, a marina with rental boats and fishing gear, a pack station with horse rentals, a restaurant, and a store. These resorts range from very rustic to very luxurious, and everything in between. Many have a loyal string of customers who come back year after year.

Last but not least in this chapter are the towns and resorts just north, west, and south of Yosemite National Park, where the Sierra foothills mark the transition zone between the low-elevation Central Valley and the high peaks of the Sierra crest. In this area, elevations range from 3,000 to 7,000 feet. Snow falls in the higher areas in winter, but doesn't hang around until June. Forests are a dense mix of pines, cedars, and firs. Streams and rivers are filled with fishing spots and swimming holes, and recreation lakes like Pinecrest Lake and Beardsley Reservoir beckon boaters, water-skiers, swimmers, and anglers.

Renting a cabin or cottage in these areas usually means a vacation centered around the water: You wear your bathing suit or fishing clothes all day, hang your beach towels to dry on your cabin's front porch, and sit outside on warm nights bragging about the day's feats on the lake.

Clearly, there's something for everybody in Yosemite and Mammoth Lakes. Check out the pages that follow to locate the perfect cabin or cottage for your getaway to this world-class setting.

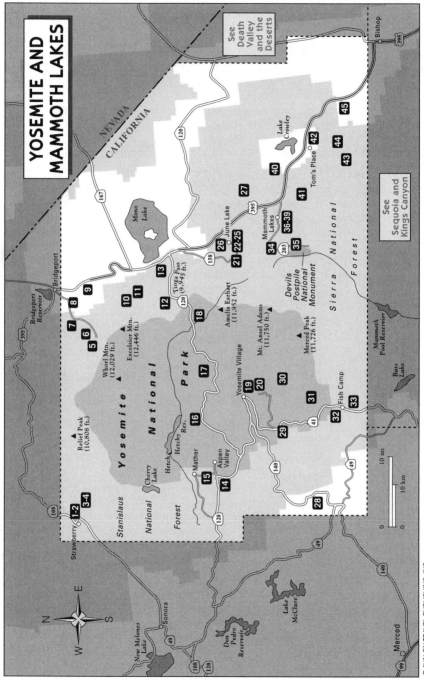

YOSEMITE AND MAMMOTH LAKES

See Death Valley and the Deserts

See Sequoia and Kings Canyon

10 mi

10 km

© AVALON TRAVEL PUBLISHING, INC.

CHAPTER 4
YOSEMITE AND MAMMOTH LAKES

1. THE RIVERS RESORT

If you're not sure where Strawberry is, think small mountain town at 5,300 feet in elevation on the South Fork Stanislaus River. Think fishing in the river, swimming and boating at Pinecrest Lake, hiking in Stanislaus National Forest, and skiing at Dodge Ridge Ski Area.

© ANN MARIE BROWN

Off Highway 108 in Strawberry

Luxury rating: 3

Recreation rating: 3

Then think about The Rivers Resort, or as they say in their brochure, The Rivers Condominium Resort. Why condominium? It's a mystery, since their accommodations consist of 10 cabins ranging in size from one to four bedrooms, which bear no resemblance to condos except for their fully equipped kitchens and cable television. Although the cabins were built in the 1950s and are older in style, many have remodeled kitchens and bathrooms.

Cabin number 3, a large four-bedroom unit for up to eight people, is right on the river. It's the preferred choice for those who want to sit on their deck and watch the water roll by. The rest are clustered nearby amid the conifers, only a stone's throw from the river. Not one of them is a bad choice.

It can get quite warm here in summer, so the resort has a 25- by 50-foot swimming pool on the grounds. Plenty of visitors cool off in the river, too. (The pool, unlike the river, is heated.) A grocery store is located right next door, so you can purchase anything you need. Across the road is a restaurant and bar at the historic Strawberry Inn.

The Rivers Resort makes a great base camp for day hikers. Among the many hikes possible in Stanislaus National Forest, one of the most fascinating is the Trail of the Gargoyles, located off nearby Herring Creek Road. It's a short walk that passes by bizarre-looking geological formations perched on a high canyon rim. Another popular day hike is the short but strenuous climb to Burst Rock and Powell Lake in the Emigrant Wilderness.

If you want to let somebody else do the walking for you, horse rentals are available at two stables within a few miles of the resort.

Facilities: There are 10 cabins ranging in size from one to four bedrooms. All cabins have fully equipped kitchens. A store and restaurant are on-site.

Bedding: Linens and towels are provided.

Reservations and rates: Reservations are recommended. Fees range from $110 to $195 per night in winter and summer, $100 to $175 per night in spring and fall. There is a two-night minimum stay. Pets are permitted in some cabins with a $150 deposit.

Directions: From Fresno, take Highway 99 north to Modesto. Turn east on Highway 108 and drive 52 miles to Sonora. Continue east on Highway 108 for 32 miles to Strawberry (past the Pinecrest turnoff). Rivers Resort is on the right, across from Strawberry Inn.

Contact: The Rivers Resort, P.O. Box 81, Strawberry, CA 95375; 209/965-3278 or 800/514-6777; website: www.gorr.com.

The Rivers Resort

2. THE CABINS AT STRAWBERRY

The Cabins at Strawberry are located right next door to the historic Strawberry Inn and are owned by the same folks. But the two accommodations have distinctly different characters. The inn, built in 1939, provides standard motel rooms and a restaurant on the river. The adjacent Cabins at Strawberry are large, modern structures that were built in the 1990s. They are perfectly suited for family vacations and group ski trips.

Off Highway 108 in Strawberry

Luxury rating: 4

Recreation rating: 3

It's not uncommon for a wedding to be held at the inn and the guests to stay at the cabins. The cabins are two-story, three-bedroom, two-bath units that can comfortably contain eight people. They are set on the South Fork of the Stanislaus River and some have river views (be sure to pay the additional 20 bucks to get one). The sound of the river greatly diminishes the sound of nearby Highway 108, which runs by the resort.

All cabins have fully furnished kitchens, gas fireplaces, cable television, and VCRs. These are clean, modern homes, not funky riverside cabins. The only downside is that they were built too close together, with only enough space around them to park a car or two.

The restaurant at Strawberry Inn is well-known for its American and California cuisine. You might not expect the food to be that great way out here in the little town of Strawberry, but this place will surprise you.

Since The Cabins at Strawberry require a three-night minimum stay, you're going to need something to do with your time. In winter, everybody heads to Dodge Ridge for skiing and snowboarding, or to Leland Meadows Sno-Park for sledding and snow play. If you're a budding Kristi Yamaguchi, drive to nearby Long Barn to ice-skate. All these options are just a few miles away. In summer, the focus is on the South Fork of the Stanislaus River for fishing, nearby Pinecrest Lake for boating, fishing, and swimming, and Stanislaus National Forest and the Emigrant Wilderness for hiking.

Facilities: There are eight three-bedroom cabins that can accommodate up to eight people. All cabins have fully equipped kitchens and gas fireplaces. A store and restaurant are on-site.

Bedding: Linens and towels are provided.

Reservations and rates: Reservations are recommended. Fees range from $160 to $180 per night. There is a three-night minimum stay. Pets are not permitted.

Directions: From Fresno, take Highway 99 north to Modesto. Turn east on Highway 108 and drive 52 miles to Sonora. Continue east on Highway 108 for 32 miles to Strawberry (past the Pinecrest turnoff). Check in at the Strawberry Inn, on the left side of the road.

Contact: The Cabins at Strawberry, P.O. Box 109, Strawberry, CA 95375; 209/965-0885 or 888/965-0885; website: www.strawberrycabins.com.

OTHER CABINS AND COTTAGES NEARBY

* Darlene's Vacation Cabins, P.O. Box 35, Long Barn, CA 95335; 800/273-0740; website: darlenesvacationcabins.com.

The Cabins at Strawberry

3. PINECREST LAKE RESORT

Got kids? Then Pinecrest Lake Resort is your ticket to vacationland. Located in Stanislaus National Forest on the edge of granite-rimmed Pinecrest Lake,

© ANN MARIE BROWN

Off Highway 108 near Sonora

Luxury rating: 3

Recreation rating: 5

THIS CABIN RANKS . . .
Best for Families

the resort caters to families with its two- and three-bedroom housekeeping cabins nestled among the sugar pines.

From the door of your cabin, walk to the lake's sandy beach for swimming and sunning. Walk to the marina to rent a boat and go fishing. Walk to the store to buy the stuff you forgot to pack. Walk to the post office to mail your postcards. Walk to the restaurant and order dinner when you can't stand grilling one more hamburger.

Pinecrest Lake Resort, and the lake itself, is a social place, where families make friends with other families. Organized activities are plentiful: a nightly movie in the outdoor amphitheater, sailboat and paddle boat rentals, bike rentals, guided nature hikes, and video games at the resort center. Even teenagers will be happy here; they'll meet all the other teenagers and talk about how boring their parents are.

In case you haven't gotten the picture yet, don't expect a tranquil, private mountain escape. A four-mile recreation trail circles Pinecrest Lake; on a July Saturday morning, it was overflowing with joggers. If you want peace and quiet, you'll have to drive down the road to the trailheads for the Emigrant Wilderness.

Or just show up in the off-season. The resort is open year-round and it's only five minutes from Dodge Ridge ski resort, which is usually snow-bound by December 1. Discounted lift tickets are available to resort guests.

Autumn is by far the quietest time. On one October trip, I was the only customer in the resort's Steam Donkey Restaurant. Built of weathered timbers from an old bridge over the Tuolumne River, the Steam Donkey's food is excellent (sandwiches and salads for lunch; a variety of entrées for dinner) and reasonably priced to boot.

The only downer at Pinecrest Lake Resort? The cabins are located right next to the resort's tennis courts, so the annoying *thwack* of tennis balls punctuates the sound of the wind in the pines.

Facilities: There are seven two- and three-bedroom housekeeping cabins, plus two- and three-bedroom townhouses and numerous motel rooms. The cabins and townhouses have fully equipped kitchens. A store and restaurant are on-site.

Bedding: Linens and towels are provided.

Reservations and rates: Reservations are recommended. Fees range from $100 to $200 per weekend night in winter and summer; $80 to $160 per weekend night in spring and fall. Sunday through Thursday nights are discounted. There is a one-week minimum stay in July and August. Pets are not permitted.

Directions: From Fresno, take Highway 99 north to Modesto. Turn east on Highway 108 and drive 52 miles to Sonora. Continue east on Highway 108 for 31 miles to the Pinecrest turnoff. Turn right and drive one mile to Pinecrest Lake Resort.

Contact: Pinecrest Lake Resort, P.O. Box 1216, Pinecrest, CA 95364; 209/965-3411; website: www.pinecrestlakeresort.com.

Pinecrest Lake Resort

4. PINECREST CHALET

Pinecrest Chalet is the closest lodging to the Dodge Ridge ski area, and for an easy winter vacation, that could be all you need to know. Winter recreation at Dodge Ridge includes family-oriented downhill and cross-country skiing, plus snowboarding, snowmobiling, ice-skating, and sledding. If you want to teach your kids how to ski, or take the love of your life somewhere where you can snowshoe far from the madding crowd, a reservation for Pinecrest Chalet fits the bill.

The resort offers a variety of cabin and townhouse accommodations, including mini chalets (one-room cabins with fully stocked kitchens and fireplaces), economy cabins (one-room housekeeping bungalows with kitchenettes), and larger deluxe cabins with two to four bedrooms, so

you can bring the whole clan. The honeymoon chalet has a king bed and whirlpool hot tub.

Pinecrest Chalet gets its share of summer visitors, too. The resort is only a couple of minutes from popular Pinecrest Lake, where fishing, boating, and swimming are the main activities. Numerous hiking trails begin within a few miles of Pinecrest Chalet at the Gianelli Cabin Trailhead for the Emigrant Wilderness. If you want to ride your mountain bike, drive west on Highway 108 to the turnoff for Lyons Reservoir. From the parking area by the lake, advanced riders should head east to Fraser Flat Bridge (10 miles one-way). Those who are less ambitious should head west on an old railroad grade to Confidence Road (only five miles, and level all the way).

Some visitors are happy just to hang around their chalet or cabin. The North Fork of the Tuolumne River flows through Pinecrest's property. A swimming pool, volleyball court, basketball court, and jungle gym can keep the kids occupied.

Off Highway 108 in Strawberry

Luxury rating: 3

Recreation rating: 5

THIS CABIN RANKS . . .

Best for Winter Sports

Facilities: There are 23 cabins and townhouses that can accommodate up to 14 people, plus an RV park. All cabins have kitchen facilities; some are fully equipped. There is a swimming pool on-site.

Bedding: Linens and towels are provided.

Reservations and rates: Reservations are recommended. Fees range from $70 to $295 per night in winter and summer and $65 to $240 per night in spring and fall. Discounted weekly rentals are available. Pets are permitted only with prior approval.

Directions: From Fresno, take Highway 99 north to Modesto. Turn east on Highway 108 and drive 52 miles to Sonora. Continue east on Highway 108 for 31 miles to the Pinecrest turnoff. Turn right, then right again for Dodge Ridge Ski Area.

Contact: Pinecrest Chalet, 500 Dodge Ridge Road, P.O. Box 1279, Pinecrest, CA 95364; 209/965-3276; website: www.pinecrestchalet.com.

Pinecrest Chalet

5. ANNETT'S MONO VILLAGE RESORT

Don't expect peace and quiet when you come to Annett's Mono Village Resort. The place is a miniature city, with cabins, motel rooms, rental trailers, a grocery store, gift shop, restaurant, cocktail lounge, marina, and 300-site campground. It's one of the busiest places on the east side of the Sierra.

Off U.S. 395 near Bridgeport

Luxury rating: 3

Recreation rating: 4

Why? Well, in addition to excellent fishing, Upper Twin Lake is one of the few lakes around that allows waterskiing, a sport that always attracts a crowd. Waterskiing is limited to the hours of 10 A.M. to 3 P.M., and during those five hours, the fast boats fly. The rest of the time, anglers can have some peace. And the fishing doesn't disappoint. The lake is regularly stocked by the Department of Fish and Game, but Mono Village supplements the plants with larger, two- to four-pound trout. Sometimes they grow really big: a 26-pound, 8-ounce brown trout was caught here in 1987.

It goes without saying that Mono Village is a full-service resort. They operate under a "something for everyone" philosophy; in addition to waterskiing and fishing, opportunities abound for swimming, hiking, road biking, deer hunting in autumn, and just plain relaxing. A major Hoover Wilderness trailhead is located at Mono Village's campground; many people just hike the trail for a mile or two to see the cascades on Horse Creek. There are also hot springs nearby.

For the best experience, rent one of the resort's newer, updated log cabins. Older, rustic models are also available, but they are on the dilapidated side. Definitely ask for a cabin with a lake view, or even better, one situated on the lakeshore. Some of the cabins are located in a busy parking lot between the bar and the store—not exactly a fantasy vacation spot.

One more tip: Smart vacationers show up in September or October, after the summer crowds have dispersed. The fishing is often best at this time and the autumn colors are outstanding.

Facilities: There are 18 cabins ranging in size that will accommodate up to six people, plus rental trailers, motel rooms, a campground, and RV resort. All cabins have fully equipped kitchens. A general store, restaurant, bar, and marina are on-site.

Bedding: Linens and towels are provided.

Reservations and rates: Reservations are recommended. Fees range from $65 to $70 per night for rustic cabins and $100 to $150 per night for newer cabins and lakeshore cabins. Pets are not permitted.

Directions: From the junction of U.S. 395 and Highway 120 in Lee Vining, drive north on U.S. 395 for 25 miles to Bridgeport. Turn left (west) on Twin Lakes Road and drive 14 miles to Annett's Mono Village (on Upper Twin Lake). Take the right fork signed for motel and cabin reservations.

Contact: Annett's Mono Village Resort, P.O. Box 455, Bridgeport, CA 93517; 760/932-7071; website: www.monovillage.com.

Annett's Mono Village Resort

6. TWIN LAKES RESORT

Twin Lakes Resort on Lower Twin Lake is a fine place to toss your line in the water, gaze up at the jagged peaks of the Sawtooth Range, and forget your troubles for a while. Located west of Bridgeport in the Twin Lakes Recreation Area of Toiyabe National Forest, Twin Lakes Resort is the quieter of the two large resorts on Twin Lakes. (Annett's Mono Village, the other resort, is a half mile up the road on Upper Twin Lake.) Twin Lakes Resort's housekeeping cottages are set across the road from the lower lake, spread out amid a large, grassy lawn. Some have partial views of the water.

© ANN MARIE BROWN

Off U.S. 395 near Bridgeport

Luxury rating: 3

Recreation rating: 4

From your cabin, you can walk 50 yards to the marina and rent a boat for the day. If you brought your own boat, you can launch it from there. If you don't like boats, you can fish from shore. If you don't like fishing, you can sit on the shore and admire the scenery. If you get bored, you can jump off the rope swing and swim in the lake. Choices, choices.

Everything about your vacation here is simple. The resort has a general store, serves three meals a day, and provides bike rentals. If you catch a big fish, they have taxidermy service. If you forgot your fishing license, they'll sell you one.

Lower Twin Lake, like its neighbor Upper Twin Lake, is famous for large and plentiful fish: rainbow and brown trout and kokanee salmon. The general rule is to fish deep. If you don't catch anything, the eye-popping Sierra scenery will more than compensate. The best views are had in late spring and early summer, when the Sawtooth Range is crowned in thick snow.

Hikers should head to the Hoover Wilderness trailhead at Upper Twin

Lake. From there, they can hike the Robinson Creek Trail steeply uphill to Barney Lake, four miles out. If you'd rather relax, there are hot springs nearby on Buckeye Creek.

Facilities: There are seven cabins that can accommodate two to six people, all with fully equipped kitchens. A small general store and restaurant are on-site.

Bedding: Linens and towels are provided.

Reservations and rates: Reservations are recommended. Fees are $99 to $156 per night for two people, plus $20 for each additional person. The resort is open year-round. Pets are permitted with a $25 fee.

Directions: From the junction of U.S. 395 and Highway 120 in Lee Vining, drive north on U.S. 395 for 25 miles to Bridgeport. Turn left (west) on Twin Lakes Road and drive 13 miles to Twin Lakes Resort on the right (by Lower Twin Lake).

Contact: Twin Lakes Resort, P.O. Box 248, Bridgeport, CA 93517; 800/407-6153; website: www.lowertwinlakesresort.com.

Twin Lakes Resort

7. DOC & AL'S RESORT

There's nothing fancy about Doc & Al's Resort, but ask yourself: Did I come here to admire the furniture or did I come here to fish?

Right answer. Doc & Al's Resort is located on Robinson Creek in the Twin Lakes Recreation Area of Toiyabe National Forest. Just up the road are a half dozen campgrounds, and everybody at those has come here to fish, too.

Doc & Al's one-room rustic cabins are a small step up from camping. You get a roof over your head, a wall heater, beds and bedding, and outdoor cooking facilities. Bathrooms are a short walk away. The tiny cabins are squeezed in tightly, each one only a few feet from the next.

Off U.S. 395 near Bridgeport

Luxury rating: 3

Recreation rating: 3

If you're smart, you'll spring for the much larger housekeeping cabins on the creek. They are more appealing in every way: spaced farther apart, bearing large decks that overlook Robinson Creek, and best of all, they have kitchens and bathrooms. Forest and Ranger are the newest cabins and best of the lot.

The resort also has a busy RV and tent camping area, and a communal lodge with a fireplace and old piano. Anglers gather here for chess, card playing, and telling lies about fish.

The surrounding terrain is a mix of aspens, Jeffrey pines, and sage at this 7,000-foot elevation. Those who can't wait to fish take their pick from fly, lure, and bait fishing for rainbows, browns, brooks, and even cutthroat trout and kokanee salmon. Robinson Creek is the main draw, since it runs right alongside the resort, but Buckeye and Eagle Creeks are also nearby. Fish are planted in Robinson Creek at the bridge by Doc & Al's Resort.

If the fish aren't biting, you can go explore a few nearby ghost towns: Masonic, Aurora, Boulder Flat, and most famous of them all, Bodie State Historic Park. Hot springs lovers will want to check out Buckeye Hot Springs, a short distance from the resort, or Travertine Hot Springs, on the east side of Bridgeport.

Facilities: There are 10 one-room cabins without bathrooms that can accommodate up to four people, and 12 housekeeping cabins with bathrooms that can accommodate up to 10 people. The housekeeping cabins have fully equipped kitchens. A campground for RVs and tents is also available. A small general store is on-site.

Bedding: Linens and towels are provided.

Reservations and rates: Reservations are recommended. The fee for rustic one-room cabins is $42 to $61 per night; the fee for housekeeping cabins is $67 to $98 per night. Pets are permitted with a $3 fee per night.

Directions: From the junction of U.S. 395 and Highway 120 in Lee Vining, drive north on U.S. 395 for 25 miles to Bridgeport. Turn left (west) on Twin Lakes Road and drive seven miles, then turn right on Buckeye Road to enter Doc & Al's Resort.

Contact: Doc & Al's Resort, 85 Twin Lakes Road, P.O. Box 266, Bridgeport, CA 93517; 760/932-7051.

Doc & Al's Resort

8. HUNEWILL GUEST RANCH

Hunewill Guest Ranch is for horse lovers. If you've seen *Black Beauty* or *The Horse Whisperer* more times than you can remember, you will be among friends here. As you drive in to the ranch, you are greeted by miles of open pasture land and dozens, sometimes hundreds, of horses and cows. That scene sums up your entire vacation.

So, pack up your cowboy boots and a big sack of apples and carrots, and head for Bridgeport. Hunewill Guest Ranch comprises 26,000 acres of meadows and sagebrush, backed by the rugged mountains of the High Sierra. The original ranch was founded by Napoleon Bonaparte Hunewill (no kidding) in 1861. The guest ranch was opened by his descendants in the 1930s. The Hunewill family has been handling horses, cattle, and visitors around here long enough to know what they're doing.

The ranch caters to families, couples, singles, and people who travel with their own horses—in short, just about everybody. They try to provide a complete ranch experience, which means a wide mix of activities: evening

Off U.S. 395 near Bridgeport

Luxury rating: 3

Recreation rating: 4

THIS CABIN RANKS . . .
Best for Horseback Riding

cookouts and square dances, home-style meals in the Victorian ranch house, trout fishing in the East Walker River, cowboy skills lessons at the 1,200-head cattle ranch, and all the horseback riding you could want. (They have 120 horses on the ranch, so if you didn't bring your own, they'll assign you one.)

The cabins, which are cozy and clean, are located near the horse pasture, so you can stand on your front porch and watch the horses to your heart's content. Some of the cabins are newer than others, but all are in excellent repair. Not surprisingly, they're decorated in Western style.

Most people sign up for a seven-day package deal, which includes housing in cabins with private baths, plus all meals and activities. This costs about $1,000 for adults and half that for children. Not bad for a week's vacation, considering you won't spend another dime once you're there—although tips for the wrangler and ranch hands are appreciated—unless you plan to use the trophy trout pond, a new feature at the ranch. If you have a serious fly fisher in your family, he or she can pack along a float tube, pay an hourly fee, and catch a few two- to seven-pound rainbow trout.

If you're an equestrian but your spouse is not, Hunewill Ranch offers reduced rates for non-riding guests. If you bring your own horse, you can subtract $117 per week. Five- and three-day packages are also available. The ranch is open from late May to October 1, and the best time to visit may be the last week of the season, when the fall colors are on display and the air is cooler.

If for some reason you have the urge to leave the property, Buckeye Hot Springs and Travertine Hot Springs are nearby.

Facilities: There are 24 cabins, each with two rooms and two bathrooms. The cabins do not have kitchens; meals are included in your stay. A small general store and restaurant are on-site.

Bedding: Linens and towels are provided.

Reservations and rates: Reservations are required. Rates range from $909 to $1,119 per week for adults, including all meals and activities. Rates for children are $200 to $781 per week, depending on their ages. Five- and three-day packages are also available. The resort is open from late May to October 1. Pets are not permitted.

Directions: From the junction of U.S. 395 and Highway 120 in Lee Vining, drive north on U.S. 395 for 25 miles to Bridgeport. Turn left (west) on Twin Lakes Road and drive four miles to Hunewill Ranch on the left.

Contact: In summer: Hunewill Guest Ranch, P.O. Box 368, Bridgeport, CA 93517; 760/932-7710. In winter: Hunewill Guest Ranch, 200 Hunewill Lane, Wellington, NV 89444; 775/465-2201; website: www.hunewillranch.com.

Hunewill Guest Ranch

9. VIRGINIA CREEK SETTLEMENT

If you want to visit the ghost town at Bodie, there's no better place to stay than Virginia Creek Settlement. This is especially true if you're traveling with kids—or kids-at-heart. Not only is Virginia Creek Settlement the closest lodging to Bodie State Historic Park, it's also designed to get you in the Old West spirit.

Off U.S. 395 near Lee Vining

Luxury rating: 2

Recreation rating: 3

THIS CABIN RANKS . . .
Best for Families
Best for Value

The place looks like a movie set. The cabins are large converted sheds with clever false fronts crafted to look like the buildings of an Old West town; kids really get a kick out of this theme. Each represents a different enterprise, including Cooper's Freight and Mercantile Company, Assay and Land Office, and Anthony Agony, M.D. Three covered wagons (also for rent) complete the scene. If you want something more conventional, the resort has motel rooms and tent sites, but why spoil the ghost town mood?

Here's the unbelievable part: These cute little cabins cost a mere 20 bucks a night for two people. What a deal.

Inside, the cabins and covered wagons are one single room with beds. A communal restroom and shower area is a few feet away. Meals are available at the settlement's historic dining room; the menu is a mix of Italian and American, including pizza and wine. Order something Italian and pretend you're in a spaghetti Western.

Most people who stay at Virginia Creek Settlement have Bodie State Historic Park on their itinerary. Bodie was a gold-mining town that saw its heyday in the 1870s, when it boasted more than 30 operating mines, 65 saloons, and a population of more than 10,000 people. Like most mining towns, it eventually suffered a complete decline, and all its residents moved elsewhere. Still, Bodie's buildings have withstood the test of time. You can walk around the old town, peek in windows, and imagine what life was like in another era. A museum is open daily, but there are no other facilities or food services in the park.

To get to Bodie, drive one mile south on U.S. 395 and turn east on Highway 270. It's 13 miles to the ghost town (the last couple miles are gravel). For advice on other recreation in the area, the Toiyabe National Forest Ranger Station is just five miles north of Virginia Creek Settlement on U.S. 395.

10. VIRGINIA LAKES RESORT

"Watch your step; sea level is 9,770 feet down," notes the sign above the door at Virginia Lakes Resort. It should warn you to check your footing because of the scenery; the neighboring peaks are so spectacular, you could trip over something while gazing upward.

© ANN MARIE BROWN

Off U.S. 395 near Lee Vining

Luxury rating: 3

Recreation rating: 5

The resort is set on Little Virginia Lake, which is right next to Big Virginia Lake and within a half-mile drive of Trumbull Lake. Behind the lakes rise a few magnificent Sierra summits: Dunderberg Peak, Mount Olsen, Virginia Peak, and Black Mountain. In addition to its cabins, Virginia Lake Resort has a store, the small but good Summit Cafe (breakfast and lunch only), and rowboat rentals. No gas motors are permitted on any of the nearby lakes.

Unlike the resorts to the north at Bridgeport, and Lundy Lake Resort to the south, Virginia Lakes Resort caters to a somewhat more upscale crowd with tidier cabins and newer furnishings. We're not talking Ritz-Carlton quality here, more like Best Western, but the place is clean, attractive, and appealing.

Nine of the cabins have lake views; the other 10 are on Virginia Creek. For the best experience, make sure you request a cabin with a fireplace and a deck overlooking the lake. Not surprisingly, the resort is wildly popular, so its cabins are rented only by the week from June 15 to Labor Day. The rest of the season, there is a three-night minimum.

And get this—in a world of instant ATMs, automatic deposits, and plastic everything, Virginia Lakes Resort does not take credit cards. Hooray for them.

The main activity at the resort is fishing. Little Virginia, Big Virginia, and Trumbull Lakes are planted weekly with rainbow trout. If you want to catch only big ones, trophy fish are stocked on a monthly basis. The three lakes, plus seven others in the basin, also contain populations of native trout—eastern brook and German brown. It's a regular fish-o-rama.

Don't like to fish? There's plenty for hikers to do around Virginia Lake, also. From the trailhead at the end of the road, you can hike to several high alpine lakes, including Blue Lake, Cooney Lake, and Frog Lakes, all in the first 1.5 miles. If you can ignore the siren call of these pretty lakes, keep climbing up to 11,110-foot Burro Pass, where the views will knock your socks off. More lakes await on the other side.

Facilities: There are 19 cabins ranging in size that will accommodate 2 to 12 people. All cabins have fully equipped kitchens. Some have fireplaces. A small general store and restaurant are on-site.

Bedding: Linens and towels are provided.

Reservations and rates: Reservations are required; deposits must be mailed by check (the resort does not take credit cards). From June 15 to Labor Day, fees are $462 to $1,517 per week, depending on the number of people and size of cabin. The rest of the season, three-night rentals are available; the fee is $77 to $252 per night. The resort is usually open from late May to late September, depending on weather. Pets are permitted with a $20 fee.

Directions: From the junction of U.S. 395 and Highway 120 in Lee Vining, drive north on U.S. 395 for 12 miles to the left turnoff for Virginia Lakes (at Conway Summit). Turn left and drive six miles to the resort.

Contact: Virginia Lakes Resort, HCR 1 Box 1065, Bridgeport, CA 93517; 760/647-6484.

Virginia Lakes Resort

11. LUNDY LAKE RESORT

Lundy Lake Resort is the opposite of fancy or showy. If you spend much time thinking about what clothes to wear or what kind of car you drive, you won't like it here.

To illustrate my point, the owner told me he has owned the resort for 10 years and he's never done a thing to the cabins. They are bare bones and rustic, although they do come furnished with linens, bedding, and cooking utensils. Electricity comes from a generator, so forget about bringing along your hair dryer or espresso-maker. They aren't going to function well here, or if they do, somebody else will be groping around in the dark.

All that is irrelevant to the people who stay at Lundy Lake Resort, because they are here for one reason: to fish Lundy Lake and the neighboring streams in Lundy Canyon. At elevation 7,800 feet, Lundy Lake is one mile in length and has 100 surface acres, with a Southern California Edison dam at one end. The lake is set among pines, quaking aspens, and breathtaking granite mountains. In the 1880s, it was the site of a historic sawmill and mining town.

© ANN MARIE BROWN

Off U.S. 395 near Lee Vining

Luxury rating: 2

Recreation rating: 4

Brown and rainbow trout are regularly planted by the Department of Fish and Game. The resort rents boats with or without motors, and plenty of folks fish from shore, too. Mill Creek, the stream that feeds Lundy Lake, is also stocked. Brook and rainbow trout can be caught by anglers who hike into Lundy Canyon.

Speaking of hiking, a trailhead is located two miles west of the resort. It's the access point for Lundy Canyon, from which you can hike into the spectacular 20 Lakes Basin in 5.4 miles, or cut your trip short and enjoy the waterfalls and wildflowers in the first two miles. Another trailhead is located at the dam at the east end of Lundy Lake; this will take you to Crystal and Oneida Lakes and a historic gold mine in 3.5 miles. Mountain bikers also use this trail.

Two natural events shouldn't be missed at Lundy Lake Resort: the riotous wildflower bloom in Lundy Canyon, which usually occurs around July, and the colorful autumn aspen show in October.

Facilities: There are six cabins that can accommodate up to five people, plus four mobile home rentals. All have fully equipped kitchens. A small general store is on-site.

Bedding: Linens and towels are provided.

Reservations and rates: Reservations are recommended. Fees are $50 to $80 per night for two people, plus $5 for each additional person. There is a three-night-minimum stay from June 15 to September 15. The resort is open from late April to November 1. Pets are permitted.

Directions: From the junction of U.S. 395 and Highway 120 in Lee Vining, drive north on U.S. 395 for seven miles to the left turnoff for Lundy Lake. Turn left and drive five miles to the resort.

Contact: Lundy Lake Resort, P.O. Box 550, Lee Vining, CA 93541; 626/309-0415.

Lundy Lake Resort

12. TIOGA PASS RESORT

You can forget about staying at Tioga Pass Resort in the summer unless you're one of those people who can plan way in advance. A year and a half in advance, to be exact. Tioga Pass Resort is heavily booked for several reasons: It's perfectly situated next to Yosemite's high country, it's extremely well-managed, and it has a loyal clientele of folks who come back year after year.

Off Highway 120 near Tioga Pass

Luxury rating: 3

Recreation rating: 5

THIS CABIN RANKS . . .
Best for Winter Sports

If you've driven to Yosemite National Park on U.S. 395, you've passed right by the resort. It's situated on Tioga Road, just two miles from Yosemite's eastern entrance, at the mighty elevation of 9,600 feet. In summer, the resort's store, café, and outdoor espresso cart are popular stops for folks driving in and out of the park.

But only a lucky few stay in the cabins. In summer, they are available for rent by the week only. To get a reservation, you need to mail in your request in January for the following summer, i.e., 18 months in advance.

From the outside, the cabins don't bowl you over. They are quaint and rustic-looking, built of logs and painted brown with yellow and green trim. They are set quite close to the road and resort parking lot, but luckily, a stream runs between them, keeping noise to a minimum.

In addition to all the wonderful hikes in neighboring Yosemite (try the short but steep tromp to Gaylor Lakes, right by the park entrance station), resort guests can take advantage of their proximity to hiking and fishing opportunities at Saddlebag Lake and the 20 Lakes Basin. Mountain bikers will want to try out the Moraines and Meadows Trail near the junction of Tioga Pass Road and U.S. 395. Folks looking for an easy stroll should walk the trail to Bennettville, the site of an ill-fated 1882 silver mining operation that led to the construction of the original Tioga Road.

You can cook in your cabin if you wish, but it's hard to justify when Tioga Pass Resort's café makes such great food. Their Tioga Burgers are legendary. Breakfasts are just what you want in the mountains—big fluffy pancakes and huge omelettes.

In winter, Tioga Pass Resort transforms into a cozy ski lodge. Most years, both deep powder and spring corn snow are in plentiful supply. The road to the resort isn't plowed in winter; you have to ski in six miles. (Consequently, this makes winter reservations easier to come by.) Guests stay in heated cabins, then get together in the main lodge for meals, which are included in the price.

Facilities: There are 10 one- and two-bedroom cabins, plus four motel rooms. All cabins have fully equipped kitchens. A small general store and restaurant are on-site.

Bedding: Linens and towels are provided in summer only; in winter, ski in with your own.

Reservations and rates: Reservations are required. Fees are $700 to $900 per week in summer (weekly rentals only) and $120 per person per night in winter (meals included). A reduced rate is offered midweek in winter. Pets are not permitted.

Directions: From U.S. 395 at Mammoth Lakes, drive north 26 miles on U.S. 395 to Highway 120. Turn west on Highway 120 and drive 12 miles to Tioga Pass Resort on the right.

Coming from the west in Yosemite National Park, take Highway 120 east. Pass the Tioga Pass entrance station, then continue two more miles to Tioga Pass Resort on the left.

Contact: Tioga Pass Resort, P.O. Box 7, Lee Vining, CA 93541; 209/372-4471; website: www.tiogapassresort.com.

Tioga Pass Resort

13. TIOGA LODGE

Considering how wonderful it is, it's a pity that Tioga Lodge suffers from an identity crisis: People keep confusing it with similarly named Tioga Pass Resort. That's partly because Tioga Lodge is the new kid in town, whereas Tioga Pass Resort has been around forever. And it's partly because the two resorts are only 15 miles apart, and both have cabins for rent.

Off U.S. 395 near Lee Vining

Luxury rating: 3

Recreation rating: 4

The lodge is located right smack on U.S. 395, which could deter from its desirability because of incessant road noise, except that its roadside setting allows open views of Mono Lake. No other cabin resort overlooks this spectacular 60,000-acre saltwater oddity, with its coral-like tufa spires and strange looking volcanic islands. If you want to see or visit Mono Lake, Tioga Lodge is your ticket.

The lodge may be newly opened, but in fact, it isn't new at all. Several of its buildings were transported here in the 1880s; they came from the nearby gold mining town of Bodie (now a state historic park). One hundred years later, the long-closed buildings had become an eyesore. But along came Walter and Lou Vint, who restored the original buildings and added new ones to Tioga Lodge. At this book's press time, these proud owners are still working at it.

The cabins are furnished with late 1800s

antiques and pine log furniture. No two cabins are alike; each has its own personality that reflects the Mono Basin area's history. None of the cabins have kitchens, so you'll eat at the lodge's excellent restaurant, or at the highly acclaimed Mono Inn just up the road. For something more casual, you can always drive south into Lee Vining and get a hamburger or a barbecue dinner.

Tioga Lodge is one of the few places north of Lee Vining that stays open year-round. The owners cater to anglers; in fact, as long as you clean your catch, they will cook and/or smoke your fish for you. The lodge also attracts skiers poised for Mammoth or June Lake, and hikers heading for Lundy Canyon and surrounding Inyo National Forest.

The most obvious attraction, of course, is Mono Lake. Tioga Lodge is just two miles north of the Mono Basin National Forest Scenic Area Visitor Center, where you can learn everything about the 700,000-year-old body of water. The lodge is across the road from Mono Lake County Park, where you can get a close look at some of the lake's tufa spires, put in your kayak or canoe, or go swimming (the salt water makes you extremely buoyant!). The most impressive group of tufas is located a few miles to the south, at the Mono Lake Tufa State Reserve.

Facilities: There are 12 one- and two-bedroom cabins, plus four motel rooms. Some cabins are duplex-style; none have kitchens. A small general store and restaurant are on-site.

Bedding: Linens and towels are provided.

Reservations and rates: Reservations are recommended. Fees are $70 to $120 per night. Seasonal discounts are available. The resort is open year-round. Pets are not permitted.

Directions: From the junction of U.S. 395 and Highway 120 in Lee Vining, drive north on U.S. 395 for 2.5 miles to Tioga Lodge on the left.

Contact: Tioga Lodge, P.O. Box 580, Lee Vining, CA 93541; 760/647-6423; website: www.tiogalodge.com.

Tioga Lodge

14. YOSEMITE LAKES

Most people who stay at Yosemite Lakes make the five-mile drive into Yosemite National Park at least once during their stay, but a surprising amount are happy to hang around on the resort's grounds and just sink into vacation mode. You know vacation mode: the operating procedure in which you get up every morning, put on your bathing suit and flip-flops, then wear them right up until bed time. In between, you read a few chapters of a book, sip cool drinks and eat Doritos, and maybe debate the merits of catch-and-release fishing with your cohorts. The hours pass quite pleasantly this way.

Yosemite Lakes is located off Highway 120, midway between Groveland and Yosemite National Park, on the South Fork of the Tuolumne River. It's just hot enough in summer that you'll probably want to hang around the

Off Highway 120 in Groveland

Luxury rating: 3

Recreation rating: 3

THIS CABIN RANKS . . .

Best for Families

river all day, but just shady enough that you'll never be too hot.

Members of the Thousand Trails/NACO camping organization have a sweet deal here; they can rent Yosemite Lakes' cabins and yurts for a 20 percent discount over the regular prices. The cabins are typical rustic wood-frame units—nice but not especially note-worthy—but the yurts are unique: They're circular, tent-like structures with a skylight and windows, and are equipped with full kitchens and baths. They even have satellite TV, for whatever that's worth. Ten yurts are clustered together in Yurt Village, but each one has an abundance of space around it. Bar-becues and picnic tables are located outside each yurt if you don't feel like cooking inside.

Recreation opportunities abound. The South Fork Tuolumne River runs through Yosemite Lakes' property and monopolizes a good portion of guests' itineraries. Kayaks, inner tubes, fishing poles, and gold pans are available for rent. Horseback riding is popu-lar from mid-May to mid-September; stables are located on the grounds. Most visitors don't do anything more ambitious than an hour-long ride through the pines, but it's great fun for families.

Facilities: There are 10 cabins and 10 yurts that can accommodate up to four peo-ple, plus hostel and inn accommodations, an RV park, and tent sites. The yurts have full kitchens; the cabins do not. A store is on-site.

Bedding: Linens and towels are provided.

Reservations and rates: Reservations are recommended. Fees range from $44 to $104 per night from May to October; $44 to $84 per night from November to April, except holidays. Thousand Trails/NACO members receive a 20 percent discount. Pets are permitted.

Directions: From Fresno, take Highway 99 north to Manteca. Turn east on High-way 120 and drive 65 miles to Groveland. From Groveland, continue east on Highway 120 for 16 miles to the sign for Yosemite Lakes on the right, at Hardin Flat Road.

Contact: Yosemite Lakes, 31191 Hardin Flat Road, Groveland, CA 95321; 209/962-0100 or 800/533-1001; website: www.1000trails.com.

OTHER CABINS AND COTTAGES NEARBY

- Sunset Inn Yosemite Guest Cabins, 33569 Hardin Flat Road, Groveland, CA 95321; 209/962-4360.

- Yosemite Pines RV Resort, 20450 Old Highway 120, Grove-land, CA 95321; 209/962-5042 or 800/368-5386; website: www.yosemitepines.com.

Yosemite Lakes

15. EVERGREEN LODGE

Most everybody in California has visited Yosemite Valley at one time or another, but not everybody has visited Hetch Hetchy Valley, Yosemite's twin in the northern section of the park. Of the five park entrance stations, Hetch Hetchy gets the fewest number of cars passing through, day after day.

Off Highway 120 in Yosemite

Luxury rating: 3

Recreation rating: 3

Hetch Hetchy Valley was flooded in 1906 to create a water supply for the city of San Francisco. It was the tragic end of a long fight for naturalist John Muir, who tried in vain to save Hetch Hetchy from the big city politicians. Remarkably, Hetch Hetchy is still beautiful today, even though it's covered with 400 feet of water.

When it's your time to visit Hetch Hetchy, book a stay at the cabins at Evergreen Lodge. Located nine miles up the Hetch Hetchy Road from Highway 120, Evergreen Lodge is only a half-hour drive from Hetch Hetchy's spectacular water-filled valley. You can spend a comfortable night in your cabin, then get up early and head to the trailhead at Hetch Hetchy's impressive dam. In a single day, you can hike out and back along the length of the reservoir, passing spectacular waterfalls, granite cliffs, and a prolific variety of trees, plants, and wildflowers. The entire round-trip is 13 miles; plenty of people just hike a portion of it. Wapama Falls, at two miles out, is a highlight. At the end of the day, you're back at Evergreen Lodge, where you can have dinner at the lodge's outdoor barbecue.

Other recreation options include a visit to pretty Carlon Falls on the South Fork Tuolumne River (a two-mile hike from the trailhead at Carlon Day-Use Area), and fishing in the Tuolumne. Don't think about fishing or swimming in Hetch Hetchy; since it's a water supply, people are strictly forbidden from going in or near the lake. However, many anglers park at Hetch Hetchy's dam and hike down to the river below.

You won't be bowled over by luxury at Evergreen Lodge; the cabins look like they haven't changed much since the 1920s, when most were built. A few are duplexes; make sure you request the individual units if it matters to you. Don't be surprised if you have a visit from Mr. Bear; several of the big furry guys make nightly raids on the lodge to see if anyone has left trash or food outside. Be sure to follow all the posted rules about food storage and garbage.

Facilities: There are 12 one- and two-bedroom cabins. A restaurant, deli, bar, and store are on-site.

Bedding: Linens and towels are provided.

Reservations and rates: Reservations are recommended. Fees range from $69 to $105 per night, and include breakfast. The lodge is open from April to October. Pets are not permitted.

Directions: From Fresno, take Highway 99 north to Manteca. Turn east on Highway 120 and drive 65 miles to Groveland. From Groveland, continue east on Highway 120 for 22 miles to the left turnoff for Evergreen Road and Hetch Hetchy. Turn left and drive nine miles to Evergreen Lodge on the left.

Contact: Evergreen Lodge, 33160 Evergreen Road, Groveland, CA 95321; 209/379-2606 or 800/935-6343; website: www.evergreenlodge.com.

OTHER CABINS AND COTTAGES NEARBY
- Yosemite Riverside Inn, 11399 Cherry Lake Road, Groveland, CA 95321; 800/626-7408; website: www.yosemiteriversideinn.com.

Evergreen Lodge

16. WHITE WOLF LODGE

The first time you glimpse the cabins at White Wolf, you sense the realization of your Yosemite lodging dreams. Set at the sweet high-country elevation of 8,000 feet, the white wooden cabins are trimmed in hunter green, with Adirondack chairs lined up on the porches to face a wildflower-filled meadow. If you think that it doesn't get any better than this, you're exactly right.

© ANN MARIE BROWN

Off Highway 120 in Yosemite

Luxury rating: 2

Recreation rating: 4

Except that you might be wrong. The trick is that not every White Wolf cabin is one of those quaint *Sunset* magazine–style jobs; only the ones visible from the parking lot fit that bill. Right behind them are dozens of typical Yosemite tent cabins—large, dirty-white tents on raised wooden platforms, almost bare inside except for a woodburning stove, candles for lighting, and a couple of beds.

There are four white wooden cabins, and they have their own bathrooms, propane heat, daily maid service, and electricity (generated only during certain hours of the day). There are 24 tent cabins, and they have none of the above. Guess which ones are harder to come by?

Regardless of which type of cabin you reserve, everything about a stay at White Wolf is easy. An excellent restaurant on the premises serves breakfast and dinner and makes box lunches to go. Dinners include steak, fish, chicken, a vegetarian entrée, and hamburgers. Prices are reasonable ($10 to $16 for entrées). A small store sells snacks, drinks, and a few minimal supplies.

Hikers can set out right from their cabins. The best options are the 2.5-mile trail to Lukens Lake and the three-mile trail to Harden Lake. The Harden Lake Trail is great for wildflowers, but the lake itself practically dries up by the end of summer. Go see it in June or July. Lukens Lake is ideal for swimming throughout the summer; the shallow water warms up to a comfortable temperature.

The big question is: How do you get one of those white-and-green cabins at White Wolf? Plan on calling at least a year in advance. Rub your rabbit's foot, then pick up the phone.

Facilities: There are four wooden cabins with private bathrooom, propane heat, and electricity that can accommodate up to four people. There are 24 tent cabins that can accommodate up to four people. A restaurant and small store are on-site.

Bedding: Linens and towels are provided.

Reservations and rates: Reservations are required. Fees are $49 per night for tent cabins; $83 per night for wooden cabins. The lodge is open from mid-June to early September. Pets are not permitted.

Directions: From Fresno, take Highway 99 north to Manteca. Turn east on Highway 120 and drive 65 miles to Groveland. From Groveland, continue east on Highway 120 for 23 miles to the Big Oak Flat entrance at Yosemite. Continue east on Highway 120 for nine miles to Crane Flat, then turn left and drive 15 miles to the White Wolf turnoff on the left.

If you're coming from U.S. 395, White Wolf is 32 miles west of the Tioga Pass entrance station to Yosemite.

Contact: Yosemite Reservations, 5410 East Home Avenue, Fresno, CA 93727; 559/252-4848; website: www.yosemitepark.com.

White Wolf Lodge

17. YOSEMITE HIGH SIERRA CAMPS

Among people who love to hike but hate to carry a heavy backpack, the Yosemite High Sierra Camps are legendary. The five camps are spaced 5.7 to 10 miles apart along a loop trail that begins at Tuolumne Meadows. With nothing on your back but a light day pack filled with water, a change of clothes, sheets, and a towel, you hike through the high country for nearly a week. Along the way, you eat first-rate meals, enjoy hot showers, and sleep in a comfortable bed in a tent cabin each night.

Not everybody does the whole loop and stays at all five camps. In fact, unless you plan a year in advance, it's virtually impossible to do so. Reservations for the High Sierra Camps are taken on a lottery basis each autumn, and only a lucky few win the lottery.

Off Highway 120 in Yosemite

Luxury rating: 2

Recreation rating: 4

THIS CABIN RANKS . . .
Best for Hiking

Still, many people manage to get reservations for an out-and-back trip to one or more of the camps. Even those who wait until the last minute have a fair chance, because each summer there are cancellations. The key is to call the High Sierra Camp desk on a regular basis; availability changes minute by minute. Another option is to sign up for organized four- and seven-day trips led by National Park Service rangers; these cost more, but you get the benefit of having a naturalist guide along on your trip. Organized horseback trips are also available.

If you aren't traveling the entire loop, the one-way hikes to the camps are as follows: Glen Aulin at 7,800 feet is five miles from the Lembert Dome Trailhead. May Lake at 9,300 feet is one mile from the May Lake Trailhead. Sunrise Camp at 9,400 feet is five miles from the Sunrise Trailhead. Vogelsang Camp at 10,300 feet is seven miles from the Tuolumne Meadows Trailhead. Merced Lake Camp at 7,200 feet is the only one that's a bit far to reach if you're not traveling from another camp on the loop; it's 15 miles from Tuolumne Meadows or 13 miles from Yosemite Valley.

The set-up is basically the same at all five camps, although each has a varying number of tent cabins, so the size of the crowd will differ. (Merced Lake Camp is the largest, with a 60-person occupancy; the others fit 30 to 40 guests at a time.) Dinner and breakfast are served in a main dining tent; box lunches can be purchased to go. Generally, the camps are very social: Meals are served family-style, and the tent cabins are spaced within a few feet of each other, so you'll get to know your neighbors. Hope they don't snore.

Speaking of snoring, one critical rule at the High Sierra Camps is that overnight accommodations are dormitory style, which means that men and women are housed in separate tents, four people to a tent. If your significant other happens to be of the opposite sex, you'll have to wave goodbye to him or her at night.

Facilities: Glen Aulin and May Lake have eight tent cabins each, Sunrise has nine tent cabins, Merced Lake has 19 tent cabins, and Vogelsang has 12 tent cabins. The cabins can accommodate up to four people. Meals are provided.

Bedding: Pillows and blankets are provided, but not linens and towels; guests may purchase sleep-sacks and trek towels by mail order from the High Sierra Camp desk, or bring their own sheets and towels.

18. TUOLUMNE LODGE

Tuolumne Lodge has the same upsides as other tent cabin resorts in Yosemite's high country: a chance to stay in convenient lodging right in the midst of Yosemite's best day hiking, fishing, and scenery-watching country, with easy access to hearty meals and necessary supplies.

Off Highway 120 in Yosemite

Luxury rating: 2

Recreation rating: 5

THIS CABIN RANKS . . .
Best for Hiking

It also has the same downsides as the other resorts: the cabins are a bit dark and dreary (canvas-covered tents on raised wood platforms with nothing but beds, candles, and a woodburning stove). Also, they are packed in so tightly that you can hear your neighbors talking, coughing, and snoring at night. At Tuolumne Lodge, it's slightly worse than at nearby White Wolf, because Tuolumne has a whopping 59 tent cabins. That's enough for a small tent cabin city.

Of course, few people who stay here ever complain. The upsides simply far outweigh the downsides. Guests come to be within a stone's throw of Tuolumne Meadows, and not for any other reason. The cabins are across the road from Lembert Dome and the Soda Springs trailhead, and within 100 yards of the John Muir Trail and Pacific Crest Trail. Hiking options are virtually unlimited. Short, long, easy, hard—whatever kind of trails you like, you can access them without needing to drive anywhere.

If hiking isn't your bag, you can always rock climb, fish, ride horses from the

Tuolumne Meadows stables, or take the free shuttle bus to other points along Tioga Road. After exploring the high country all day, you'll sit down to a hearty dinner at the Tuolumne Meadows Lodge dining tent alongside the Tuolumne River. The food is excellent and prices are reasonable, especially considering the spectacular setting.

If you prefer something more casual, the Tuolumne Meadows Grill is a half mile down the road by the Tuolumne Meadows campground and store. They make great buckwheat pancakes, plus the usual burgers and fries.

Facilities: There are 59 tent cabins that can accommodate up to four people. A restaurant and small store are on-site.

Bedding: Linens and towels are provided.

Reservations and rates: Reservations are required. Fees are $56 per night. The lodge is open from mid-June to mid-September. Pets are not permitted.

Directions: From Fresno, take Highway 99 north to Manteca. Turn east on Highway 120 and drive 65 miles to Groveland. From Groveland, continue east on Highway 120 for 23 miles to the Big Oak Flat entrance at Yosemite. Continue east on Highway 120 for nine miles to Crane Flat, then turn left and drive 39 miles to the Tuolumne Meadows Lodge turnoff on the right, just past Lembert Dome.

If you're coming from U.S. 395, Tuolumne Meadows Lodge is 6.5 miles west of the Tioga Pass entrance station to Yosemite.

Contact: Yosemite Reservations, 5410 East Home Avenue, Fresno, CA 93727; 559/252-4848; website: www.yosemitepark.com.

Tuolumne Lodge

19. CURRY VILLAGE CABINS

Many visitors have a love-hate relationship with Curry Village in Yosemite Valley. On the one hand, they love Curry Village because it's centrally located in the Valley and it comes with all the amenities: lodging, food, parking, bus shuttles, stores, etc. On the other hand, they hate Curry Village because it embodies the worst of Yosemite Valley on its most hectic summer days: too many people, too crowded, too noisy.

That said, make sure you know what you are signing up for when you book a stay at Curry Village. In the off-season (or even in summer if you plan way in advance), you could be fortunate enough to rent one of Curry Village's private, cozy, wooden cabins. If you were born under a lucky star, you might even get one of the cabins with private bath, which will save you from a hike to the restroom in the middle of the night.

But most of the time, and for the vast majority of visitors, the only cabins available at Curry Village are the 400-plus tent cabins. The two facts you need to know about these cabins are that they are made of

© ANN MARIE BROWN

Off Highway 140 in Yosemite Valley

Luxury rating: 3

Recreation rating: 5

THIS CABIN RANKS . . .
Best for Families

canvas and they are placed about nine inches apart. This is convenient if you want to stay up late and learn a new language from the bevy of international visitors. Of course, it's inconvenient if you enjoy sleeping. The tent cabins have electric lights, and some of them are heated. Other than that, don't expect much other than a couple of beds with linens.

Regardless of how much sleep you get, you are situated in the most glorious national park in California, so you can't complain all that much. Every imaginable form of outdoor recreation is right outside your door—hiking, biking, fishing, rock-climbing, waterfall watching, horseback riding, you name it. Curry Village is ideally situated near the Happy Isles trailhead, where the spectacular hikes to Vernal and Nevada Falls, and the arduous trek to the summit of Half Dome, begin.

In winter, Curry Village's ice-skating rink is open daily. In summer, naturalist programs are held every evening, and bicycle and raft rentals are available. One of the greatest ways to see Yosemite Valley in early summer is to take a lazy float down the Merced River in an inflatable raft.

Facilities: There are 102 wooden cabins with private baths, 80 wooden cabins without a private bath, and 427 canvas tent cabins, plus 19 standard motel rooms. None of the cabins have kitchens. A restaurant, café, store, swimming pool, and equipment rentals are on-site.

Bedding: Linens and towels are provided.

Reservations and rates: Reservations are recommended. Fees are $48 to $58 per night for tent cabins and $74 to $102 per night for wooden cabins. Pets are not permitted.

Directions: From Merced, take Highway 140 east for 75 miles to the Arch Rock entrance station at Yosemite. Continue east into Yosemite Valley for 11.5 miles to Curry Village on the right.

Contact: Yosemite Reservations, 5410 East Home Avenue, Fresno, CA 93727; 559/252-4848; website: www.yosemitepark.com.
Curry Village Cabins

20. GLACIER POINT SKI HUT

If you like the sound of an overnight stay at a cross-country ski hut, but think that getting there may be beyond your abilities, the Glacier Point Ski Hut will ease your fears about your snow skills. Although the distance to be covered on skis or snowshoes is a substantial 10 miles from where you leave your car, the going is easy, and you have almost nothing to carry.

Off Glacier Point Road in Yosemite

Luxury rating: 2

Recreation rating: 3

If you've driven to Glacier Point in summer, you've seen the Glacier Point Ski Hut. Except in summer, it's not a ski hut, it's an impressive log building that houses a snack shop a few yards from one of the West's most spectacular viewpoints. While savoring the incomparable view of Half Dome and the valley floor 3,000 feet below, you can buy a snow cone here in August or make a snowman here in February—take your pick. Completely renovated in 1997, the ski hut building is a lovely structure in any season, with its massive timber beams and huge stone fireplace. In winter, Yosemite Concession Services (YCS) removes the store shelves and cash registers and puts in bunk beds, then leads guided ski trips with an overnight stay at the hut.

The fact that the trip requires a guide makes it suitable even for beginners. Although YCS requests that you are at least an intermediate-level cross-country skier, plenty of beginners make the trip. It's doable because the 10-mile route from Badger Pass is on a well-groomed track that follows Glacier Point Road all the way. With one guide in front of your group and one in back, everybody skis at their own pace and nobody gets left behind.

It's also doable for beginners because you carry almost nothing on your back. YCS issues each skier his or her own lightweight liner to stuff inside the hut's sleeping bags. You carry that and some water and snacks for the trip; the guides take care of the rest, including all meals and wine.

The minimum number of people for a night at Glacier Point Ski Hut is five; the maximum is 20. On weeknights, you and your family or friends can have the place to yourselves (plus your guides, of course). On weekends, you're likely to share the place with company, unless you managed to convince 20 people to go with you.

Facilities: There is one ski hut that can accommodate 5 to 20 people. Meals are provided.

Bedding: Sleeping bags and liners are provided.

21. SILVER LAKE RESORT

Of all the real estate for sale in the June Lake area, the toughest properties to buy are those on the shore of Silver Lake. They almost never come up for sale. Why? Because most people agree that 110-acre Silver Lake is the prettiest of the four lakes on the June Lake Loop, and having a piece of it is too good to give up.

Off Highway 158 in June Lake

Luxury rating: 3

Recreation rating: 4

Luckily, there's Silver Lake Resort, where anybody can get a little piece of Silver Lake, at least for a few days or a week. Silver Lake Resort is a full-service operation with a general store, cabins, café, RV park, and boat rentals. It was established in 1916, which makes it the oldest resort in the eastern Sierra.

The resort has plain, brown, log-style cabins—rustic-looking on the outside, but clean and well cared for on the inside. Many have remodeled interiors, including new curtains and bedding. None have telephones, and only a few have televisions. The cabins are set amid a grove of aspens, giving the illusion of seclusion even though they are close together. All cabins are only a stone's throw from the lake; a few have lake views.

Most resort guests take advantage of fishing on Silver Lake; motorboats and canoes are for rent by the hour or the day. If you want to hike, the Rush Creek Trailhead is about 100 yards away, from which a spectacular day hike can be taken to Agnew and Gem Lakes. If you have the urge to ride Old Paint, a pack station is located next door to the resort.

Facilities: There are 17 cabins ranging in size that can accommodate two to eight people. All cabins have fully equipped kitchens. A general store, café, and RV park are on-site.

Bedding: Linens and towels are provided.

Reservations and rates: Reservations are recommended. Fees are $70 to $195 per night, depending on cabin size. For the eight-person cabins, a five-night minimum stay is required. The resort is open from June to October, weather permitting. Pets are not permitted.

Directions: From U.S. 395 at the Highway 203/Mammoth Lakes turnoff, drive 15 miles north on U.S. 395 to Highway 158, the southern turnoff for the June Lake Loop. Turn west on Highway 158 and drive 7.5 miles to Silver Lake Resort on the left.

Contact: Silver Lake Resort, P.O. Box 116, June Lake, CA 93529; 760/648-7525; website: silverlakeresort.net.

Silver Lake Resort

22. REVERSE CREEK LODGE

"Our family welcomes yours" is the motto at Reverse Creek Lodge. The Reverse Creek Lodge (similarly—but not quite literally—named after Reversed Creek) family is David and Denise Naaden and their 12 children, whom they call their "cleaning crew." With that many kids, the place ought to be clean as a whistle, and sure enough, it is.

Off Highway 158 in June Lake

Luxury rating: 3

Recreation rating: 4

The Naadens took over the lodge and its cabins and A-frame chalets in 1995. The rustic cabins are set in the pines along Reversed Creek, but the modern A-frame chalets are the more popular rentals. Located down the street about 100 yards from the rest of the resort, the chalets are perched above Reversed Creek in a cluster of pines. Some have a fair view of 10,909-foot Carson Peak, a mammoth granite landmark in June Lake.

The only disadvantage is that the five chalets are a bit cramped, each one only a few feet from the next. Like the cabins, the A-frames have fully stocked kitchens, cable TV, VCRs, gas fireplaces, gas barbecues, and all the other amenities of home. For big groups, the resort has a private residence cabin with four bedrooms and two full baths.

At Reverse Creek Lodge, all the recreation opportunities of the June Lake area are at your disposal. The ski resort is only a half mile away, fishing is possible in four lakes (June, Silver, Gull, and Grant) and several streams, horses and bicycles can be rented, and so on. Hikers can head for the Yost Creek Trail, located next door to the resort. Featuring a hearty climb, the trail leads to Yost and Fern Lakes. The last mile to Fern Lake is the steepest; if you want something a little easier, take the left fork to Yost Lake. Both are scenic, high alpine lakes.

Facilities: There are eight cabins with one or two bedrooms, five A-frame chalets that can accommodate up to six people, and one large four-bedroom house. All have fully equipped kitchens. A store and restaurant are nearby.

Bedding: Linens and towels are provided.

Reservations and rates: Reservations are recommended. Fees are $65 to $100 per night for the cabins, $125 to $140 per night for the chalets, and $245 per night for the four-bedroom house. The resort is open year-round. Pets are not permitted.

Directions: From U.S. 395 at the Highway 203/Mammoth Lakes turnoff, drive 15 miles north on U.S. 395 to Highway 158, the southern turnoff for the June Lake Loop. Turn west on Highway 158 and drive 4.5 miles to Reverse Creek Lodge on the left.

Contact: Reverse Creek Lodge, Route 3, Box 2, June Lake, CA 93529; 760/648-7535 or 800/762-6440; website: www.reversecreeklodge.com.

Reverse Creek Lodge

23. FERN CREEK LODGE

All of the cabin resorts in June Lake are clean, serviceable, and well-situated for recreation enthusiasts. But some simply have more character than others, and Fern Creek Lodge is in that category. Maybe it's because the lodge has been around since 1927 (it's the oldest year-round lodge on the June Lake Loop), or maybe it's that each of its cabins is completely different in style and appearance. There's just something about this resort that makes it cozy and appealing.

The cutest cabin is the green-and-white Old Schoolhouse, a tiny little house for two people only. It's situated at the back of the property, farthest from the road. Dutch Lady and Heart Tree are the largest cabins; they're both two-story units with four bedrooms, two bathrooms, and a sundeck around the front.

A modern hot tub is set in the middle of the cabins; guests take turns using it. The main lodge area has a selection of games and—get this—Internet access. A common barbecue area and fish-cleaning facilities are available. If you don't feel like cooking, you can always drive down the road a half mile to the Carson Peak Inn, a popular dinner spot in June Lake.

© ANN MARIE BROWN

Off Highway 158 in June Lake

Luxury rating: 3

Recreation rating: 4

For recreation, take your pick from all that June Lake has to offer: trout fishing in four good-sized lakes, water sports, and swimming in summer; downhill skiing, cross-country skiing, snowboarding, and snowmobiling in winter; and watching the aspens turn bright gold in autumn. Hiking and biking in the area are excellent any time the ground is snow-free. The lodge is located a half mile from June Mountain Ski Area and midway between Gull and Silver Lakes. Basically, nothing you might want to do is more than five miles away.

Facilities: There are 10 cabins ranging in size from one to four bedrooms, plus four apartment units. All cabins have fully equipped kitchens. A hot tub and small store are on-site; a restaurant is nearby.

Bedding: Linens and towels are provided.

Reservations and rates: Reservations are recommended. Fees are $50 per night for the one-bedroom cabins, $110 to $120 per night for the two-bedroom cabins, and $210 per night for the four-bedroom cabins, which can accommodate up to 14 people. (Rate is based on eight people; add $8 per night for each additional person.) The resort is open year-round. Pets are permitted with an $8 fee per night.

Directions: From U.S. 395 at the Highway 203/Mammoth Lakes turnoff, drive 15 miles north on U.S. 395 to Highway 158, the southern turnoff for the June Lake Loop. Turn west on Highway 158 and drive five miles to Fern Creek Lodge on the right.

Contact: Fern Creek Lodge, 4628 Highway 158, Route 3, Box 7, June Lake, CA 93529; 760/648-7722 or 800/621-9146; website: www.ferncreeklodge.com.

Fern Creek Lodge

24. FOUR SEASONS

If the idea of looking out your cabin's floor-to-ceiling windows at 10,909-foot Carson Peak appeals to you, you'll enjoy staying at the Four Seasons. The resort's A-frame chalets are located just off the road at the base of Carson Peak, across the street from the popular restaurant at Carson Peak Inn.

From the front, they don't look like much. The six chalets are packed in like sardines (they're almost touching each other). But once you're inside, you remember why you came here: The view of Carson Peak's snow-covered granite is truly stunning.

Each chalet is identical: 800 square feet in size, with an enclosed master bedroom, plus a loft bedroom that overlooks the living room. The living room has the giant windows with the view. If you want an even better view, go sit outside on your chalet's sundeck. In summer, you can flip hamburgers while you gaze at the scenery; the chalets have gas barbecues. If you prefer to cook indoors, the kitchens are fully stocked with everything you need except food.

Off Highway 158 in June Lake

Luxury rating: 3

Recreation rating: 4

Just about every kind of recreation imaginable is possible from your Four Seasons chalet. Within a 10-minute drive are the four lakes of the June Lake Loop (including five marinas and a swimming beach). A horse stable is just down the road, as are several hiking trailheads. Cyclists enjoy riding the 21-mile June Lake Loop (it's wise to get an early morning start, especially on weekends, before the traffic gets going). In winter, June Mountain Ski Area provides the fun. Or, if you strap on a pair of snowshoes or cross-country skis, you can explore the closed-in-winter section of the June Lake Loop.

Only one element is missing from a vacation at Four Seasons: Although the chalets have old-fashioned wood stoves, the resort doesn't provide firewood. You have to buy your own.

Facilities: There are six chalets that can accommodate up to seven people. All cabins have fully equipped kitchens. A store and restaurant are nearby.

Bedding: Linens and towels are provided.

Reservations and rates: Reservations are recommended. Fees are $89 for two people, plus $20 for each additional person (maximum is seven at $189). Rates are slightly higher in August and during summer and winter holidays. A three-night minimum stay is required. The resort is open year-round. Pets are not permitted.

Directions: From U.S. 395 at the Highway 203/Mammoth Lakes turnoff, drive 15 miles north on U.S. 395 to Highway 158, the southern turnoff for the June Lake Loop. Turn west on Highway 158 and drive five miles to the Four Seasons on the left.

Contact: Four Seasons, Star Route 3, Box 8-B, June Lake, CA 93529; 760/648-7476; website: www.junelake.com/lodging/foursns.

OTHER CABINS AND COTTAGES NEARBY

• Gull Lake Lodge, P.O. Box 25, June Lake, CA 93529; 760/648-7516 or 800/631-9081.

• June Lake Pines Cottages, P.O. Box 97, June Lake, CA 93529; 760/648-7522 or 800/481-3637.

• June Lake Motel and Cabins, P.O. Box 98, June Lake, CA 93529; 760/648-7547 or 800/648-6835; website: www.junelake.com/jlmotel.

• Lake Front Cabins, P.O. Box 696, June Lake, CA 93529; 760/648-7527; website: www.lake-front-cabins.com.

• Whispering Pines Motel and Cabins, Route 3, Box 14-B, June Lake, CA 93529; 760/648-7762 or 800/648-7762; website: www.junelake.com/wpines.

Four Seasons

25. DOUBLE EAGLE RESORT

When the Double Eagle Resort opened in 1999, most June Lake regulars weren't sure what to think of it. It was (and is) far more upscale than other local resorts, or even those in nearby Mammoth Lakes. Would people want to stay there? Would all that money spent on a fancy restaurant, health spa, picture-perfect cabins, and trophy trout ponds go to waste? And what would it mean for the future of June Lake? Would it change the character of the place?

Off Highway 158 in June Lake

Luxury rating: 5

Recreation rating: 4

THIS CABIN RANKS . . .
Most Luxurious

Well, a few years have gone by, and after all the hubbub, it seems that little is different in June Lake, except now the town has a really plush cabin resort and a great restaurant, and the locals can join the resort's health club for a discounted fee. The Double Eagle owners are well-respected for bringing in more business to the June Lake Loop.

No doubt about it, the Double Eagle is the most luxurious place to stay in June Lake. It features brand-new, two-bedroom cabins with fully equipped kitchens and fireplaces. They are tastefully decorated and large enough to fit four to six people. All the extra amenities are provided: microwave oven, barbecue, TV and VCR, and the like. They even have telephones, a rarity in the cabin world.

Additionally, the resort features the Creekside Spa and Fitness Center, which includes a gorgeous 60-foot indoor pool and hot tub and all kinds of fitness equipment and classes. There is even a full-service salon for guests who want to get their nails or hair done, or have a facial treatment or massage. Honestly, that's about the last thing I would do on vacation in June Lake, but whatever floats your boat.

Then there's the Eagle's Landing Restaurant, which serves the best food in town, and offers a scenic view besides. Every table has a look at Carson Peak and Reversed Creek. In addition to the regular menu, the restaurant offers a spa menu, just in case you're taking this fitness thing seriously.

So when you've finally finished your pedicure, aromatherapy massage, tai chi class, and gourmet lunch, what's next? You can head outside and try out the resort's trophy trout pond, which is stocked with trout up to 18 pounds. What, you don't know how to fly-fish? No matter, they offer lessons daily. There's even a fly-fishing pond just for kids. Full guide service is available, plus a fly-fishing shop.

There's so much to do at Double Eagle Resort, not to mention in the surrounding June Lake area, you should probably stay at least a week. Otherwise, you won't have time for one of the best activities: sitting on your cabin's deck and staring at the view of Carson Peak and Carson Falls. In case you haven't guessed, this resort was built on some spectacular property.

Facilities: There are 13 two-bedroom cabins that can accommodate up to six people, plus one group cabin that can accommodate up to 12 people. All cabins have fully equipped kitchens and fireplaces. A restaurant, spa, and fitness center are on-site.

Bedding: Linens and towels are provided.

Reservations and rates: Reservations are recommended. Fees are $211 to $271 per night. Some weekday and five-night discounts are available. The resort is open year-round. Pets are permitted in a limited number of cabins.

Directions: From U.S. 395 at the Highway 203/Mammoth Lakes turnoff, drive 15 miles north on U.S. 395 to Highway 158, the southern turnoff for the June Lake Loop. Turn west on Highway 158 and drive six miles to Double Eagle Resort on the left.

Contact: Double Eagle Resort, 5587 Highway 158, Route 3, Box 14C, June Lake, CA 93529; 760/648-7004 or 877/648-7004; website: www.double-eagle-resort.com.

Double Eagle Resort

26. BIG ROCK RESORT

When Southern Californians think of taking a serious skiing or snowboarding trip, they bypass all their local ski areas and load up their sport utility vehicles for the long drive to Mammoth. There's nothing wrong with the ski resorts in the nearby San Gabriel and San Bernardino Mountains; they just aren't the eastern Sierra.

The majority of those SUVs head for the glamour runs on Mammoth Mountain and the town of Mammoth Lake's popular hotels, restaurants, and nightlife. But there's a less visited ski mountain, just 30 miles to the north, in the town of June Lake. If you want to have a skiing vacation in a place that doesn't feel like a transplanted Los Angeles, give June Lake a try.

At June Mountain Ski Area, you'll find less crowds and cheaper lift tickets. You'll have snowmobiling, sledding, snowshoeing, and cross-country skiing options. And best of all, you'll be sharing a quiet, winter wonderland vacation with your loved ones in a lakeside cabin at Big Rock Resort.

The cabins at Big Rock are a perfect destination in any season. Because they're perched next to large June Lake, they allow summer visitors easy access to excellent trout fishing, sailing, and boating. The resort pro-

Off Highway 158 in June Lake

Luxury rating: 3

Recreation rating: 5

THIS CABIN RANKS . . .
Best for Fishing

vides motorboat and paddleboat rentals, or cabin guests can bring their own boat and launch it for free.

Cyclists can saddle up at their cabin and ride the spectacular June Lake Loop. For hikers, a trailhead is located across the street from Big Rock Resort by the June Lake Firehouse. From there, you can hike five miles through flower-filled Yost Meadows and the June Mountain Ski Area to Yost Lake.

In winter, 2,500 vertical feet of skiing are available on June Mountain, just 1.5 miles from Big Rock Resort. Many snowboarders insist that the boarding is better here than at neighboring Mammoth Mountain. One thing is certain: The lines at the chair lifts are shorter.

The one- to three-bedroom cabins at Big Rock Resort have everything you need for either a winter or summer vacation. Some of the cabins are duplexes, however, so make sure you request a single unit if you don't want to share exterior walls.

Facilities: There are eight cabins ranging in size from one to three bedrooms, all with fully equipped kitchens. A small store and restaurant are on-site.

Bedding: Linens and towels are provided.

Reservations and rates: Reservations are recommended. Fees range from $80 to $160 per night, depending on cabin size. Reduced rates are available in September, October, and May, excluding holidays. The resort is open year-round. Pets are permitted with advance permission, a $50 deposit, and a $5 fee per night.

Directions: From U.S. 395 at the Highway 203/Mammoth Lakes turnoff, drive 15 miles north on U.S. 395 to Highway 158, the southern turnoff for the June Lake Loop. Turn west on Highway 158 and drive 2.5 miles to Big Rock Road on the right. Turn right and drive to the resort.

Contact: Big Rock Resort, P.O. Box 126, 1 Big Rock Road, June Lake, CA 93529; 760/648-7717 or 800/769-9831; website: www.junelake.com.

Big Rock Resort

27. ALPERS OWENS RIVER RANCH

If you don't know what Alpers means, you won't know why a stay at Alpers Owens River Ranch is so special. Tim Alpers is the name of a man who raises world-class trophy trout. Alpers trout, known for their size, beauty, and feisty nature, are planted in many waters of the eastern Sierra, including the trophy ponds of several resorts.

© ANN MARIE BROWN

Off U.S. 395 near Mammoth Lakes

Luxury rating: 3

Recreation rating: 3

THIS CABIN RANKS . . .

Best for Fishing

That same man owns Alpers Owens River Ranch, where nine cabins, a lodge, and general store surround two miles of the Owens River. Quite simply, guests come here because they are passionate about fly fishing for trout.

When you enter the main lodge, the first thing you notice is an enormous stuffed beaver on the coffee table, accompanied by a sign that reads: Don't pet the dam beaver. As your eyes adjust to the dim light, you discover lots more: old black-and-white photographs, taxidermied trout, and assorted bric-a-brac and antiques from earlier days. There is much dust, and even some rust. But it's infinitely charming.

Alpers Owens River Ranch is a throwback to the old days, let's say the 1920s. It doesn't try to be anything else. Take Cabin 6, for example. It's the most luxurious cabin on the ranch, which means it has a propane refrigerator and stove. All of the furniture looks like it's been sat on by a herd of elephants. Sound like a fishing camp? Yes, this is a fishing camp.

Cabin 6 is the preferred rental choice because it's six feet from the Owens River. You can practically fly-fish off your porch. Of course, that's after you've had your try at the trophy pond or the headwaters of the Owens River (barbless fly fishing for native trout). River access, and access to artificially constructed Alpers Creek (bait fishing and fly fishing for stocked, one- to two-pound rainbows), is included in your stay. To access the four-acre trophy pond, you pay $35 for three hours. Make a reservation for a three-hour slot, then inflate your float tube while you're waiting.

Two other cabins are also right on the river. If any of the riverfront cabins are available, don't even think of renting the others, which are clustered near the main lodge and parking lot.

What do non-anglers do at Alpers Owens River Ranch? Not much except sit on the porch with a good book or seek out nearby hot springs. But around here, a non-angler is a rare species.

Facilities: There are nine cabins ranging in size that can accommodate two to 10 people. All cabins have kitchens.

Bedding: Linens and towels are provided.

Reservations and rates: Reservations are required. Fees are $45 per person per night. If there are more than two in your party, the fee is $40 per person per night. The resort is open from April to October. Pets are not permitted.

Directions: From U.S. 395 at the Highway 203/Mammoth Lakes turnoff, drive seven miles north on U.S. 395 to Owens River Road on the right. Turn right (east) and drive three miles to Alpers Owens River Ranch on the left.

Contact: Alpers Owens River Ranch, Route 1, Box 232, Mammoth Lakes, CA 93546; 760/648-7334 (summer) or 760/647-6652 (winter).

Alpers Owens River Ranch

28. KOA YOSEMITE-MARIPOSA

You can say what you want about a place that spells cabins with a K, but the KOA Yosemite-Mariposa is a godsend for Yosemite travelers. Located in the town of Midpines, 10 minutes from Mariposa and 45 minutes from Yosemite Valley, this unit of the national KOA campground chain has 12 Kamping Kabins that serve as a home away from home for about 50 bucks a night. That's right, 50 smackers for a one-room cabin accommodating a family of four.

© ANN MARIE BROWN

Off Highway 140 near Mariposa

Luxury rating: 2

Recreation rating: 2

THIS CABIN RANKS . . .
Best Value

The cabins are the same as what you'll find at most KOAs across America. They are one-room log buildings, with two working windows and a locking front door. Inside are a log-frame double bed and log-frame twin bunk beds, complete with mattresses but not bedding, plus a tiny table/shelf to set your stuff on. Amazingly, there is still enough room left so you can walk around.

Each cabin has electric lights and a small heater, plus a front porch with a swing wide enough for two. With a barbecue grill and picnic table right outside your door, you can cook your dinner at your cabin if you wish.

Probably the only downer to a KOA Kabin is the lack of a private bathroom, resulting in occasional hikes to the restroom in the middle of the night. But hey, what do you expect for 50 bucks? At the KOA Mariposa, the central restrooms are bright, clean, and have plenty of hot water in the showers.

The KOA also has a swimming pool, fish

pond, real train caboose with video games inside, TV lounge with Yosemite videos, and a small store. The current owners, who took over the place in March 2000, make a real effort to keep the place clean, safe, and friendly. They're nice folks who will gladly help you plan a visit to nearby Yosemite.

One last bonus at the KOA Kamping Kabins: In spring and summer, when everything in or near Yosemite is booked, you have a decent chance of finding lodging at the KOA. I've called several times on a Thursday or Friday and been lucky enough to get a cabin for the weekend.

Facilities: There are 12 cabins that can accommodate up to four people, plus RV and tent sites. Each cabin has a barbecue but no kitchen. A small store and swimming pool are on-site.

Bedding: Linens and towels are not provided; bring your own, plus sleeping bags or blankets and pillows.

Reservations and rates: Reservations are recommended. Fees are $48 per night for two persons plus $5 per additional person. Children under eight years old are free. Pets are not permitted in the cabins, but they are permitted in the campground.

Directions: From Fresno, take Highway 99 north to Merced. Turn east on Highway 140 and drive 37 miles to Mariposa, then continue for six more miles to Midpines. The KOA is on the left.

Contact: KOA Yosemite-Mariposa, P.O. Box 545, 6323 Highway 140, Midpines, CA 95345; 209/966-2201 or 800/562-9391.

OTHER CABINS AND COTTAGES NEARBY

• Meadow Creek Ranch, 2669 Triangle Road, Mariposa, CA 95338; 209/966-3843 or 800/853-2037.

• Little Valley Inn, 3483 Brooks Road, Mariposa, CA 95338; 209/742-6204 or 800/889-5444; website: www.little valley.com.

KOA Yosemite-Mariposa

29. YOSEMITE WEST

Yosemite National Park is packed with people every day all summer long, but over at Yosemite West you can hear a pin drop on your cabin's deck. Oh, you haven't heard of Yosemite West? Chances are you drove right by its turnoff on your last trip to the park. Yosemite West is an in-holding—privately owned property within the federal park boundary. It's a collection of private homes, most of which are for rent, located on a hillside right across from the junction of Highway 41 and Glacier Point Road.

You couldn't have a better location for exploring the Glacier Point area of Yosemite, which features the best easy day hiking in the park. The short, mostly level trails to spectacular valley overlooks at Dewey Point,

Taft Point, and Sentinel Dome are less than a 30-minute drive from your Yosemite West cabin. If you choose to drive into the valley, it's less than an hour away.

Off Highway 41 in Yosemite

Luxury rating: 4

Recreation rating: 5

A cabin at Yosemite West is also the best choice for a winter Yosemite vacation, because it's the closest lodging to the downhill runs at Badger Pass ski area (a 20-minute drive). Badger Pass serves as the starting point for snowshoeing and cross-country skiing trails, too, including the spectacular day trip to Dewey Point for a view of the valley below. Rentals and skiing lessons are available.

The rental homes at Yosemite West are on the upscale, modern side. They vary in size and shape, and most come with one or more extras like a hot tub, barbecue, pool table, or home entertainment center. Most have fireplaces and free firewood is provided. The homes' lot sizes are fairly large, so you probably won't hear or see much of your neighbors. This place is for those who want peace, quiet, and seclusion.

Several companies, as well as private individuals, offer homes for rent in Yosemite West (see the list below). This is a bonus for vacationers; if you strike out for reservations with one company, phone another.

Facilities: There are more than 140 vacation home rentals ranging in size from two to six bedrooms. All have fully equipped kitchens. Most have fireplaces.

Bedding: Linens and towels are provided.

Reservations and rates: Reservations are recommended. Fees range from $125 to $365 per night, depending on size of accommodations. Off-season rates are available midweek between September and April, excluding holidays. Pets are not permitted.

Directions: From Fresno, take Highway 41 north for 65 miles to the Wawona/southern entrance station at Yosemite National Park. Continue north on Highway 41 for 16.5 miles to the left turnoff for Yosemite West, just south of Glacier Point Road. Turn left and drive approximately one mile to your Yosemite West rental office.

Contact: Several companies handle rentals in Yosemite West, including Yosemite West Cottages, 559/642-2211 or website: www.yosemitewestreservations.com; Yosemite's Scenic Wonders, 800/296-7364 or 888/967-3648 or website: www.scenicwonders.com; and Yosemite's Four Seasons, 209/372-9000 or 800/669-9300 or website: www.yosemitelodging.com.

Yosemite West

30. OSTRANDER SKI HUT

You have to earn your stay at the Ostrander Ski Hut. It's not for everybody; it's only for those who are strong and skilled enough to ski or snowshoe 10 miles on mostly ungroomed track. But for those who make the snowy journey, the reward is a warm night in a two-story stone cabin perched on the edge of Ostrander Lake at 8,500 feet in elevation.

Off Glacier Point Road in Yosemite

Luxury rating: 1

Recreation rating: 3

Still reading? Good. The Ostrander Ski Hut is operated by the Yosemite Association, a nonprofit educational organization. It's open each year from mid-December to mid-April, depending on snow conditions. The hut sleeps 25 people and has bunks, mattresses, a wood stove, solar lights, a kitchen with gas stove for cooking, and assorted cooking and eating utensils. For drinking water, you walk 100 feet down to Ostrander Lake, fill up a bucket, then bring it back and filter it.

You're on your own for your trek to Ostrander Ski Hut, so you must possess some winter backcountry skills. Skiers should be at least intermediate level and in good physical shape. You'll need to carry quite a few items with you: sleeping bag, sleeping pad, head lamp, water filter, water bottle, snow emergency gear, food, and so on.

Even with all these prerequisites, reservations for Ostrander Ski Hut can be tough to come by. The Yosemite Association starts taking reservations in the fall. If you don't get the dates you want at that time, try phoning later on to see if there are cancellations. Of course, your chances are much better midweek than on weekends.

Facilities: There is one ski hut that can accommodate up to 25 people. It has a minimally equipped kitchen. Drinking water must be filtered.

Bedding: Linens and towels are not provided.

Reservations and rates: Reservations are required and are made by lottery in early November; some reservations are available by phone after December 1. The fee is $20 per person per night. Pets are not permitted.

Directions: From Fresno, take Highway 41 north for 65 miles to the Wawona/southern entrance station at Yosemite National Park. Continue north on Highway 41 for 17 miles to the right turnoff for Glacier Point Road. Turn right and drive six miles to Badger Pass Ski Area. Ski trails lead from there.

Contact: Yosemite Association, Ostrander Reservations, P.O. Box 545, Yosemite, CA 95389; 209/372-0740.

Ostrander Ski Hut

31. THE REDWOODS CABINS

The Wawona area of Yosemite is like the poor cousin of Yosemite West (see listing, this chapter) up the road. Like Yosemite West, it's an inholding within the national park, where anyone can own (or rent) a home. But unlike at Yosemite West, the homes in the Wawona area are clustered tightly together on small lots. Many of the houses are truly cabins—meaning they're a bit on the rustic side.

© ANN MARIE BROWN

Off Highway 41 in Yosemite

Luxury rating: 3

Recreation rating: 5

However, being the poor cousin isn't necessarily a bad thing. The Wawona cabins, collectively known as The Redwoods Vacation Home Rentals, are beautifully situated at the southern entrance to the park. This is perfect for Southern Californians making the long drive north to Yosemite. Within moments of passing through the park gates, you pull up to your rental cabin. After a good night's sleep, you're perfectly situated to hike the eight-mile round-trip to Chilnualna Falls (trailhead is five minutes from your cabin), or take a shorter walk around the spectacular Giant Sequoias of the Mariposa Grove.

In addition, the many trailheads and attractions of Glacier Point Road are only 30 minutes away; Yosemite Valley is an hour away. On hot summer days, Flat Rocks and Swinging Bridge swimming holes in the nearby South Fork of the Merced River offer a chance to cool off. Sometime during your stay, be sure to visit the Pioneer History Center in Wawona to gain a glimpse at different periods of Yosemite's history.

Another advantage to being the poor cousin is that The Redwoods cabins are a real bargain. For as little as $82 per night in winter, two people can rent a small cabin complete with linens, cookware, dishes, barbecue, and firewood. (Rates go up by about 20 percent in summer.) Larger houses that can accommodate a whole family or large group are also available. Every home is privately owned and reflects the owner's personal tastes and requirements, so there should be one that suits you, too.

To make it easy, The Redwoods has arranged its 130 vacation rentals into categories. Category C includes the smallest, least expensive cabins with the least amenities (no fireplace, for example). Category U contains the priciest cabins; these may have as many as six bedrooms, plus amenities like satellite TV, a dishwasher, or a gas grill. Every kind of cabin in between falls into one of four other categories.

Facilities: There are 130 cabins and vacation homes, all with fully equipped kitchens. A store and restaurant are nearby.

Bedding: Linens and towels are provided.

Reservations and rates: Reservations are recommended. Fees are $82 to $325 per night in winter, and $121 to $482 per night in summer, depending on the size and luxury level of the rental. There is a three-night minimum stay in summer and on holidays and a two-night minimum stay in the off-season. Pets are permitted in some cabins.

Directions: From Fresno, take Highway 41 north for 65 miles to the Wawona/southern entrance station at Yosemite National Park. Continue north on Highway 41 for seven miles to Chilnualna Falls Road in Wawona. Turn right and drive one mile on Chilnualna Falls Road to the Redwoods rental office on the right.

Contact: The Redwoods Cabins, P.O. Box 2085, Wawona Station, Yosemite, CA 95389; 209/375-6666; website: www.redwoodsinyosemite.com.

The Redwoods Cabins

32. OWL'S NEST CABINS

Some people are well-suited for the jobs they do, and that's certainly true for Bob and Barbara Taylor. The couple runs Owl's Nest Cabins in Fish Camp, just south of the southern entrance to Yosemite National Park. When I first met them, they had just returned from a day's exploration in the wilds of Sierra National Forest. Barbara was very excited about the huge marmot she'd seen, and Robert wanted to talk about the old mining cabins they'd discovered.

© ANN MARIE BROWN

Off Highway 41 in Fish Camp

Luxury rating: 3

Recreation rating: 3

The Taylors love living in Fish Camp, and they enjoy having visitors come stay at their three cabins, located just across the street from their house. The cabins are all completely different; one is a small upstairs unit above a utility room, another is a large chalet for a family, and the third is a rounded A-frame, sized just right for two people. All three have fully furnished kitchens, plus a barbecue grill outside. Each includes a TV and VCR, but since it's too mind-numbing to sit around and watch game shows and re-runs, the Taylors have provided a stock of videotapes about Yosemite.

The Taylors will happily supply guests with information about what to do and see in Yosemite (two miles north) and Sierra National Forest (all around to the south and east). A stream runs behind the Taylors' main house, and visitors can fish in it or just enjoy its coursing flow.

Because Fish Camp is located so close the southern entrance to Yosemite, you might think it's logical to spend all your vacation time there, visiting the Wawona and Mariposa Grove areas and hiking the many trails on Glacier Point Road. But don't neglect the many attractions to the south, including the Nelder Grove of Giant Sequoias and Fresno Dome in Sierra National Forest. Another must is a hike along the Lewis Creek National Recreation Trail, located three miles south of Fish Camp. The trail follows the historic Madera Sugar Pine Lumber flume route, passing Corlieu Falls, Red Rock Falls, and a wide variety of wildflowers in early summer.

Facilities: There are three cabins that can accommodate up to six people. All have fully equipped kitchens. A store and restaurant are nearby.

Bedding: Linens and towels are provided.

Reservations and rates: Reservations are recommended. Fees are $85 to $125 per night for two people, plus $15 for each additional person (up to six). Pets are not permitted.

Directions: From Fresno, take Highway 41 north for 63 miles to Fish Camp (two miles south of the Wawona entrance to Yosemite). Owl's Nest Cabins are on the left side of the road in the center of town (look for the owl statues).

Contact: Owl's Nest Cabins, 1237 Highway 41, P.O. Box 33, Fish Camp, CA 93623; 559/683-3484; website: www.owlsnestlodging.com.

OTHER CABINS AND COTTAGES NEARBY

• Chalet for Two, 1191 Highway 41, P.O. Box 130, Fish Camp, CA 93623; 559/683-7962.
Owl's Nest Cabins

33. APPLE TREE INN

The Apple Tree Inn is one of the nicest places to stay in the town of Fish Camp, but because it's only a few years old, surprisingly few people know of it. Set on seven pine-covered acres, the inn is a peaceful spot right off Highway 41, just two miles from Yosemite's southern gate.

Fish Camp, elevation 5,000 feet, is the home of the Yosemite Mountain Sugar Pine Railroad, an attraction that brings to life memories of long-gone logging camps. On the same route where sturdy flumes once transported lumber from Fish Camp to Madera, visitors today can ride an authentic narrow-gauge steam train (The Logger) through scenic woodlands. The Apple Tree Inn is located only a half mile from the railroad, which also features special moonlight rides, a museum, gift shop, and evening barbecues.

The other obvious draw for guests at Apple Tree Inn is southern Yosemite National Park. After only a 10-minute drive, visitors can be gazing upward

Off Highway 41 in Fish Camp

Luxury rating: 4

Recreation rating: 3

at the Giant Sequoias in the Mariposa Grove, or they can head farther into the park to explore the sights and trails of Glacier Point Road or Yosemite Valley.

Those who choose to hang around the resort's 11 acres will find an indoor swimming pool, hot tub, and racquetball court. The cottages are new-looking and prettily decorated in Laura Ashley fabrics; each comes with convenient amenities like hair dryers and coffeemakers. Each unit also has a gas fireplace.

Most guests don't attempt to make dinner in their very limited kitchenette (small refrigerator and microwave). Instead, they walk the short footpath to the restaurant at neighboring Tenaya Lodge. A complimentary continental breakfast is served each morning in the Apple Tree's dining room.

Facilities: There is one freestanding cottage at Apple Tree Inn, plus 53 duplex- and triplex-style cottages. The cottages have refrigerators and microwaves, plus fireplaces. An indoor pool and hot tub are on-site. A store and restaurant are nearby.

Bedding: Linens and towels are provided.

Reservations and rates: Reservations are recommended. Fees are $120 to $180 per night midweek from September through mid-May, and $160 to $210 per night the rest of the year and on all weekends and holidays. A continental breakfast is included. Pets are permitted in some cottages with a $50 fee.

Directions: From Fresno, take Highway 41 north for 63 miles to Fish Camp (two miles south of the Wawona entrance to Yosemite). Apple Tree Inn is on the right side of the road, a half-mile north of the Yosemite Mountain Sugar Pine Railroad.

Contact: Apple Tree Inn, 1110 Highway 41, Fish Camp, CA 93623; 559/683-5111 or 888/683-5111; website: www.appletreeinn-yosemite.com.

Apple Tree Inn

34. MAMMOTH MOUNTAIN CHALETS

For people who love to ski or snowboard but don't like to drive to the lifts, Mammoth Mountain Chalets are ideal. They're located right across the street from Chairs 1 and 11 at Mammoth Mountain Ski Area, so you can literally ski to the lifts. The 11,053-foot summit of Mammoth Mountain is easily accessible via a glass-paneled gondola.

By the same token, for people who love to mountain bike but don't like a long drive to the trailhead, Mammoth Mountain Chalets are ideal.

They're located right across the street from Mammoth Mountain Bike Park, the summer persona of the ski resort. The park is famous for its occasional pro races, when all the big-name mountain bikers show up. Most of the time, though, it's just regular vacationers cruising around the trails, which run the full spectrum from easy to extremely difficult. Bike rentals are available if you don't bring your own.

Off Highway 203 in Mammoth Lakes

Luxury rating: 4

Recreation rating: 5

THIS CABIN RANKS . . .
Best for Winter Sports

Mammoth Mountain's A-frame chalets are big enough for a whole group. Most have two or three bedrooms, plus assorted extra beds to accommodate up to 10 people. They're modern in style, and include amenities like dishwashers, phones, televisions, and fireplaces. In winter, you can't drive right up to your chalet; instead, you park at the main lodge and a snowcat carries you and your gear to your front door.

Everything, absolutely everything, can be purchased in the town of Mammoth Lakes, so don't worry if you forgot all your belongings except the clothes on your back. Next door to the chalets are a huge lodge and restaurant complex, where you'll find many shops and places to eat.

Other area highlights include a summer day trip to Devils Postpile National Monument. A shuttle bus runs from the lodge every 30 minutes. Or, if you leave before 7:30 A.M. or after 5:30 P.M., you can drive your own car into the park. (Traffic is restricted in the park because of its narrow, winding road.) Once there, you can hike to the columnar basalt formation known as the Devils Postpile, plus view spectacular Rainbow Falls and Lower Falls.

Another must is enjoying a sunset at Minaret Vista, a Forest Service overlook that is within walking distance of your cabin. The vista takes in the entire sawtooth range of the Minarets, including 12,936-foot Banner Peak and 13,143-foot Mount Ritter. It's a popular spot at any time, but especially at the close of the day.

Last but not least, try bathing in the nearby springs at Hot Creek.

Facilities: There are 20 chalets that can accommodate 4 to 10 people. All have fully equipped kitchens and fireplaces. Stores and restaurants are nearby.

Bedding: Linens and towels are provided.

Reservations and rates: Reservations are recommended. Fees are $135 to $170 per night in summer (higher during bike race events) and $207 to $337 per night in winter (higher on holidays). There is a two-night minimum stay; three nights on holidays. The resort is open year-round. Pets are not permitted.

Directions: From U.S. 395 at Mammoth Lakes, take the Highway 203 turnoff and drive west for four miles, through the town of Mammoth Lakes, to the intersection of Highway 203 and Lake Mary Road. Turn right on Highway 203 (Minaret Road) and drive five miles to Mammoth Mountain Chalets across from the ski area.

Contact: Mammoth Mountain Chalets, P.O. Box 513, Mammoth Lakes, CA 93546; 760/934-8518 or 800/327-3681.

OTHER CABINS AND COTTAGES NEARBY

• Zwart House, P.O. Box 174, Mammoth Lakes, CA 93546; 760/934-2217.

• Pine Cliff Resort, P.O. Box 2, Mammoth Lakes, CA 93546; 760/934-2447.

• Edelweiss Lodge, P.O. Box 658, Mammoth Lakes, CA 93546; 760/934-2445 or 877/233-3593.

Mammoth Mountain Chalets

35. RED'S MEADOW RESORT

With all the people who pour into Devils Postpile National Monument during the few short months it's open each year, it's surprising how few know about the cabins at Red's Meadow Resort. Red's is the only commercial service in the park; they run a pack station, small store, and café, plus rent out eight cabins and 10 motel rooms. Technically, the resort is just outside the park in Inyo National Forest, but nobody ever notices the difference.

© ANN MARIE BROWN

In Devils Postpile National Monument

Luxury rating: 2

Recreation rating: 4

THIS CABIN RANKS . . .
Best for Horseback Riding

The cabins are A-frames, older in style but clean and serviceable inside. They have small kitchens with a stovetop but no oven (don't plan on basting a turkey). Meals are also available at the resort's Mule House Cafe.

Chances are you won't spend much time at your cabin because there's much to do in surrounding Devils Postpile and Inyo National Forest. Fishing enthusiasts head for Starkweather Lake, Sotcher Lake, and the Middle Fork of the San Joaquin River (good for fly fishing). Hikers can walk the short and easy Rainbow Falls Trail from the trailhead right next to the resort; the 1.5-mile pathway leads to a spectacular 101-foot waterfall on the San Joaquin River. And yes, Rainbow

Falls does have a rainbow, but to see it clearly you must show up in the late morning, when sunlight hits the fall's spray just right.

From Rainbow Falls, you can hike downstream to Lower Falls, or upstream to Devils Postpile, a spectacular display of columnar basalt left from an ancient lava flow. First-time visitors always walk away from it shaking their heads; it's like nothing you've seen anywhere else. For a more ambitious trek, start hiking at Agnew Meadows and head past Olaine Lake to large and beautiful Shadow Lake at 8,737 feet. The round-trip is about seven miles, with some unforgettable Sierra scenery.

Red's Meadow Resort's big business is its pack station; in addition to two-hour, half-day, and full-day horseback rides, they run a dizzying array of multiday trips into the wilderness. Many are oriented toward fishing, often with an experienced guide. Where do the pack trips go? Just about everywhere in the surrounding John Muir and Ansel Adams Wilderness Areas, where more than 100 lakes and many miles of streams are within a day's ride. Some trips allow riders as young as five years old, making an ideal outing for families.

Facilities: There are eight cabins ranging in size that can accommodate two to eight people, plus 10 motel rooms. All cabins have kitchenettes (stovetop but no oven). A small general store and restaurant are on-site.

Bedding: Linens and towels are provided.

Reservations and rates: Reservations are recommended. Rates are $89 per night or $540 per week for two people, plus $30 for each additional person. Motel rooms are $59 per night for two people. The resort is open from mid-June to early October, weather permitting. Pets are permitted.

Directions: From U.S. 395 at Mammoth Lakes, take the Highway 203 turnoff and drive west for four miles, through the town of Mammoth Lakes, to the intersection of Highway 203 and Lake Mary Road. Turn right on Highway 203 (Minaret Road) and drive five miles to the Mammoth Mountain ski area, then continue beyond it for 10 miles to the resort. (Because you are staying at Red's Meadow, you do not have to ride the shuttle bus into the monument.)

Contact: Red's Meadow Resort, P.O. Box 395, Mammoth Lakes, CA 93546; 760/934-2345 or 800/292-7758; website: www.reds-meadow.com.

Red's Meadow Resort

36. TAMARACK LODGE RESORT

Twin Lakes in the town of Mammoth Lakes was once two separate lakes that are now adjoined by a marshy area. Set in a granite-lined bowl, the large, hourglass-shaped body of water is continually replenished by the rushing cascade of 250-foot Twin Falls. The lake is also continually replenished by the Department of Fish and Game, which keeps it filled with rainbow trout all summer long. This makes Twin Lakes a favorite spot of both fishing enthusiasts and scenery-lovers.

If you want to hang around the lake for a few days, book a stay at Tamarack

Lodge Resort, which has 25 cabins spaced on six acres along the shore of Twin Lakes. The only resort on Lake Mary Road that is open year-round, Tamarack is a classic 1924 mountain lodge with a big stone fireplace and log-lined walls. Only some of its cabins have views of Twin Lakes, but if you don't stay in one of them, your disappointment will disappear when you see that with a few footsteps, you're standing on its shoreline.

Off Highway 203 in Mammoth Lakes

Luxury rating: 3

Recreation rating: 5

THIS CABIN RANKS . . .
Best for Winter Sports
Best for Fishing

The list of outdoor activities at Tamarack Lodge is long enough to fill an entire book. The winter list includes skiing and snowboarding at Mammoth Mountain Ski Resort, and cross-country skiing and snowshoeing right from your cabin door on more than 45 kilometers of groomed track. Equipment rentals and instructions are available. The summer list includes trout fishing in Twin Lakes and neighboring lakes, swimming in Horseshoe Lake, mountain biking at Mammoth Ski Area's summer bike park, and discovering nearby hot springs.

Plus hiking, hiking, hiking. The best trails near Tamarack Lodge are the short hike to Panorama Dome and the strenuous hike to Mammoth Mountain Summit. Panorama Dome Trail begins off Lake Mary Road, just past the turnoff to Twin Lakes. It's an easy half-mile hike to the top of a rocky dome with stunning summit views. The Mammoth Mountain Summit Trail starts in the west loop of Twin Lakes Campground, then climbs 2,500 feet over four miles to the 11,053-foot summit. If you tire out, Seven Lakes Point is a spectacular overlook and potential turnaround at 1.3 miles out.

One final highlight of Tamarack Lodge is its restaurant. It's easy to imagine that an old fishing and skiing lodge would serve little besides steak and potatoes, or burgers and fries, but not so at Tamarack's dining room, The Lakefront. Its French-California cuisine has a reputation that has spread far beyond Mammoth Lakes; it's been written up in *Sunset* and *Bon Appétit* magazines. For something different, try the elk or wild boar medallions.

Facilities: There are 25 cabins ranging in size from studios to three bedrooms, all with fully equipped kitchens. Lodge rooms are also available. A restaurant and general store are on-site.

Bedding: Linens and towels are provided.

Reservations and rates: Reservations are recommended. Fees range from $120 to $330 per night ($185 to $405 on holidays) depending on cabin size. The resort is open year-round. Pets are not permitted.

Directions: From U.S. 395 at Mammoth Lakes, take the Highway 203 turnoff and drive west for four miles, through the town of Mammoth Lakes, to the intersection of Highway 203 and Lake Mary Road. Continue straight on Lake Mary Road for 2.2 miles, then bear right on Twin Lakes Road and follow it for a quarter mile to Tamarack Lodge Resort.

Contact: Tamarack Lodge Resort, P.O. Box 69, Mammoth Lakes, CA 93546; 760/934-2442; website: www.tamaracklodge.com.

Tamarack Lodge Resort

37. CRYSTAL CRAG LODGE

It's confusing, but let's try to get this straight: Crystal Crag Lodge doesn't have a view of 10,377-foot Crystal Crag; Woods Lodge (see listing, this chapter) does. Crystal Crag Lodge faces Mammoth Mountain and Red Mountain. It's geographically below Crystal Crag but not within sight of it.

© ANN MARIE BROWN

Off Highway 203 in Mammoth Lakes

Luxury rating: 3

Recreation rating: 4

Despite its misleading name, Crystal Crag Lodge is just right for many visitors. The lodge is located across the road from 140-acre Lake Mary, the largest of the lakes in Mammoth Lakes Basin, where you can fish from shore or by boat for brown, rainbow, and brook trout. A bonus is that the lodge rents 14-foot aluminum boats.

Hikers can easily access the Sky Meadows Trail, which begins at neighboring Coldwater Campground. The path is short and easy to rocky Emerald Lake, then it continues to Sky Meadows, where the summer wildflowers bloom with enthusiasm. Many other trails for hikers and bikers are located nearby. There are also several hot springs nearby, which can make for a nice side trip.

The cabins are surprisingly modern and updated inside, considering their bland exteriors. I rented the resort's smallest and least expensive cabin, Twin, which was quite spacious: two main rooms (bedroom and combined kitchen/living/dining area with a big fireplace) plus a large bathroom. Like the resort's other cabins, it has a very workable kitchen, complete with a microwave, toaster, and coffeemaker.

Some cabins are directly across from the lake, so be sure to request one. Twin is at the back of the resort, farthest from the lake, but this wasn't a minus: On a busy Memorial Day weekend, it was quiet and peaceful. Noisy neighbors could potentially be a problem at Crystal Crag Lodge because the resort packs 20 large A-frame cabins into a small space.

Facilities: There are 20 cabins ranging in size from one to four bedrooms. All have fully equipped kitchens. A general store is on-site.

Bedding: Linens and towels are provided.

Reservations and rates: Reservations are recommended. Fees are $112 to $232 per night, depending on cabin size. The resort is open from late May to early October. Pets are permitted with an $8 fee per night.

Directions: From U.S. 395 at Mammoth Lakes, take the Highway 203 turnoff and drive west for four miles, through the town of Mammoth Lakes, to the intersection of Highway 203 and Lake Mary Road. Continue straight on Lake Mary Road for 3.5 miles to Crystal Crag Lodge on the left.

Contact: Crystal Crag Lodge, P.O. Box 88, Mammoth Lakes, CA 93546; 760/934-2436; website: www.mammothweb.com/lodging/crystal.

Crystal Crag Lodge

38. WOODS LODGE

Woods Lodge qualifies as one of my fantasy cabin vacations. It's the kind of getaway spot your mind drifts to again and again when you're immersed in the pedestrian details of everyday life.

Off Highway 203 in Mammoth Lakes

Luxury rating: 4

Recreation rating: 4

Woods Lodge is located in Mammoth Lakes Basin at George Lake, one of four lakes at the end of Lake Mary Road. All four lakes are breathtaking, but few would disagree that Lake George is the most breathtaking of them all. At 9,200 feet in elevation, it is deep blue and lined with granite, but what sets it off is Crystal Crag, a spectacular chunk of rock in the lake's background. You see it for the first time and you say, "Wow."

Woods Lodge is also one of the classier cabin resorts in the Mammoth area. It is owned and managed by the Schotz family, the same folks who run Wylderie Resort (see next listing) on Lake Mamie. They've owned Woods Lodge since 1950. Their longevity is easy to understand; who would give up this place?

The cabins are one- to three-bedroom models, with full kitchens and outside barbecues. Their furnishings are clean and simple. Because they are set on a hill overlooking Lake George, each one has a view from its deck of the lake and Crystal Crag.

Unlike at many resorts, the cabins at Woods Lodge are spaced a good distance apart. The ambience is more like a nice neighborhood of private homes than a pack-'em-in cabin resort. The cabins are situated on a separate driveway from the main access road and parking area for Lake George, so you won't have a lot of anglers and hikers driving past your cabin. There's no traffic at all except from the cars belonging to the two dozen other cabins.

What's there to do at Woods Lodge? Fishing is a big draw, both at Lake George and the neighboring Mammoth lakes. Equally convenient are the two hiking trails that start almost at your Woods Lodge cabin door. You can hike to Barrett and T.J. Lakes in an easy half mile, or Crystal Lake and the Mammoth Crest in a much steeper three miles. Crystal Lake is hidden at the base of magnificent Crystal Crag (1.75 miles out); Mammoth Crest provides 360-degree views of the surrounding countryside. If you're up to driving a bit, there are hot springs nearby at Hat Creek.

Facilities: There are 25 cabins ranging in size from one to three bedrooms. All have fully equipped kitchens.

Bedding: Linens and towels are provided.

Reservations and rates: Reservations are recommended. A seven-night minimum is required on advance reservations. Fees are $504 to $1,512 per week, depending on cabin size. One-night rentals are $78 to $236 per night. The resort is open from late May to early October. Pets are permitted in some cabins with an $8 fee per night.

Directions: From U.S. 395 at Mammoth Lakes, take the Highway 203 turnoff and drive west for four miles, through the town of Mammoth Lakes, to the intersection of Highway 203 and Lake Mary Road. Continue straight on Lake Mary Road four miles to the Lake George turnoff. Turn left and drive a half mile to Woods Lodge.

Contact: Woods Lodge, P.O. Box 108, Mammoth Lakes, CA 93546; 760/934-2261; website: www.mammothweb.com/lodging/woodslodge.

Woods Lodge

39. WILDYRIE RESORT

The same smart folks who run Woods Lodge (see previous listing, this chapter) on Lake George also run Wildyrie Resort on Lake Mamie, located about two miles away. Like Woods Lodge, Wildyrie Resort has a genteel, but not stuffy, air to it. It feels like an older, established vacation resort.

The high points about Woods Lodge also apply here at Wildyrie: The cabins are perched on a hillside overlooking a lake—this one being deep blue Lake Mamie, which is apt, considering that "wildyrie" is an old Scottish word for "eagle's nest." The cabins are spaced far enough apart for privacy and quiet, and because they are located behind the main lodge and off the road, they are safe from road noise. Each cabin has a front deck and most have a lake view, although it is somewhat obscured by trees. The best views are from cabins 5, 6, and 7, which are all two-bedrooms.

Wildyrie Resort rents rowboats on Lake Mamie (a 100-foot walk to the

Off Highway 203 in Mammoth Lakes

Luxury rating: 4

Recreation rating: 4

dock from your cabin). No motorboats are permitted on the lake, which is filled with rainbow, brown, and brook trout.

If you don't want to fish, there's plenty to do within walking distance of your cabin. Bike rentals are available at Pokonobe Country Store on Lake Mary. Mammoth Lakes Pack Outfit is nearby; guided horseback rides are available. Twin Falls picnic ground is across the street from Wildyrie, and Horseshoe Lake is a quarter mile away. A trailhead at Horseshoe Lake leads to McLeod Lake in a half mile. More ambitious hikers can walk four miles downhill to Red's Meadow at Devils Postpile National Monument, then turn around and hike back up (a moderate 1,700-foot gain). While at Red's Meadow, you can ride the free shuttle bus to other points in the monument.

If you're up to venturing farther from the resort, hot springs are nearby at Hat Creek.

Facilities: There are 11 cabins ranging in size from one to four bedrooms, plus lodge rooms and apartments. All cabins have fully equipped kitchens.

Bedding: Linens and towels are provided.

Reservations and rates: Reservations are recommended. A seven-night minimum is required on advance reservations. Fees are $672 to $1,533 per week, depending on cabin size. One-night cabins rentals are $104 to $231 per night. Lodge rooms and apartments are $75 to $140 per night. The resort is open from late May to early October. Pets are not permitted.

Directions: From U.S. 395 at Mammoth Lakes, take the Highway 203 turnoff and drive west for four miles, through the town of Mammoth Lakes, to the intersection of Highway 203 and Lake Mary Road. Continue straight on Lake Mary Road for three miles, then turn right, and quickly right again, at the sign for Lake Mamie and Horseshoe Lake. Wildyrie Resort is on the left.

Contact: Wildyrie Resort, P.O. Box 109, Mammoth Lakes, CA 93546; 760/934-2444; website: www.mammothweb.com/lodging/wildyrieresort.

Wildyrie Resort

40. HOT CREEK RANCH

Hot Creek Ranch is where fly fishers should go when their spouses don't like to fly-fish. For one thing, the non-fishing spouse can sit around and admire the modern cabin they're inhabiting, which is nicer, and has a much better view, than the average suburban home. For another, a wealth of recreation alternatives abound.

Let's start with the fly fishing, since that is the big draw at Hot Creek Ranch. The ranch is located along Hot Creek in the Owens River Valley, which is well-known for two things: trout and hot springs. The trout in Hot Creek are not easy to catch; this is for experienced fly fishers only. When you catch them, you don't keep them: this is barbless-fly-only, catch-and-release fishing with a zero limit. On the private stretch of stream owned by the ranch, an additional restriction is in effect: dry flies only.

Off U.S. 395 near Mammoth Lakes

Luxury rating: 5

Recreation rating: 4

THIS CABIN RANKS . . .
Best for Fishing

Hot Creek originates as an underground creek, formed from a combination of 11 different springs. It bubbles forth from a fissure in volcanic rock, then runs down a narrow gorge, creating excellent habitat for wildlife, including wild rainbow and brown trout. How big are the fish? The standard trout is at least 12 inches; fish in excess of 20 inches are not unusual.

So what are non–fly fishing partners to do? When they get tired of admiring the view of Mammoth Mountain and the Minarets beyond, they can scan the sky for bald eagles and osprey (both are fairly common). They can drive down the road 1.5 miles (or hike on the trail beside Hot Creek) to the Hot Creek Geologic Area, a public hot springs run by the Forest Service. The springs bubble up from the middle of the river, so bathers alternate between hot and cold water with just one swimming stroke. Hot Creek is a popular, family-oriented spot that is usually filled with swimmers from sunup to sundown.

Non-anglers can also head into Mammoth Lakes, just six miles away, and take advantage of myriad hiking, biking, swimming, and boating opportunities. Some years, the Mammoth Mountain Ski Area is open until the beginning of July, well into fly fishing season.

The cabins at Hot Creek Ranch aren't really cabins at all, more like small private homes. With only nine cabins total at the ranch, guests aren't saddled with a passel of neighbors. And because the ranch has a gated driveway, nobody drives in unless they have a reservation. Each cabin has electric heat and appliances, an enclosed carport, a spectacular view, and an outdoor barbecue. Even better is what they don't have: televisions and phones.

Facilities: There are nine cabins that can accommodate four people and one apartment for one person. All cabins have fully equipped kitchens.

Bedding: Linens and towels are provided.

Reservations and rates: Reservations are required. Fees are $150 per night for two people on weekdays with a minimum two-night stay. The weekend rate is $495 for two people, Friday to Monday. The weekly rate is $950.

Each additional person is $75 per night (but only three fly fishers are permitted per cabin). The one-person apartment is $90 per night. The resort is open from the end of April to the end of October. Pets are not permitted.

Directions: From U.S. 395 at Bishop, drive north for 36 miles to Hot Creek Hatchery Road (it's 2.7 miles south of the Mammoth Lakes turnoff). Turn right (east) and drive 1.7 miles to the ranch on the left.

Contact: Hot Creek Ranch, Route 1, Box 206, Mammoth Lakes, CA 93546; 760/924-5637 or 888/695-0774; website: www.hotcreekranch.com.

Hot Creek Ranch

41. CONVICT LAKE RESORT

The first question that rises to mind as you drive up the road to Convict Lake Resort is something like, "What is that incredible peak looming in the background?"

It's 12,277-foot Mount Morrison.

© ANN MARIE BROWN

Off U.S. 395 near Mammoth Lakes

Luxury rating: 3

Recreation rating: 5

THIS CABIN RANKS . . .

Best for Fishing

Next question: How did Convict Lake get its name?

A group of convicts escaped from a Nevada prison in 1871. They were sighted camping at Monte Diablo Lake, which quickly became known as Convict Lake. The convicts shot it out with a posse on the shores of the lake; one of the posse, Robert Morrison, was killed. Mount Morrison (see the previous question) was named in his honor.

Final question: How can I live at Convict Lake Resort for the rest of my life?

You'll have to figure that one out for yourself.

Convict Lake Resort is set at 7,600 feet in elevation, just south of the town of Mammoth Lakes in the eastern Sierra. It's about 150 yards from Convict Lake, a 168-acre, half-mile wide, one-mile-long lake. The lake's water is remarkably clear blue and stunning, partly because much of the lake is more than 100 feet deep. Its deepest point is 140 feet.

Nestled in a grove of aspens, many of the resort's cabins bear fishing-related names, like Steelhead, Cutthroat, Golden, and Rainbow. If you get to choose among them, pick Golden. It's the most private and also the most scenic, with a wide-open view of Mount Morrison and surrounding peaks. Unfortunately, none of the cabins have lake views, but the mountain views are fair compensation.

Fishing is the main task of vacationers here. The lake is stocked weekly with rainbow trout, and they share the waters with some trophy-size brown trout. Convict Creek, which runs by the resort, is also stocked. The resort rents motorboats, pontoon boats, rowboats, and canoes, and its store sells bait and tackle as well as basic groceries.

Perhaps more notable than even the fishing is the restaurant at Convict Lake Resort. Open for dinner year-round, it's the only four-diamond restaurant in Mono or Inyo Counties. The "country French" menu includes entrées and appetizers such as quail, salmon, rack of lamb, mussels, escargot, scallops, and other gourmet items. The food isn't cheap (entrées are $22 to $32), but if you want to save money you can select from an alternate café menu. The restaurant's martini bar brags of having the stiffest cocktail in the Sierra.

If you tire of fishing and eating, you can rent horses at Convict Lake pack station and take a guided horseback ride along the lakeshore, or a longer ride into the John Muir Wilderness. Or you can do your own walking: An easy and level trail travels the lakeshore for a mile, then starts to ascend with a vengeance to Mildred Lake and Lake Dorothy (five and six miles out). Or, if you want water that's naturally hot and perfect for soaking in, hot springs are located nearby at Hat Creek.

Since Convict Lake is primarily a fishing resort, it's surprising that it stays open year-round, but it does. Winter visitors use the resort as their base for cross-country skiing at local snow parks, plus downhill skiing at Mammoth Mountain (it's a 25-minute drive to the lifts). After a rigorous day on the slopes, it's nice to have a four-diamond dinner to look forward to.

Facilities: There are 23 cabins ranging in size that can accommodate up to 10 people, plus large group houses for 13 to 30 people. All have fully equipped kitchens. A store and restaurant are on-site.

Bedding: Linens and towels are provided.

Reservations and rates: Reservations are recommended. Fees range from $85 to $290 per night for cabins, depending on cabin size. Weekly discounts are available. Group houses for 13 to 30 people are $450 to $650 per night. There is a two-night minimum stay on weekends. The resort is open year-round. Pets are permitted with a $10 fee.

Directions: From U.S. 395 at Bishop, drive north for 35 miles to the Convict Lake turnoff (it's 3.7 miles south of the Mammoth Lakes turnoff). Turn left (west) and drive two miles to the resort.

Contact: Convict Lake Resort, Route 1, Box 204, Mammoth Lakes, CA 93546; 760/934-3800 or 800/992-2260; website: www.convictlake.com.

Convict Lake Resort

42. TOM'S PLACE RESORT

Crowley Lake is the huge, shallow-looking lake on the east side of U.S. 395 midway between Bishop and Mammoth Lakes. The largest lake in the eastern Sierra at 5,183 acres, Crowley is essentially a flooded valley that's loaded with fish. Anglers share the waters with sail boaters, windsurfers, personal watercraft riders, and water skiers, and it all adds up to a big party on the lake on summer days.

Off U.S. 395 in Tom's Place

Luxury rating: 2

Recreation rating: 3

Tom's Place Resort is 3.5 miles south of Crowley Lake, and that is the primary reason why anyone would stay there. Unlike most lakes in the eastern Sierra, Crowley Lake doesn't have a resort nestled on its shoreline, so unless you're camping, Tom's Place is the closest possible lodging.

Tom's Place Resort has a lodge, store, café, and bar. The bar is a historic watering hole that brags of its "world-famous Bloody Marys." The café serves three meals a day—basic food like ham and eggs for breakfast, patty melts for lunch, and pork chops for dinner. The cabins are scattered around the property; some are in sight of U.S. 395, so steer clear of those. All are fairly rustic, but there is one luxury: some are surrounded by lilac bushes that deliver an intoxicating scent in early summer.

The resort has been open since 1917, long before U.S. 395 was a paved road. It has an interesting history as a stopover for Southern Californians traveling to Yosemite, but otherwise it is unremarkable except that it provides bargain-priced access to the outdoors, particularly Crowley Lake and Lower Rock Creek. Quite simply, it's a cheap place to stay if you want to fish, boat, or windsurf. How cheap? Try 55 bucks a night for a cabin for two, or 90 bucks a night for a cabin for six.

The money you'll save will be spent at Crowley Lake. Operated by the Los Angeles Department of Water and Power (the largest reservoir in its aqueduct system), Crowley Lake's fees are $6 per day to park, or $15 per day to park and launch a boat. Boat rentals and a tackle shop are available.

Fishing rules are a bit complicated: Trout season runs the usual end-of-April to end-of-October schedule, but starting August 1, no bait fishing is allowed—only barbless lures or flies. The planted trout run the gamut from Kamloop rainbows, Eagle Lake rainbows, and Coleman rainbows to browns and cutthroats. Perch fishing follows the same schedule (no bait fishing after August 1) and a big Perch Derby is held each August. The largest perch ever caught in California was hauled out of Crowley Lake—a three-pound, 10-ouncer.

If you get too hot hanging out in the boat all day, you're out of luck. No swimming or diving is ever permitted at the lake.

Facilities: There are 12 cabins ranging in size from one to three bedrooms, plus seven lodge rooms. All cabins have fully equipped kitchens. A store, café, and bar are on-site.

Bedding: Linens and towels are provided.

Reservations and rates: Reservations are recommended. Fees range from $50 to $100 per night, depending on size of cabin and number of people. Lodge rooms are $45 to $55 per night. The resort is open year-round. Pets are permitted in some cabins with a $5 fee per night.

Directions: From Bishop, drive 25 miles north on U.S. 395 to Tom's Place, at the junction with Rock Creek Drive (on the left).

Contact: Tom's Place Resort, HCR 79 Box 22-A, Crowley Lake, CA 93546; 760/935-4239; website: www.tomsplaceresort.com.

Tom's Place Resort

43. ROCK CREEK LAKES RESORT

If you can get a cabin at Rock Creek Lakes Resort, you must have been born under a lucky star. The resort is located right across the road from Rock Creek Lake in gorgeous Rock Creek Canyon, and with all that scenery, its cabins are booked up most all the time.

© ANN MARIE BROWN

Off U.S. 395 near Tom's Place

Luxury rating: 3

Recreation rating: 4

THIS CABIN RANKS . . .
Best for Hiking

Still, if you can live spontaneously, you have a chance. The resort keeps a waiting list for cancellations, and if you are willing to pack up and go on short notice, you'll get your cabin. I tried the waiting-list technique one summer and was offered two different weeks. Another option is to visit on weekdays, especially before or after the main summer season.

Why is Rock Creek Lakes Resort so popular? Two reasons: fishing and hiking. For starters, you can walk from your cabin to the boat dock at Rock Creek Lake and fish your heart out all week long. Rock Creek Lake is stocked all summer with rainbow trout. Small boats are for rent (trolling motors only), but many anglers float around in rubber rafts and kayaks or fish from the shore. If you want to fish other waters, the Owens River, Crowley Lake, McGee Creek, and Hot Creek are a short drive away.

If hiking appeals to you, Rock Creek Lakes Resort is ideally located for accessing the John Muir Wilderness, a dramatic landscape of

13,000-foot peaks, permanent snow fields, and gem-like lakes. The Hilton and Davis Lakes trailhead is a quarter mile from the cabin turnoff; you could walk to the trailhead and then hike four miles to the Hilton Lakes or five miles to Davis Lake. Or drive one mile to the Mosquito Flat trailhead at the end of Rock Creek Road. At 10,300 feet, it's one of the highest trailhead elevations in California. Set off on the easy, level trail through Little Lakes Valley and you'll see dozens of small lakes, one after another about every half mile. For something more ambitious, follow the Mono Pass Trail to Ruby Lake and beyond, heading steeply uphill to 12,400-foot Mono Pass.

If you have a choice when you make your reservation at Rock Creek Lakes Resort, ask for one of the higher numbered cabins. All cabins are secluded and in the trees, but numbers 1, 2, and 3 are the closest together. The cabins are on the modern side, painted a cheerful red and fully furnished with kitchens, bathrooms, linens, and everything you need for your stay except food.

The resort has a small lunch counter that is renowned for its homemade pies and soups. (The list of pies is longer than the list of main courses.) Their soups are outrageously good, as are their breakfasts, but you're on your own for dinner.

Facilities: There are 10 cabins ranging in size from one to three bedrooms. All have fully equipped kitchens. A lunch counter and general store are on-site.

Bedding: Linens and towels are provided.

Reservations and rates: Reservations are required. Fees range from $98 to $240 per night, depending on cabin size. The resort is open from mid-May to mid-October. Pets are not permitted.

Directions: From Bishop, drive 24 miles north on U.S. 395 to the Rock Creek turnoff near Tom's Place. Turn west on Rock Creek Road and drive nine miles to Rock Creek Lakes Resort on the right.

Contact: Rock Creek Lakes Resort, P.O. Box 727, Bishop, CA 93515; 760/935-4311; website: www.rockcreeklake.com.

Rock Creek Lakes Resort

44. ROCK CREEK LODGE

From November to May, Rock Creek Lodge is the only resort in spectacular Rock Creek Canyon that is open for business. Cross-country skiers are grateful for those extra winter months, because at 9,373 feet in elevation, midway between Bishop and Mammoth Lakes, Rock Creek Canyon is snow heaven.

Rock Creek Lodge was founded in the 1920s as one of the first ski resorts in America. Although summer is busy at Rock Creek Lodge, with hordes of visitors showing up for the plentiful fishing and hiking opportunities, the winter season has always been Rock Creek Lodge's special niche.

Here's how a winter visit works: First, you confirm your cabin reservation, then drive to the town of Tom's Place. At a prearranged time, you leave your car at the East Fork Sno-Park and a snowmobile shuttles you the last two miles to your cabin. (Rock Creek Road is not plowed beyond East Fork in winter.) From the moment you arrive, you strap on your skis and glide wherever you wish.

Off U.S. 395 near Tom's Place

Luxury rating: 3

Recreation rating: 4

THIS CABIN RANKS . . .
Best for Winter Sports

Even if you've never cross-country skied before, you won't be left out in the cold; equipment rentals and lessons are available. Experienced skiers can go off on their own and even stay overnight at a backcountry hut.

Since you can't drive anywhere once the snowmobile has dropped you off, the resort is fully equipped. A beautiful log cabin serves as the restaurant. Inside are long wooden tables where you eat hearty meals and meet all your neighbors. You don't choose from a menu; instead, you eat whatever they are serving that night. During our visit, it was lasagna on Saturday, teriyaki chicken on Sunday, enchiladas on Monday, and so on.

The lodge has both "modern" and "rustic" cabins. Modern means they have their own showers; rustic means you walk to a separate building for showers. The cabins are spaced well, with plenty of breathing room between them. You must bring your own sleeping bag and towels (pillows and pillowcases are provided).

It's hard to pin down the best part of a winter trip to Rock Creek Lodge, but after debating it a while, I settled on this: The road is closed, so there are no cars visible anywhere in this snowy wonderland. Civilization? You'll quickly forget all about it.

Facilities: There are 14 cabins that can accommodate two to eight people. Eight cabins have full bathrooms and showers. All cabins have kitchenettes. A restaurant and general store are on-site.

Bedding: Pillows and pillowcases are provided; bring your own sleeping bag and towels.

Reservations and rates: Reservations are required. Winter fees range from $90 to $115 per night per person, including breakfast and dinner; children under 12 stay for reduced rates. Summer fees range from $75 to $140 per night for two people. Pets are permitted in summer only; $10 fee per night.

Directions: From Bishop, drive 24 miles north on U.S. 395 to the Rock Creek turnoff near Tom's Place. Turn west on Rock Creek Road and drive eight miles to Rock Creek Lodge on the left. In winter, drive six miles on Rock Creek Road and park at the East Fork lot. A snowmobile will meet you and take you the final two miles to the lodge.

Contact: Rock Creek Lodge, Route 1, Box 12, Mammoth Lakes, CA 93546; 760/935-4170 or 877/935-4170; website: www.rockcreeklodge.com.

Rock Creek Lodge

45. PARADISE RESORT

A stay at Paradise Resort is a different kind of vacation experience than others in the eastern Sierra. The resort is set along Lower Rock Creek in the arid, desert-like Owens Valley, quite a few miles from the nearest set of high mountain peaks. If you're looking for sawtooth ridges or an alpine lake right outside your cabin door, this isn't the place.

© ANN MARIE BROWN

Off U.S. 395 near Bishop

Luxury rating: 3

Recreation rating: 3

On the other hand, if fishing is your bag, this *is* the place. Right outside your cabin is what the resort calls "family-style fishing," which means you drop a line in Lower Rock Creek and hope that something with fins swims past. Lower Rock Creek is regularly stocked with trout, so your chances are pretty good, especially early in the year. Experienced anglers head for the myriad lakes and streams in the area, including Lake Sabrina, North Lake, South Lake, Rock Creek Lake, Crowley Lake, and the Owens River.

Hikers can drive to the nearby John Muir Wilderness trailheads in Rock Creek Canyon or try out the Lower Rock Creek Trail. A section of it runs right by Paradise Resort. The trail is popular with both hikers and mountain bikers, especially in the early summer when wildflowers are blooming. (Bikers, take note: This isn't a trail for amateurs.) Other great side trips include a drive east out of Bishop to visit the White Mountains and the Ancient Bristlecone Pine Forest. Here, you'll find the oldest living trees on earth.

Paradise Resort's cabins are set close together along the river, with a few RVs sprinkled among them. They're nothing fancy, to say the least: one or two bedrooms, a serviceable kitchen and bathroom, and a small front porch where you can sit outside and listen to the creek gurgle. They have no views, except of the other cabins and of something that appears like a mirage in the dry Owens Valley—a large expanse of green lawn, with Lower Rock Creek coursing through the middle of it. At first, I mistook it for a golf course, but Paradise Resort's owners call it a "picnic-and-play meadow."

If you don't catch any fish, you can pay a visit to Paradise Resort's restaurant, which serves far more than typical lodge fare. The menu includes Alaskan snow crab (reportedly flown in fresh), various gourmet cuts of beef, and a good selection of wine. If a more rustic meal appeals to you, you can always use the barbecue outside your Paradise cabin to prepare some blackened hot dogs and roasted marshmallows.

Facilities: There are 17 cabins ranging in size from one to two bedrooms. All have fully equipped kitchens. RV sites are also available. A restaurant is on-site.

Bedding: Linens and towels are provided.

Reservations and rates: Reservations are recommended. Fees range from $65 to $130 per night with a two-night minimum stay. The resort is open year-round; rates are discounted in winter. Pets are permitted with a $10 fee.

Directions: From Bishop, drive north on U.S. 395 for 12 miles to the turnoff for Paradise/Lower Rock Creek Road/Gorge Road. Turn left (west), then turn right immediately and drive two miles north on Lower Rock Creek Road to the resort.

Contact: Paradise Resort, Route 2, Bishop, CA 93514; 760/387-2370; website: www.theparadiseresort.com.

Paradise Resort

CHAPTER 5

Sequoia
and Kings Canyon

*L*ocated on the western slope of the Sierra Nevada Mountains, Sequoia and Kings Canyon National Parks are famous for their Giant Sequoia groves, tall mountains, deep canyons, roaring rivers, and spectacular hiking trails with views of the jagged peaks of the Great Western Divide. Often referred to as "Yosemite without the masses," these two side-by-side national parks offer classic Sierra scenery without the infamous overcrowding that plagues that great park to the north. Kings Canyon and Sequoia have been managed jointly by the National Park Service since 1943.

The parks abound with superlatives. The highest peak in the contiguous United States, Mount Whitney at 14,494 feet, is found in Kings Canyon. Several other park summits top out at more than 14,000 feet. The largest living tree in the world, the Sherman Tree, is found in Giant Forest in Sequoia. At 275 feet tall and with a 103-foot circumference at the ground, the massive tree is still growing; every year, it adds enough wood to make another 60-foot-tall tree. The Sherman Tree is estimated to be 2,300 to 2,700 years old.

The second and third largest trees in the world, named Washington and General Grant, respectively, are also found in Sequoia and Kings Canyon. The easiest way to visit these record-holders is to reserve a stay at Grant Grove Lodge, situated less than a mile from the General Grant Tree, or at Montecito Sequoia Lodge, near Giant Forest.

Three powerful rivers course through the boundaries of Sequoia and Kings Canyon: the Kings, Kern, and Kaweah. The steep and barren canyons through which these rivers flow are as awe-inspiring as the raging waters themselves. The canyon of the

Kings River is carved to a depth of 8,000 feet below the summit of neighboring Spanish Mountain. This makes Kings Canyon deeper than the Grand Canyon or any other canyon in North America. One cabin resort, Kings Canyon Lodge, is found along the Kings River canyon. Several more are located along the Kaweah in the town of Three Rivers, just outside the parks.

Less visited areas in the parks include the South Fork and Mineral King Valley areas of Sequoia. Mineral King is a glacier-carved bowl surrounded by massive peaks, topped by the distinct pointed pinnacle known as Sawtooth Peak. Reaching the 7,800-foot valley requires a circuitous 25-mile drive from the foothills of Three Rivers, the same route that was taken by miners seeking their fortune in the 1880s. The easiest way to visit Mineral King is to reserve a stay at the cabins at Silver City Resort or Paradise Canyon Cabins.

In December 2000, a new national park joined the borders of Sequoia and Kings Canyon: Giant Sequoia National Monument. Administered by the Forest Service, not the National Park Service, the new national monument contains two non-contiguous land areas, both designed to increase protection for the last remaining Giant Sequoia groves in the world. (Although Sequoias once ranged across the planet, today they are found only in a narrow strip of land, approximately 40 miles wide and 150 miles long, in the Sierra Nevada.) Several cabins can be rented in both parts of the new national monument, including four historic fire stations belonging to the U.S. Forest Service.

The recreation options don't stop at the national park and monument borders. Boaters and anglers head to Bass Lake, Shaver Lake, and Huntington Lake in Sierra National Forest for warm summer days on the water. Skiers and snowboarders enjoy uncrowded lift lines at Sierra Summit near Huntington Lake and Shirley Meadows near Kernville. White-water rafters flock to the Kern and Kaweah Rivers. Fly fishers head for the Kern River north of Kernville. And hikers can walk through magnificent and much less visited Giant Sequoia groves in national forest and state forest lands near Dinkey Creek (McKinley Grove), Oakhurst (Nelder Grove), and Springville (Mountain Home State Forest).

In each of these places, you can look forward to choosing from a variety of interesting places to spend the night, including the cabins and cottages listed in the pages that follow.

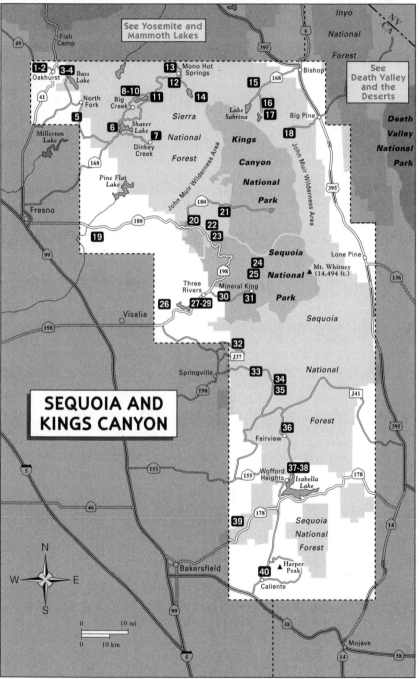

CHAPTER 5
SEQUOIA AND KINGS CANYON

1. THE HOMESTEAD

Cindy Brooks and Larry Ends are the perfect kind of people to run a resort for outdoor enthusiasts, because they are outdoor lovers themselves. In 1992, they left their desk jobs and big-city life in Los Angeles and moved to Ahwahnee to open The Homestead, an oak-dotted resort on 160 acres.

Off Highway 49 in Ahwahnee

Luxury rating: 4

Recreation rating: 4

The Homestead's five cottages are all newly built and beautifully appointed. (Cindy and Larry did much of the construction themselves.) The interiors are lined with Saltillo tiles, warm pine wood, and simple but tasteful furnishings. Each cottage, including an above-the-barn "star gazing loft," has a fully equipped kitchen and a fireplace. They also have air-conditioning, a real bonus in the summer at this 2,000-foot elevation.

If horses are your thing, and you like to travel with yours, you'll be all set at The Homestead. In addition to its cottages, The Homestead has a corral where your horse can go on vacation. Cindy and Larry will provide you with information on all the local horseback riding trails.

If you are traveling sans horse, a great place to start your exploration of the area is on the Sierra Vista National Scenic Byway, a driving loop that begins near Bass Lake. The road ascends as high as 7,300 feet to a land of big conifers, imposing granite domes, and wide-angle vistas of the Sierra Crest and surrounding wilderness areas.

Another option is to head a few miles north on Highway 41 to Sky Ranch Road, from which you can access the Nelder Grove of Giant Sequoias and the lovely Shadow of the Giants National Recreation Trail, or the short and scenic trail to the top of Fresno Dome (wow, what a view). Heading north on Highway 41, you'll find a trailhead for Lewis Creek Trail (great wildflowers and two small, pretty waterfalls). Or head farther north to Fish Camp and the Yosemite Mountain Sugar Pine Historical Railroad, where you can relive history with a ride on its narrow-gauge steam trains. A few miles beyond Fish Camp is the southern entrance to Yosemite National Park.

Needless to say, there's much to do. Let Larry and Cindy at The Homestead provide you with maps and brochures, then get out there and get busy.

Facilities: There are five one-bedroom cottages, all with fully equipped kitchens, fireplaces, and air-conditioning.

Bedding: Linens and towels are provided.

Reservations and rates: Reservations are recommended. Fees are $129 to $189 per night for two adults. There is a two-night minimum stay on weekends. The resort is open year-round. Pets are not permitted.

2. HOUNDS TOOTH INN

Hounds Tooth Inn's location might discourage potential guests: It's set within a few yards of busy Highway 41 in Oakhurst. But in actuality, its placement is one of its assets: From the door of your Hounds Tooth Inn cottage, all the recreation opportunities of the Bass Lake and southern Yosemite area await. It's not so much *what* Hounds Tooth Inn is, but *where* it is, that makes it work.

© ANN MARIE BROWN

Off Highway 41 in Oakhurst

Luxury rating: 4

Recreation rating: 4

That said, Hounds Tooth Inn is a lovely new lodging with one separate 850-square-foot cottage and 12 guest rooms. It looks like a country inn that was moved out of the country. The Hounds Tooth does a fair job of concealing its roadside location: It's set below the highway and out of its sight line, and its three-acre grounds are beautifully landscaped with walkways, trees, and foliage.

The cottage features a large suite with a king bed, spa, fireplace, and small kitchenette, plus its own private patio with a garden and small waterfall. It is frequently used for honeymoons, but can also fit a small family. The kitchenette is a bit of a disappointment for people who like to cook, but because the town of Oakhurst is a mere two minutes away, you probably won't starve. Also, a complimentary breakfast and afternoon tea are served each day at the main building.

For recreation, Bass Lake is a mere 10 minutes away and the southern entrance to Yosemite is 20 minutes away. Horseback riding in the area is popular, as are mountain biking, hiking (maps are available at the inn), fishing, all water sports, and all winter sports.

Facilities: There is one one-bedroom cottage with a kitchenette (microwave and refrigerator), fireplace, and patio, plus 12 guest rooms.

Bedding: Linens and towels are provided.

3. THE FORKS RESORT

Bass Lake fits the bill for anybody who likes boating or fishing. The lake is situated at 3,500 feet in elevation in Sierra National Forest, and if that makes you think of warm summer days and waterskiing, you're thinking clearly.

Off Highway 41 on Bass Lake

Luxury rating: 3

Recreation rating: 4

THIS CABIN RANKS . . .
*Best for Boating
& Water Sports*

Bass Lake is only 14 miles from the southern entrance to Yosemite National Park, but the folks who come here usually don't head for Yosemite. Instead, they while away their days on the big, pretty lake, which covers more than 1,000 acres when full. Although waterskiing is the main attraction, personal watercraft riders, anglers, and swimmers also share the waters.

The Forks Resort is one of the old-style resorts on the lake; it's been owned and operated by the same family for three generations. It has cabins of varying sizes, a good general store, its own dock with boat rentals (patio boats, motorboats, rowboats, and canoes), and a café that looks like the kind of place where the waitresses are all named Thelma. Seriously, "the home of the world-famous Forks Burger" is right out of the 1950s. Order a milk shake or a root beer float while you're there.

The cabins at The Forks Resort are unremarkable, but they make the perfect base camp for a Bass Lake vacation. Only a handful have lake views, but all are right across the road from the water's edge, about a two-minute walk. Each cabin has a fully equipped kitchen, plus a porch with a barbecue grill so you can cook up all the fish you catch. The one-bedroom cabins have two double beds; you can squeeze in four people. The one-bedroom suite cabins have an extra room. The two-bedroom cabins can accommodate as many as six people. In addition to the extra space, you also get a fireplace and a microwave.

The Forks Resort is a family-oriented place, and it's reinforced by a "no party" policy. That keeps the ambience quiet and peaceful, even though this is a very busy and popular resort. You won't be woken up at 2 A.M. by a bunch of drunkards next door.

Facilities: There are 20 cabins ranging in size from one to two bedrooms; they can accommodate up to six people. All cabins have fully equipped kitchens and a porch with barbecue. A general store and café are on-site.

Bedding: Linens and towels are provided.

Reservations and rates: Reservations are recommended. Fees range from $85 to $135 per night. The resort is open year-round. Pets are permitted with a $25 fee.

Directions: From Fresno, drive north on Highway 41 for 45 miles to Oakhurst, then turn east (right) on Road 426 (Crane Valley Road). Drive seven miles on Road 426, then turn left at the sign for Bass Lake. Drive one mile; The Forks Resort will be on your left at the junction with Road 222.

Contact: The Forks Resort, 39150 Road 222, Bass Lake, CA 93604; 559/642-3737; website: www.theforksresort.com.

OTHER CABINS AND COTTAGES NEARBY
- The Pines Resort, P.O. Box 109, Bass Lake, CA 93604; 800/350-7463; website: www.basslake.com.
- Bass Lake Vacation Rentals, P.O. Box 507, Bass Lake, CA 93604; 559/642-2211.
- Bass Lake Realty (vacation cabins), P.O. Box 349, Bass Lake, CA 93604; 559/642-3600; website: www.basslakerealty.com.

The Forks Resort

4. MILLER'S LANDING

Bass Lake has so much development around its edges that it can seem like a small city. With several campgrounds, restaurants, and resorts, plus numerous places to rent boats or buy fishing equipment, the lakeshore is more like a vacation town than a peaceful mountain retreat.

That's why a stay at Miller's Landing is so refreshing. Located at the southern edge of the lake, Miller's Landing has easy access to the lake's commercial services but is far from the hubbub of the busy Pines Village area. The resort is self-contained—it features cabins, a restaurant, and its own marina with boat rentals (patio boats, ski boats, Waverunners, fishing boats,

Off Highway 41 on Bass Lake

Luxury rating: 3

Recreation rating: 4

THIS CABIN RANKS . . .

***Best for Boating
& Water Sports***

kayaks, and canoes)—so you don't need to go anywhere else if you don't feel like it.

The cabins at Miller's Landing run the gamut from bare-bones to more elaborate. The most deluxe cabins sleep eight; they have two bedrooms, two baths, satellite television, and a full-size kitchen with all the accoutrements. My personal favorites are cabins 3 through 6, which are two-bedroom rustic cabins with a full kitchen. You must use restroom and shower facilities located a short walk away, and you have to bring your own linens, bedding, dishes, pots, and pans, but you get a roof over your head and a fair amount of space for 45 bucks a night. A picnic table and fire ring are right outside your door. Cabin 2 is of the same minimalist ilk, but even smaller and less expensive.

A nice day hike is possible from the trailhead at neighboring Spring Cove Campground. Follow Spring Cove Trail uphill to join Goat Mountain Trail, which connects with Goat Mountain Road and leads to an operating fire lookout tower perched at 4,675 feet. The entire round-trip is 8.4 miles; views of the lake and surrounding forest are exceptional.

Fishing is good at Bass Lake, but not necessarily for bass, as the lake's name leads you to believe. Instead, trout fishing is popular in winter and spring; the Department of Fish and Game drops in heavy plants of rainbows. In summer, people catch a little bit of everything: catfish, bluegill, bass, crappie, and trout.

Facilities: There are 13 cabins ranging in size that can accommodate two to eight people. Some cabins have fully equipped kitchens; rustic cabins have refrigerators and stoves only, and no cooking or eating utensils or private restrooms. A general store and café are on-site.

Bedding: Linens and towels are provided in some cabins; for cabins 2 through 6, you must bring your own.

Reservations and rates: Reservations are recommended. Fees range from $35 to $45 per night for rustic cabins without plumbing and $130 to $170 per night for cabins with baths and full kitchens. The resort is open year-round. Pets are permitted with a $25 fee.

Directions: From Fresno, drive north on Highway 41 for 45 miles to Oakhurst, then turn east (right) on Road 426 (Crane Valley Road). Drive seven miles on Road 426, then turn left at the sign for Bass Lake. Drive one mile to Road 222; turn right and drive three miles to Miller's Landing Resort on the right.

Contact: Miller's Landing, 37976 Road 222, Wishon, CA 93669; 559/642-3633; website: www.millerslanding.com.
Miller's Landing

5. BONNIE B RANCH

A lot of people have a private fantasy about owning their own ranch . . . the kind of place with horses grazing on the grounds, a big house with extra bedrooms for your friends, and maybe even a few fishing ponds sprinkled around the property.

Off Highway 41 near North Fork

Luxury rating: 4

Recreation rating: 4

THIS CABIN RANKS . . .
Best for Horseback Riding

You can dream about having a place like this, or you can rent Bonnie B Ranch and make it real. Here's how to do it: Gather up a group of five to eight people—invite your family, your friends, or what the heck, even your boss; tell them to pack up their fishing gear, outdoor clothes, and a week's worth of groceries; then head to the town of North Fork, just southeast of Oakhurst and Bass Lake, and begin your private ranch vacation.

You need your friends because you're paying to rent an entire ranch house and the 440 acres surrounding it. This doesn't come cheap; current rates are $350 per night or $2,300 per week. At the weekly rate, a group of six people will pay about $55 each per night. For that price, they get lodging in a beautiful 3,000-square-foot ranch house, plus all the horseback riding and catch-and-release fishing they can stand. The ranch has five small lakes that are loaded with hand-raised bass, bluegill, and crappie. The largest lake can be fished by float tube or pram (bring your own); the rest are for shore fishing. Hikers and equestrians can choose from 16 miles of trails on the property.

If you're wondering if you'll be staying in a run-down barn, here are some details on the house: It's a three-bedroom, three-bath home perched on a hill, with a fully equipped country kitchen and wrap-around deck, plus a large living area with fireplace and giant picture windows. From the living room, you can gaze at the ranch's largest pond, or the horses grazing in the pasture, or the high mountains of the Sierra. It's so scenic that the property has been used as a location for countless movies, including the films *Mousetrap* and *The Giant of Thunder Mountain*. Spring wildflowers are breathtaking, maple and oak trees bring autumn colors, and winter snow turns the ranch into a white wonderland.

The ranch dates back to 1891. On the property, you will find a covered bridge, historic gristmill, stonework, and split-rail cedar fences. A staff person lives in a separate building on the premises to help with the horses and make sure everything runs smoothly during your stay.

Facilities: There is one three-bedroom, three-bath ranch house with a fully equipped kitchen, fireplace, and deck. It can accommodate up to eight people. There is access to 440 acres, including hiking and horseback riding trails and fishing ponds.

Bedding: Linens and towels are provided.

Reservations and rates: Reservations are required. Fees range from $350 per night to $2,300 per week, and include horseback riding and fishing in five private ponds. A $150 cleaning fee is charged (nonrefundable), and a refundable $400 security deposit is required. Weeklong stays are required from June to August; there is a two-night minimum the rest of the year. Pets are not permitted.

Directions: From Fresno, drive north on Highway 41 for 25 miles to Road 200 (North Fork Road) and turn right. Drive northeast on Road 200 for 17 miles, past the turnoff for Road 221, to the left turnoff at Bonnie B Road. (If you reach the town of North Fork, you've gone too far.) Turn left on Bonnie B Road and enter the ranch.

Contact: Kerry Bryant, Bryant Farms/Bonnie B Ranch, 323 26th Street, Manhattan Beach, CA 90266; 310/546-3792; website: www.bonnieb.com.

Bonnie B Ranch

6. SHAVER LAKE LODGE

People who have never been to Shaver and Huntington Lakes usually think of them as a package deal. They're both big reservoirs, both owned by Southern California Edison, and both are popular for fishing and boating. They're located just 20 miles apart on Highway 168 in the southern Sierra.

But those who vacation at Shaver Lake and those who vacation at Huntington Lake are unlikely to belong to the same club, because Shaver Lake is known for fast boats and waterskiing and Huntington Lake is known for sailing.

Other differences? Shaver is smaller than Huntington, but the fishing is more reliable, especially in its sheltered coves. Shaver is set at 5,500 feet in elevation, while Huntington is nearly 2,000 feet higher, so Shaver is a bit warmer for swimming and water sports. And Shaver Lake has much less development along its edges. In fact, other than two Forest Service campgrounds, the only place you can spend the night at Shaver Lake is in the cabins at Shaver Lake Lodge.

When you call to make your reservation, be sure to ask for a cabin numbered between 7 and 14. These are the cabins with the best lake views. Some of the higher numbered cabins are clustered too close together on the hillside and have views of the other cabins. Cabin 9 is the best of the lot.

If you plan on setting up housekeeping, be forewarned that the cabins do not have full kitchens. They have a small refrigerator and a microwave, but that's all; it's just enough to make your oatmeal and coffee in the

Off Highway 168 on Shaver Lake

Luxury rating: 3

Recreation rating: 4

THIS CABIN RANKS . . .
**Best for Boating
& Water Sports**

morning. Dishes and utensils are not provided; bring your own from home.

The Shaver Lake Lodge Marina rents all kinds of boats: kayaks, canoes, sailboats, fishing boats, personal watercrafts, pontoon boats, and so on. If everything is rented out, Sierra Marina at Shaver Lake is up the road a mile.

Shaver Lake's cabins sit right next to the lodge restaurant, which features an extensive menu for lunch and dinner. The food is well-prepared, priced fairly, and served in mountain-sized portions. Dinner entrées include prime rib, pork chops, halibut, and chicken breast, as well as more casual food like hamburgers and salads. In summer, you can sit outside on the deck overlooking the lake and linger over long meals.

The lodge is also open in winter. Downhill skiers stay in the cabins and drive 15 miles up Highway 168 to Sierra Summit Ski Area. Cross-country skiers and snowmobilers head for Tamarack Winter Sports Area, where miles of snow-covered trails are available.

Facilities: There are 20 single and duplex cabins ranging in size from studios to two bedrooms. Most have microwaves and small refrigerators; none have full kitchens. A restaurant, small store, and marina are on-site.

Bedding: Linens and towels are provided.

Reservations and rates: Reservations are recommended. Fees range from $55 to $105 per night. The lodge is open year-round. Pets are not permitted.

Directions: From Fresno, drive north on Highway 41 for six miles to the Highway 168/Clovis turnoff. Turn east on Highway 168 and drive 47 miles to the town of Shaver Lake. Continue two miles past the town; the resort is on the right side of the road.

Contact: Shaver Lake Lodge, 44185 Highway 168, Shaver Lake, CA 93664; 559/841-3326.

OTHER CABINS AND COTTAGES NEARBY
• Shaver Lake Vacation Rentals, P.O. Box 349, Shaver Lake, CA 93664; 800/422-4102.
Shaver Lake Lodge

7. DINKEY CREEK INN

If you've heard about the Dinkey Lakes Wilderness your whole life but somehow never managed to make the trip, here's the perfect way to do it without joining the hordes of backpackers who infiltrate the area. Book a stay at the Dinkey Creek Inn, then spend a few days hiking, fishing, swimming, and exploring the territory.

Off Highway 168 near Shaver Lake

Luxury rating: 3

Recreation rating: 4

The inn's chalets were built in 1992, so they are modern in style, with fully equipped kitchens and baths, woodburning stoves, and satellite TV. Each one is nestled in the conifers, with a redwood deck out front that is perfect for barbecuing and dining al fresco. You don't need to worry about packing everything for your vacation; a small store is on the premises and almost anything you can think of can be purchased in the town of Shaver Lake, 13 miles away.

The chalets are located within a few hundred feet of Dinkey Creek and its historic trestle bridge, the only free-span redwood bridge in California. The McKinley Grove of Giant Sequoias is only six miles from the chalets. Closer to home is Honeymoon Pool, a granite-lined, 20-foot-deep swimming and fishing hole in Dinkey Creek, located at the upper end of the neighboring Forest Service campground.

The beauty continues as you head for the Dinkey Lakes Wilderness, a short drive away via Rock Creek Road and Forest Service Road 9S10. (Be prepared for two miles of rough road at the end.) A perfect day hike is the seven-mile loop to First Dinkey Lake, which also passes Mystery, Swede, and South Lakes. From First Dinkey Lake, you can loop back to the parking lot, or backtrack a short distance toward South Lake and continue on to Second Dinkey Lake, Island Lake, Rock Lake, and so on. The trail is remarkably level; you cover a surprising amount of ground in little time.

In winter, cross-country skiing, snowmobiling, and snowshoeing are all possible right outside the door of your chalet. Downhill skiers can drive up the highway to Sierra Summit Ski Area, about 40 minutes away.

Facilities: There are five chalets that can accommodate up to six people. All have fully equipped kitchens. Three rustic hiker's cabins are also available, without kitchens, baths, or linens. A store and lunch counter are on-site.

Bedding: Linens and towels are provided.

Reservations and rates: Reservations are recommended. Fees range from $75 to $100 per night; weekly rates are discounted. The chalets are open year-round. Pets are permitted with a deposit.

Directions: From Fresno, drive north on Highway 41 for six miles to the Highway 168/Clovis turnoff. Turn east on Highway 168 and drive 47 miles to the town of Shaver Lake. Turn right on Dinkey Creek Road and drive 13 miles. The resort is on the right side of the road.

Contact: Dinkey Creek Inn, 53861 Dinkey Creek Road, Shaver Lake, CA 93664; 559/841-3435; website: www.dinkeycreek.com.

Dinkey Creek Inn

8. CEDAR CREST RESORT

Cedar Crest Resort has "old-fashioned" written all over it. It's obvious that this lakefront establishment has been around a long time, and that it knows how to do vacations right.

© ANN MARIE BROWN

Off Highway 168 on Huntington Lake

Luxury rating: 3

Recreation rating: 4

The cabins at Cedar Crest are beautifully situated on a steep hill above Huntington Lake. This is one of the few area resorts that is located far off the road that circles the lake; that guarantees a quiet atmosphere. Guarded by dense pines and firs, the cabins offer the rare gift of privacy.

Completely furnished for housekeeping, each cabin has a full kitchen, one or two bedrooms, and private bathroom. Make sure you pay a few extra bucks for the "AA Plan" cabins, which have fireplaces, electric kitchens instead of butane, and the best lake views. If you are on a strict budget, you can settle for the tent cabins, which have beds, electricity, a woodstove for cooking, and a picnic table outside. Bathrooms are a short walk away.

The resort is full service; it has a restaurant, small store, and boat rentals at their marina. The boats are basic aluminum jobs with outboard motors. If you want something fancier, go to one of the larger marinas on the lake.

You probably won't want to do much but hang out on your cabin's deck, gaze at the lake, and listen to the wind in the pines. If you can tear yourself away, fishing and swimming are obvious options. For the energetic, some of the best hikes in the area begin at nearby Upper Billy

Creek Campground. A strenuous 2,300-foot climb over five miles will take you to Nellie Lake, a beautiful subalpine lake. From the same trailhead, the easy Lower Kaiser Loop offers a look at Line Creek's cascades and stunning wildflowers in early summer. Another option is to walk the Coarsegrass Meadow Trail along Home Camp Creek (trailhead is near Huntington Lake Resort's marina). It's five miles round-trip to flower-lined Coarsegrass Meadow, or you can add on a steep two miles to Aspen Meadow.

Facilities: There are 14 cabins ranging in size that can accommodate up to six people. All cabins have fully equipped kitchens. Cabana units without kitchens and tent cabins without baths and kitchens are also available. A small general store, restaurant, and boat rentals are on-site.

Bedding: Linens and towels are provided except in tent cabins.

Reservations and rates: Reservations are recommended. Fees range from $84 to $109 per night for up to four people in "A Plan" and "AA Plan" cabins. Tent cabins are $20 per night for one bed and $5 per night for each additional bed (up to three). Cabanas are $20 per night. The resort is open from late May to early September. Pets are permitted with a $5 fee per night.

Directions: From Fresno, drive north on Highway 41 for six miles to the Highway 168/Clovis turnoff. Turn east on Highway 168 and drive 70 miles, past Shaver Lake and Sierra Summit Ski Area, to the left turn for Huntington Lake. Bear left on Huntington Lake Road and drive 3.5 miles to Cedar Crest Resort on the left side of the road.

Contact: Cedar Crest Resort, P.O. Box 163, Lakeshore, CA 93634; 559/893-3233; website: www.cedarcrestresort.com.

Cedar Crest Resort

9. HUNTINGTON LAKE RESORT

Most cabins are rustic, plain, serviceable. Most cabins don't even try to be anything but . . . well, cabins. The cabins at Huntington Lake Resort are the exception. They're cute. They have a green-and-white gingerbread paint job on the outside, and a homey sweetness on the inside. Heck, they're adorable.

The cabins are set on Huntington Lake's west end, not far from the dam. Located across the road from the lake, but up high on the hillside, some are granted partial lake views. You can cook your catch of the day in your kitchen or on the barbecue by your front door, and eat it outside on your deck.

Since you're staying at the lake's west end, you're in perfect position for a few day trips. One of the best is driving up scenic Forest Service Road 8S32 for 4.5 miles to Mushroom Rock Vista and Black Point Trail. Mushroom Rock Vista delivers exactly what it promises—a big rock that looks oddly like a mushroom. Beyond the rock is the vista, a long-dis-

*Off Highway 168 on
Huntington Lake*

Luxury rating: 3

Recreation rating: 5

tance view of the forested slopes of the San Joaquin River Canyon and Shaver Lake. Black Point Trail, a half mile beyond Mushroom Rock, is a steep, half-mile hike to a spectacular overlook of Huntington Lake, Shaver Lake, Kaiser Ridge, and the San Joaquin River Canyon.

Anglers and sailors can rent a boat from the Huntington Lake Resort Marina. The marina provides sailboat and fishing boat rentals, plus fishing tackle and supplies, and a no-nonsense snack shop and café. Many anglers don't bother with a boat; instead, they fish from shore or the lake's dam. The usual catch is small stocked trout, plus occasional kokanee salmon. Home Camp Creek, which flows right next to the resort's cabins, is also a fair trout stream.

Although the western stretch of Huntington Lake Road is not plowed in winter, Huntington Lake Resort stays open year-round for those who are willing to snowmobile or ski in four miles. The resort owners will bring in your luggage and gear by sled. Once you're there, you can take your pick from miles of snow-covered roads and trails, then ski, snowshoe, or snowmobile to your heart's content.

Facilities: There are 10 cabins ranging in size that can accommodate two to eight people. Most have fully equipped kitchens.

Bedding: Linens and towels are provided.

Reservations and rates: Reservations are recommended. Fees range from $50 to $90 per night. The resort is open year-round. Pets are permitted with prior approval and a $5 fee per night.

Directions: From Fresno, drive north on Highway 41 for six miles to the Highway 168/Clovis turnoff. Turn east on Highway 168 and drive 70 miles, past Shaver Lake and Sierra Summit Ski Area, to the left turn for Huntington Lake. Bear left on Huntington Lake Road and drive five miles to the west end of the lake. Huntington Lake Resort is on the right side of the road.

Contact: Huntington Lake Resort, P.O. Box 257, Lakeshore, CA 93634; 559/893-3226.

Huntington Lake Resort

10. LAKEVIEW COTTAGES

There's only one sensible choice at Lakeview Cottages: Rent the large two-bedroom cabins on the front of the property, facing the lake. Sure, they cost a little more, but as you spend day after day on your cabin's deck, gazing at azure blue Huntington Lake, you won't feel bad about the extra money.

Off Highway 168 on Huntington Lake

Luxury rating: 3

Recreation rating: 4

Lakeview Cottages are similar to, and completely different from, other cabin resorts at Huntington Lake. They are similar in that they are set across the road from the five-mile long lake, and are fully furnished with kitchens and bathrooms for vacation housekeeping. They are different in that their lake views are nearly unobstructed. And because they are located near the end of a dead-end road, very few cars will pass by your cabin. This area of Huntington Lake is as quiet as it gets.

The cottages are rented by the week for most of the summer, but in the slower months (usually June and September) you can often get one for a shorter stay. They come with all the necessities of living except towels. Also, if you're the type who gets cold at night, bring a few extra blankets, because each bed only has one.

Rowboats and motorboats are also for rent by the week or the day, so you can fish to your heart's content. Plus all of Huntington's other outdoor recreation options are yours to choose from: swimming, hiking, horseback riding, cycling, sailing, you name it.

Facilities: There are 10 cabins ranging in size that can accommodate up to six people. All cabins have fully equipped kitchens.

Bedding: Linens are provided but not towels.

Reservations and rates: Reservations are recommended. Fees range from $325 to $390 per week for one-bedroom cabins and $520 to $585 per week for two-bedroom cabins. Shorter stays are sometimes available for $50 to $90 per night. The resort is open from June to September. Pets are permitted with a $6 fee per night.

Directions: From Fresno, drive north on Highway 41 for six miles to the Highway 168/Clovis turnoff. Turn east on Highway 168 and drive 70 miles, past Shaver Lake and Sierra Summit Ski Area, to the left turn for Huntington Lake. Bear left on Huntington Lake Road and drive six miles to the west end of the lake, past the dam. Turn left on Huntington Lodge Road and drive one mile to Lakeview Cottages on the right.

Contact: Lakeview Cottages, P.O. Box 177, Lakeshore, CA 93634; 559/893-2330 (summer) or 562/697-6556 (winter). *Lakeview Cottages*

11. LAKESHORE RESORT

Of all the big lakes in Sierra National Forest that are open for recreation, Huntington Lake is the most versatile of the lot. Although sailing is Huntington's big claim to fame, you'll find plenty of people fishing, boating, camping, hiking, picnicking, and sunbathing as well. The lake is big—five miles long and a half mile wide—so it almost never seems too crowded, even on summer weekends.

© ANN MARIE BROWN

Off Highway 168 on Huntington Lake

Luxury rating: 3

Recreation rating: 5

THIS CABIN RANKS . . .
*Best for Boating
& Water Sports*

The cabins at Lakeshore Resort are about as versatile as the lake itself. With a grand total of 26 cabins, and no two exactly alike, you're bound to find one that suits your needs. They are located behind Lakeshore's restaurant, store, and saloon, only a short walk from the lake (but with no lake views).

Lakeshore Resort is open year-round. In summer, spend your time hiking, boating, fishing, or waterskiing. In winter, try snowmobiling, snowshoeing, and downhill or cross-country skiing. Only 10 minutes away is Sierra Summit Ski Area, where you can tackle the slopes of Chinese Peak.

Serious hikers won't want to miss the chance to bag Kaiser Peak, via a 10-mile round-trip trail. Not-so-ambitious hikers can walk the beautiful easy trails to Rancheria Falls or Indian Pools, or take a pleasant walk along the edge of Huntington Lake. A moderate six-mile hike leads to Twin Lakes via scenic Potter Pass. George Lake lies another 1.5 miles beyond the upper Twin Lake, requiring a nine-mile round-trip.

Of course, at this 7,000-foot elevation, some people find hiking a bit too strenuous. If you're in this camp, the sure-footed steeds at neighboring D & F Pack Station will escort you on two-hour trail rides, half-day rides, or longer fishing and pack trips.

Many visitors opt to leave the landlubbers behind and spend all their vacation time on Huntington Lake. If you don't have your own boat, you can rent one at Rancheria Cove Marina, less than a quarter mile from your cabin. They have small fishing skiffs, large patio boats, skiing boats, various personal watercrafts, and canoes and kayaks. Trout fishing is decent from the shoreline but better while trolling; many anglers circle Big Creek Cove or work their way up and down the lake's long edges. Every few days someone catches a kokanee salmon, but most of the time it's small planted trout.

Facilities: There are 26 cabins ranging in size from one to three bedrooms. Most have fully equipped kitchens. A general store, restaurant, and saloon are on-site.

Bedding: Linens and towels are provided; rates are discounted if you bring your own.

Reservations and rates: Reservations are recommended. Fees range from $78 to $150 per night. There is a two-night minimum stay on weekends; three-night minimum stay on long holidays. The resort is open year-round. Pets are permitted with a $15 fee per night.

Directions: From Fresno, drive north on Highway 41 for six miles to the Highway 168/Clovis turnoff. Turn east on Highway 168 and drive 70 miles, past Shaver Lake and Sierra Summit Ski Area, to the left turn for Huntington Lake. Bear left on Huntington Lake Road and drive one mile. Lakeshore Resort is on the right side of the road.

Contact: Lakeshore Resort, P.O. Box 197, Lakeshore, CA 93634; 559/893-3193; website: www.lakeshoreresort.com.

Lakeshore Resort

12. MONO HOT SPRINGS RESORT

Mono Hot Springs Resort is a place where it seems time has stood still. The road to reach it is long, narrow, and winding, with no gasoline or services along the way. Electricity is available only when the generator runs. Telephones are nonexistent.

Off Kaiser Pass Road near Huntington Lake

Luxury rating: 3

Recreation rating: 3

THIS CABIN RANKS . . .
Most Unusual

The resort's raison d'être is its natural warm mineral waters. A sign outside the communal bathhouse informs you how many parts per million of carbonates, bicarbonates, chloride, and sulfates are in the water. The bathhouse has six private bathing tubs where you can soak away your cares for just a couple of bucks. The tubs vary from old-fashioned clawfoot to modern fiberglass. All are rustic; don't expect the enamel to be sparkling white. If you prefer to bathe al fresco, there's a small outdoor mineral pool that's just big enough for two or three bathers.

Be sure to reserve one of the resort's modern cabins or stone housekeeping cabins instead of the "rustic" ones. The modern and stone cabins are built of native cobblestone and come with bathrooms and full kitchens. Some even have their own showers and electricity. The rustic wood cabins cost half as much, but they are a tad too rustic. In addition to no electricity nor heat, they have no cooking facilities except an outside fire pit, and no bathrooms. You share a nearby outhouse and pay extra for showers or baths at the bathhouse.

The resort store sells basic groceries if you want to cook in your cabin. If not, Mono's Indian Camp Fine Food Cafe serves buffalo steaks and buffalo burgers in addition to the regular kind, and even offers a few veggie dishes. The restaurant is a friendly, casual place.

Hikers can set out from the resort and walk to Doris and Tule Lakes, both popular for swimming and fishing for trout and bass. Doris Lake is only one mile from the cabins, so even small children can make the trip. Other trails lead into the John Muir and Ansel Adams Wildernesses from nearby Edison Lake and Florence Lake.

Anglers, take note: Stream fishing is excellent in Mono Creek, Bear Creek, and the South Fork of the San Joaquin River (all within hiking distance). Lake fishing is first-rate in nearby Edison and Florence Lakes. Boat rentals are available at both lakes.

Facilities: There are 15 cabins ranging in size from studios to two bedrooms. The modern cabins have fully equipped kitchens and bathrooms; the rustic cabins do not. A bathhouse and outdoor mineral pool, plus restaurant, general store, and post office, are on-site.

Bedding: Linens and towels are provided in the modern cabins but not the rustic cabins.

Reservations and rates: Reservations are recommended. Fees range from $45 to $85 per night. The resort is open from late May to late October. Pets are permitted with a $4 fee per night.

Directions: From Highway 168 at the eastern edge of Huntington Lake, turn right on Kaiser Pass Road and drive 17 miles (narrow and winding) to a fork in the road. Bear left for Mono Hot Springs and Edison Lake, drive 1.6 miles and turn left again. You'll reach the resort in a quarter mile. (Note that trailers and motor homes are not recommended on Kaiser Pass Road.)

Contact: Mono Hot Springs Resort, General Delivery, Mono Hot Springs, CA 93642; 559/325-1710; website: www.monohotsprings.com. (Winter address: P.O. Box 215, Lakeshore, CA 93634.)

Mono Hot Springs Resort

13. VERMILION VALLEY RESORT

Let's get it straight: Before you make the trip to Vermilion Valley Resort at Lake Thomas A. Edison, make sure you are fully prepared. The place is 40-plus miles from the nearest town (Shaver Lake), and you won't want to make the trip more than once per vacation. It's 20 winding miles from Shaver Lake to Huntington Lake, then another 17 curving miles over 9,200-foot Kaiser Pass to Mono Hot Springs, then a final 6.5 twisting miles to Vermilion Valley Resort at Lake Thomas A. Edison.

When you reach the place, you find that it isn't exactly the Hilton, but it has all the basics. Vermilion Valley Resort's cabins are tent cabins—big tents with wood floors and twin bunk beds with mattresses, plus a table, chairs, and dresser. They have no heat, no kitchen facilities, and no electricity. Make sure you bring your sleeping bags and flashlights.

Off Kaiser Pass Road on Lake Thomas A. Edison

Luxury rating: 2

Recreation rating: 4

If you get tired of cooking meals on your camp stove or over a campfire, you can eat at the resort's café. It has an open kitchen, a few tables and chairs, trophy trout mounted on the walls, and some of the nicest people in the world working there. Breakfast is the café's claim to fame: big stacks of buttermilk pancakes, eggs, sausage, and bacon.

Edison Lake is a big trout producer, so the conversation at all meals usually revolves around who's catching what with which tackle. Unfortunately, the water level of the big lake fluctuates like most Nasdaq stocks. Up, down, up, down. It's not the most beautiful lake you've seen when it's drawn down, although it's a stunner when full, backed by the rugged 12,000-foot peaks of the high Sierra. The lake is at 7,700 feet in elevation.

Hikers can access the Pacific Crest Trail from Edison Lake, either by hiking the Mono Creek Trail along the lake's north edge or taking the ferry across the lake. An excellent day hike is the Devils Bathtub Trail from the resort; it's five miles one-way to a rocky, beautiful alpine lake. Or hike the Mono Creek Trail south from Edison Lake to Mono Hot Springs, stopping to admire beautiful Mono Meadow and Doris Lake along the way. Hot springs lovers can drive to nearby Mono Hot Springs Resort and bathe in the soothing waters.

Facilities: There are 10 tent cabins, plus four motel rooms with kitchenettes. A café and general store are on-site.

Bedding: Linens and towels are not provided; bring your own.

Reservations and rates: Reservations are recommended. Fees for the tent cabins are $40 to $45 per night. Fees for the motel rooms are $65 to $85 per night. The resort is open from June to September. Pets are permitted.

Directions: From Highway 168 at the eastern edge of Huntington Lake, turn right on Kaiser Pass Road and drive 17 miles (narrow and winding) to a fork in the road. Bear left for Mono Hot Springs and Edison Lake and drive 6.5 miles to Vermilion Valley Resort. (Note that trailers and motor homes are not recommended on Kaiser Pass Road.)

Contact: Vermilion Valley Resort, P.O. Box 258, Lakeshore, CA 93634; 559/259-4000; website: www.edisonlake.com.

Vermilion Valley Resort

14. MUIR TRAIL RANCH

If you have a big family or like to vacation with a group of friends, you are in the perfect position for a fantasy-level high Sierra vacation at your own private mountain ranch. Where? In the John Muir Wilderness. How? By renting the Muir Trail Ranch for a week. Want to know more? Keep reading.

Off Kaiser Pass Road in John Muir Wilderness

Luxury rating: 3

Recreation rating: 5

THIS CABIN RANKS . . .
Most Secluded

First, let's talk location. The Muir Trail Ranch is on 200 acres of private land near Florence Lake in Sierra National Forest, completely surrounded by the John Muir Wilderness. Getting to the ranch requires driving from Fresno to Huntington Lake, then taking narrow and winding Kaiser Pass Road to Florence Lake, then taking the water taxi across the lake, then hiking or horse packing five miles from the taxi drop-off point to Muir Trail Ranch. Sounds remote and hard to get to? It is.

Next, let's talk money. Renting the ranch for one week will cost you $8,925. Yes, it sounds expensive, but that rate is for 15 to 20 people, which works out to less than $100 per person per night. Twenty people will not overcrowd the ranch; in fact, you'll be housed with room to spare in eight log cabins and four tent cabins. The tent cabins are set on the river and equipped with electric lights and outlets; the log cabins have wash basins and toilets.

In addition to exclusive use of the cabins and surrounding land, you also have access to the ranch's big kitchen and dining room for preparing all your meals. You must pack in all your groceries for the week.

So what do you do during your stay at your own private ranch in the Sierra? Well, here at 7,700 feet in elevation, the wildflowers are pretty, fly fishing is excellent in the San Joaquin River, and hiking trails wind deep into the John Muir Wilderness. Thirty horses are available at the ranch, and one is always willing to hike to a pretty lake with you.

A few staff members live and work at the ranch. They take care of basic facility maintenance, generating electricity, and keeping the horses fed and happy. They also run a small ranch store with fishing supplies and other necessities, and will guide you on horseback trips into the wilderness.

One of Muir Trail Ranch's greatest features is its two enclosed hot springs, which everyone uses for bathing purposes as well as pure hedonistic pleasure. One bath is about 105°F; the other is a cooler 98 degrees. If it's too hot outside for a hot bath, you can always go jump in the San Joaquin River, located about 100 feet away from the tent cabins.

Facilities: There are eight log cabins at Muir Trail Ranch, plus four tent cabins. The entire ranch accommodates 15 to 20 people. A kitchen is available. Horseback riding and hot springs are available.

Bedding: Linens and towels are not provided; bring your own.

Reservations and rates: Reservations are required. The fee is $8,925 for 15 to 20 people for one week. Horses are available for $50 per day. The ranch is open from June to September. Pets are not permitted.

Directions: From Highway 168 at the eastern edge of Huntington Lake, turn right on Kaiser Pass Road and drive 17 miles (narrow and winding) to a fork in the road. Bear right for Florence Lake and drive six miles to the lake and store. From there, you will either hike to Muir Trail Ranch, ride a horse, or take the water taxi across the lake and hike the remaining five miles. (Note that trailers and motor homes are not recommended on Kaiser Pass Road.)

Contact: From October to May, contact Muir Trail Ranch at P.O. Box 700, Ahwahnee, CA 93601-0700; 209/966-3195; website: www.muirtrailranch.com. (Summer address: P.O. Box 176, Lakeshore, CA 93634-0176; no phone number is available in the summer.)

Muir Trail Ranch

15. CARDINAL VILLAGE RESORT

Historic Cardinal Village Resort is a destination in itself. Part of an old mining claim, its buildings date back to the late 1890s, when miners settled here and worked the neighboring Cardinal Gold Mine. The original town of Cardinal Village boasted a post office, store, schoolhouse, and about 100 cabins. A few of those buildings still stand and can be rented for your vacation.

© ANN MARIE BROWN

Off U.S. 395 near Bishop

Luxury rating: 3

Recreation rating: 4

Each structure has been beautifully restored. The most popular cabin is Golden Trout, which was originally a stable. It is large enough for 8 to 16 people and is often reserved a year in advance. For smaller parties, there are one-, two-, and three-bedroom cabins, each one unique, though some are more modern.

All cabins at Cardinal Village have fully equipped kitchens, but if you don't want to cook, breakfast and lunch are served daily in the resort café. Saturday is Old West–style steak barbecue night. You're on your own for dinners the rest of the week.

Cardinal Village is set in a grove of aspens along Bishop Creek, where you can try your luck at trout fishing. The resort also has Cardinal Pond, a small natural pond that is stocked with trophy trout. Other fishing opportunities abound in Bishop Creek Canyon; the closest are those at Sabrina Lake and North Lake. Sabrina Lake has a full-service boat landing with rental boats and excellent fishing for rainbow, brown, and brook trout. Much smaller North Lake is reserved for shore anglers and those in float tubes and rafts. Both lakes feature a stunning backdrop of high mountain peaks, lodgepole pines, and quaking aspens.

In summer, guests can rent horses at Cardinal Village and take trail rides up the old road to Cardinal Mine. Little remains of the mine except a few building foundations and parts of its main shaft, but it's interesting to close your eyes and imagine the old days.

Hikers seeking a challenge should follow the Piute Pass Trail from North Lake Campground to Loch Leven Lake, Piute Lake, and spectacular Piute Pass. The scenic pass is six miles out, but the lakes are closer in at 2.3 and 3.5 miles out. Alternatively, you can hike from the Lake Sabrina trailhead to photogenic Blue Lake in three miles. Each of these hike-in lakes is higher than 10,000 feet in elevation.

Facilities: There are nine cabins ranging in size that can accommodate up to 16 people, all with fully equipped kitchens. A café and general store are on-site.

Bedding: Linens and towels are not provided; bring your own or rent them for $5 per night.

Reservations and rates: Reservations are recommended. Fees range from $90 to $250 per night, depending on cabin size, and one can accommodate up to 16 people. Pets are not permitted.

Directions: From Bishop on U.S. 395, turn west on Highway 168/West Line Street. Drive 17 miles on Highway 168 to Cardinal Village Resort. (Don't bear left at the South Lake fork; continue straight ahead.)

Contact: Cardinal Village Resort, Route 1, Box A-3, Bishop, CA 93514; 760/873-4789; website: www.cardinalvillageresort.com.

Cardinal Village Resort

16. BISHOP CREEK LODGE

The lodge dining room at Bishop Creek has a wagon wheel suspended from the ceiling, fishing lures hanging everywhere like Christmas ornaments, and a chainsaw-carved wooden cowboy propped up in the corner. Hunting and fishing trophies cover every inch of the walls—the heads of several long-departed deer, an antelope, a moose, an elk, and the lifelike bodies of a few big trout.

Bishop Creek Lodge makes no pretenses: It's a fish camp, a base for people heading to South Lake or Sabrina Lake to catch trout all day. Situated at the lofty elevation of 8,300 feet, the place also attracts hikers who want to traipse the myriad trails of Bishop Creek Canyon and the John Muir Wilderness.

The resort's cabins were built by pioneers in 1928. They're rustic, not fancy. Each cabin comes with a fully stocked kitchen and bathroom, plus electricity and heat. Because supplies are minimal at the resort store, you should buy your groceries in advance. (Either that or eat Power Bait for dinner.) If you don't want to cook, you can eat at Bishop Creek's café. The menu is limited—hamburgers and sandwiches served all day, steak and chicken for dinner. The service is delightfully informal.

Off U.S. 395 near Bishop

Luxury rating: 3

Recreation rating: 4

THIS CABIN RANKS . . .
Best for Fishing

A downer for some early-morning types is that hot breakfasts are not served at the lodge. However, there is a free continental breakfast (cereals, muffins, juice, and coffee), but it isn't served until 8 A.M.—late for most serious anglers.

The primary activity at Bishop Creek is fishing at South Lake (five miles away), either along the shoreline or from a rented boat. If you don't catch anything at South Lake, head over to Sabrina Lake, just 10 miles away. Both lakes are known for their trophy brown trout. Many anglers also fish Bishop Creek; bring your fly-fishing gear.

Hikers head for the spectacular John Muir Wilderness. A trailhead is located near South Lake (try the six-mile loop hike to Ruwau, Bull, and Chocolate Lakes, or the shorter out-and-back trip to Long Lake). Another trailhead is found at the Bishop Creek Bridge (try the seven-mile round-trip to the four Tyee Lakes).

When you reserve your cabin at Bishop Creek Lodge, know that they are not all created equal. Five cabins are right on the road, which can be noisy in the early morning when trucks race up to the lake. If there are only two of you, cabin number 6 is the best bet. It's up on a hill, far from the road and set apart from the other cabins.

Facilities: There are 12 cabins ranging in size that can accommodate up to eight people. All have fully equipped kitchens and private bathrooms. A café and general store are on-site.

Bedding: Linens and towels are provided.

Reservations and rates: Reservations are recommended. Fees range from $90 to $205 per night, with a two-night minimum stay. A continental breakfast is included. Pets are permitted with a $10 fee per night.

Directions: From Bishop on U.S. 395, turn west on Highway 168/West Line Street. Drive 14 miles on Highway 168 to the South Lake turnoff. Turn left and drive 2.5 miles to Bishop Creek Lodge.

Contact: Bishop Creek Lodge, Route 1, South Lake Road, Bishop, CA 93514; 760/873-4484; website: www.bishopcreekresorts.com.

Bishop Creek Lodge

17. PARCHERS RESORT

Parchers Resort is owned and operated by the same folks who run Bishop Creek Lodge down the road, but Parchers is newer and just a little more posh than 70-year-old Bishop Creek.

Off U.S. 395 near Bishop

Luxury rating: 3

Recreation rating: 4

THIS CABIN RANKS . . .
Best for Fishing

Tucked in between two streams—Bishop Creek and Green Creek—and set among lodgepole pines and aspens, the cabins at Parchers Resort are pleasantly secluded and partially hidden from the road. They come in two styles: standard and rustic. The standard cabins house as many as four people. Each has a fully equipped kitchen and small dining area, separate bedroom with a queen or double bed, and a living area with a couple of extra twin beds. The rustic cabins are smaller but offer the same amenities, including a kitchen. A couple can save money by renting a two-person rustic cabin with no kitchen; they're half the price of the other cabins.

Parchers Resort is located only 1.2 miles from big, beautiful South Lake at 9,750 feet in elevation, which is well-stocked with rainbow and brown trout. South Lake's marina has fishing boats for rent, or you can try your luck on the shoreline.

Hikers have access to numerous trails. To get a taste for the area, try the six-mile round-trip to the five Treasure Lakes. The route begins at South Lake on the Bishop Pass Trail; after an initial climb of nearly a mile, bear right on Treasure Lakes Trail. The first two lakes are easy to reach; the remaining three require some route-finding. Many people stop at the first Treasure Lake and are satisfied; it's a sparkling gem surrounded by jagged peaks. Be sure to pick up a trail map from the resort before you head out.

After a day of hiking and fishing, you might not have energy left for cooking, so eat at Parchers' South Fork Restaurant. Dinner is the main event; it's the most well-prepared grub you can find anywhere in Bishop Creek Canyon. Backpackers come off the Bishop Pass Trail and head straight for the restaurant; most of them have already decided what they will order 10 miles back.

Facilities: There are 10 one-bedroom cabins that can accommodate up to four people. Some have fully equipped kitchens. A restaurant and general store are on-site.

Bedding: Linens and towels are provided.

Reservations and rates: Reservations are recommended. Fees range from $75 to $145 per night and include a continental breakfast. The resort is open from May to October, depending on weather conditions. Pets are not permitted.

Directions: From Bishop on U.S. 395, turn west on Highway 168/West Line Street. Drive 14 miles on Highway 168 to the South Lake turnoff. Turn left and drive six miles to Parchers Resort on the left.

Contact: Parchers Resort, 2100 South Lake Road, Bishop, CA 93514; 760/873-4177; website: www.bishopcreekresorts.com.

Parchers Resort

18. GLACIER LODGE

Glacier Lodge suffered a devastating fire in May 1998 and has not yet returned to its original splendor. The blaze, caused by a malfunctioning water heater, was a major financial setback for Glacier's owners, who have not rebuilt the historic 1917 lodge and restaurant building. Luckily, Glacier's cabins were untouched and are still available for rent.

Off U.S. 395 near Big Pine

Luxury rating: 2

Recreation rating: 4

Despite this tragic turn of events, Glacier Lodge still offers one of the best access points for outdoor recreation in the eastern Sierra. The cabins are backed up against the mountains at 8,000 feet in elevation, just before the land becomes the John Muir Wilderness. The cabins are rustic in style, but they come with the critical luxuries: bathrooms, showers, electricity (from a generator), and tiny kitchens. The kitchens are nothing to brag about, but you can cook in them, which is important since the lodge's wonderful restaurant is gone.

What do visitors do at Glacier Lodge? Serious anglers fish Big Pine Creek, particularly the pools below First Falls. If you're willing to hike, fly fishing is excellent farther up the canyon. If you have young kids with you, you can get them hooked on fishing at the small stocked pond right by the lodge.

Hikers head for the spectacular trails in Big Pine Canyon. An easy walk to First and Second Falls on the North Fork Trail begins right at the lodge. For a longer trip, head beyond the falls to Big Pine Lakes. If you take the left fork, you'll reach First Lake at four miles out. Try to make it all the way to Third Lake, five miles from the lodge and at 10,400 feet in elevation. The lake has a beautiful milky turquoise color caused by water flowing directly from Palisade Glacier, the southernmost glacier in the United States. The glacial silt is so fine that it does not settle out in the water, producing the lake's vivid, cloudy, blue-green color.

Hard-core mountaineers can make the trek all the way to Palisade Glacier, 8.5 miles from the lodge and at 12,400 feet in elevation. It's a long, hard hike, and when you near the glacier, you need climbing equipment and skills. Most people are happy if they get close enough to get a good look at it. The Palisade Crest is considered to have some of the finest alpine climbing in all of California, but it's not for the inexperienced.

Facilities: There are 10 one-bedroom cabins, all with fully equipped kitchens. A small store is on-site.

Bedding: Linens and towels are provided.

Reservations and rates: Reservations are recommended. Fees range from $70 to $100 per night. Pets are permitted with a $15 fee per stay.

Directions: From Big Pine on U.S. 395, turn west on Crocker Street and drive 10.5 miles to the end of the road and Glacier Lodge. (The road becomes Glacier Lodge Road.)

Contact: Glacier Lodge, P.O. Box 370, Big Pine, CA 93513; 760/938-2837; website: www.395.com/glacierlodge.

Glacier Lodge

19. SEQUOIA VIEW VINEYARD

Jim and Debbie Van Haun retired from the urban life in Orange County and moved to a 20-acre vineyard just off the Blossom Trail in the Sierra foothills. Located 40 minutes from Kings Canyon and Sequoia National Parks, the Van Haun's farm has a separate guest house where visitors, too, can pursue the dream of a life in the country.

The guest house, which is located about 70 yards from the Van Haun's home and is partially hidden in the grape fields, is a 1948 farmhouse that has been lovingly restored with wide pine floors, updated bathroom, and artistic touches such as country quilts and colorful wall stencils. With three good-sized bedrooms, the house could comfortably hold a family of six. The entire house is yours for the duration of your rental; you simply pay according to the number of people in your party and how many bedrooms you use.

The guest house is operated as a bed-and-breakfast, so a full gourmet meal is served each morning in the main house dining room. This is a chance for visitors to discuss the grape crop with Jim and Debbie, or test out the ripeness of the fruit from eight acres of nectarines trees. Debbie loves to cook, so expect a gourmet meal with entrées such as French toast cobbler, cast iron breakfast pie, or sourdough pancakes. And of course, fresh-squeezed orange juice from the Van Haun's trees. You won't go away hungry.

The Van Hauns recently started making their own wine and will gladly

© ANN MARIE BROWN

Off Highway 180 near Squaw Valley

Luxury rating: 4

Recreation rating: 3

serve and sell it to guests. The grapes on the Van Haun's vineyard are the rare Alicante Bouschet variety, one of the only red grapes that produces red juice (even without the skins). The grapes are currently sold to premium wineries in Sonoma and Santa Cruz Counties.

One of the best times to visit Sequoia View Vineyard is "blossom season" from the end of February to mid-March. During this time, cyclists and drivers take to the area's back roads to witness the beauty of fruit tree orchards in bloom. The Blossom Trail is well-signed, but brochures and maps are available at the guest house.

Spring is also the season for white-water rafting on the nearby Kings River. Any time of year is just right for a visit to Kings Canyon and Sequoia National Parks, where a multitude of trails and one of nature's greatest wonders, the Giant Sequoia trees, await.

Facilities: There is one three-bedroom guest house with a kitchenette (microwave and refrigerator).

Bedding: Linens and towels are provided.

Reservations and rates: Reservations are required. Fees are $95 for two people, $145 for four people, and $195 for six people, and include breakfast. Pets are not permitted.

Directions: From Fresno, drive east on Highway 180 for 19 miles to just east of Centerville and Minkler. Turn right on Frankwood Avenue and drive a quarter mile to Sequoia View Vineyard on the left.

Contact: Sequoia View Vineyard, 1384 South Frankwood Avenue, Sanger, CA 93657; 559/787-9412; website: www.svbnb.com.

Sequoia View Vineyard

20. GRANT GROVE LODGE

If you think there is no place left in California's national parks where you can rent a rustic cabin and partake in an old-fashioned nature experience, think again. Many of the cabins at Grant Grove Lodge in Kings Canyon National Park look and feel like a throwback to the 1930s, and some are only a small step above camping. Maybe that's the way it should be.

Here's the scoop on Grant Grove Lodge's cabins. The nine most luxurious "bath cabins" have electricity, propane heat, carpeting, and private baths. Twenty-four "rustic" cabins are without private baths, but have propane heat, woodburning stoves, battery lamps, and a patio with a picnic table for outdoor cooking. Some have electricity and carpeting. Restroom and shower facilities are located nearby.

Grant Grove also has 23 tent cabins with woodburning stoves and battery lamps. These cabins are spaced quite close together; a stay in one is much like car camping.

Off Highway 180 in Kings Canyon

Luxury rating: 2

Recreation rating: 4

THIS CABIN RANKS . . .
Best for Hiking
Best Value

None of the cabins have kitchens or any kind of indoor cooking facilities, so bring a camp stove and outdoor cooking utensils and dishes, or plan to eat in the restaurant at Grant Grove. It's basically a large coffee shop, but the food is passable and affordable.

The cabins are open year-round, and it's hard to say which is the best season for a visit. If you like conifers covered in snow and cross-country skiing, plan on a winter trip. Some of the park's prettiest ski trails are in Grant Grove and Giant Forest, where you can see the cinnamon-colored Giant Sequoias crowned in snow. (The General Grant Tree, the third largest tree in the world, is located less than a mile from the cabins.) Rangers lead beginner-level guided snowshoe walks, and 75 miles of marked cross-country trails are available.

If you visit Grant Grove during the hiking season, a wide array of trails are nearby. Start with the 2.5-mile Sunset Trail, which leads from Sunset Campground downhill to two pretty waterfalls on Sequoia Creek then continues to Sequoia Lake. Don't miss Panoramic Point and Park Ridge Trail, which begins two miles from the cabins. The trail offers far-reaching views and a visit to an operating fire lookout tower.

Many more trailheads can be accessed by driving north or south into Giant Sequoia National Monument, or taking Highway 180 to its end at Cedar Grove. The Grant Grove Visitor Center is a few steps away from the Grant Grove cabins, so you have easy access to all the park and trail information you want.

Facilities: There are nine one-room cabins with private baths, propane heat, and electricity, 24 rustic cabins without baths or electricity but with propane heat, and 23 tent cabins (summer only). None have kitchen facilities. A restaurant, store, post office, and visitor center are on-site.

Bedding: Linens and towels are provided.

Reservations and rates: Reservations are recommended. Fees range from $42 to $88 per night for two people, plus $10 for each additional person. Pets are not permitted.

Directions: From Fresno, drive east on Highway 180 for 55 miles to the Big Stump Entrance Station at Kings Canyon National Park. Continue 1.5 miles and turn left for Grant Grove. Drive 1.5 miles to Grant Grove Village.

Contact: Kings Canyon Park Services Company, 5755 East Kings Canyon Road, Suite 101, Fresno, CA 93727; 866/522-6966 or 559/335-5500; website: www.sequoia-kingscanyon.com.

Grant Grove Lodge

21. KINGS CANYON LODGE

There's nothing terribly special about the cabins at Kings Canyon Lodge— no fireplaces, no extra amenities, and darn little in the way of decorative charm—but they do have a great location. They're situated right along Highway 180, the only road that runs deep into the spectacular canyon of Kings Canyon National Park.

Off Highway 180 in Kings Canyon

Luxury rating: 2

Recreation rating: 3

Driving east on Highway 180, you know you're approaching the lodge when you see a hand-painted sign that reads Caution: Ice Cream Ahead. Since there is little else on this stretch of highway, plenty of people slam on their brakes for some ice cream.

Kings Canyon Lodge makes a remarkably picturesque snapshot, with its rustic buildings and old-fashioned, gravity-fed gas pumps out front. But it's wise to know a few things before you stay there. Only a few of the rustic, wood-frame cabins have kitchens. Try to reserve one that does. If yours doesn't, be prepared to eat at the lodge's grill or drive many miles for food. The grill serves little else besides hamburgers, but luckily the restaurant at Grant Grove (14 miles away) and the snack bar at Cedar Grove (18 miles away) have more extensive menus.

Also, make sure you avoid the one duplex cabin. Each side of the duplex is impossibly small and has paper-thin walls. Insist on a single unit; the best of the lot is cabin 4. Also, don't expect much customer service during your stay. The folks running the lodge do so on a laissez-faire basis.

The South Fork Kings River is across the highway from the lodge; the best access is via nearby Yucca Point Trail. It's a steep downhill path that leads to excellent wild trout fishing early in the year and swimming later in the summer. Boyden Cave is down the road about six miles, where you can go on a tour of a fascinating limestone cavern, or hike the Windy Cliffs Trail from the cave entrance. You'll gain marvelous views of the Kings River Canyon far below, and its towering granite walls.

Many visitors stop at the picnic area at Grizzly Falls, a beautiful 80-foot waterfall right by the highway that rushes into the Kings River. It's a nice break on your way to Cedar Grove and the "End of the Road," where Highway 180 stops and the wilderness begins. Trailheads are plentiful in Cedar Grove, including the popular eight-mile round-trip to Mist Falls, or the incredibly scenic 1.5-mile Zumwalt Meadow Loop. Plenty of anglers try their luck in the South Fork Kings River from along this path.

Facilities: There are 12 cabins ranging in size from studios to two bedrooms. Some have kitchens. A café, bar, and gasoline are on-site.

Bedding: Linens and towels are provided.

Reservations and rates: Reservations are recommended. Fees range from $79 to $129 per night. The resort is open from late April to October. Pets are not permitted.

Directions: From Fresno, drive east on Highway 180 for 55 miles to the Big Stump Entrance Station at Kings Canyon National Park. Continue 1.5 miles and turn left for Grant Grove and Cedar Grove. Drive 17 miles on Highway 180 to Kings Canyon Lodge on the right.

Contact: Kings Canyon Lodge, P.O. Box 820, 67751 Highway 180, Kings Canyon National Park, CA 93633; 559/335-2405. (The phone is not answered in the off-season.)   *Kings Canyon Lodge*

22. BIG MEADOWS GUARD STATION

Big Meadows Guard Station is one of four secluded Forest Service cabins available for rent in Giant Sequoia National Monument. (For information on the others, see listing for Mountain Home Guard Station in this chapter.) It's the only one that is located near Kings Canyon and Sequoia National Parks, giving you the chance to explore the parks and surrounding national forest land from your own private rustic cabin.

© ANN MARIE BROWN

Off Highway 180 in Giant Sequoia National Monument

Luxury rating: 3

Recreation rating: 5

Like most guard stations built in the 1930s, Big Meadows cabin is 900 square feet in size. It has a queen bed, twin bunk beds, and a double sofa sleeper, so six people can sleep comfortably. Up to 12 people are permitted with each reservation, but the extra six will have to spend the night on the floor. The cabin has electricity, running water, and a bathroom with hot shower. Its kitchen has an adequate supply of dishes and utensils, even a coffeepot. All you need to bring are your clothes, food, and basic supplies.

Big Meadows' location couldn't be better. You drive through Grant Grove in

Kings Canyon National Park to reach it, so that gives you a clue about the pleasure ahead. The cabin is only a couple of miles from the Fox Meadow trailhead for Jennie Lakes Wilderness, from which pretty Weaver Lake can be reached in 1.5 miles. Larger, lovelier Jennie Lake can be reached in nine miles round-trip. The ambitious can hike to the summit of Mitchell Peak, elevation 10,365 feet, for rewarding views of the Great Western Divide and the Silliman Crest. It's a fine spot to catch your breath.

Anglers don't have to hike far to fish; Big Meadows Creek runs right across the street from the cabin.

For a quick thrill, take a drive over to Buck Rock Fire Lookout, about 10 minutes from the guard station. Climb the stairs to the tower, which is perched high atop Buck Rock, and have a chat with the lookout person while you admire the far-reaching view.

Facilities: There is one cabin that can accommodate up to 12 people. It has a fully equipped kitchen, electricity, and bathroom.

Bedding: Linens and towels are not provided; bring your own.

Reservations and rates: Reservations are required. The fee is $100 per night. The cabin is currently open from May 15 to November 15. Pets are not permitted.

Directions: From Fresno, drive east on Highway 180 for 55 miles to the Big Stump Entrance Station at Kings Canyon National Park. Continue straight 1.5 miles and turn right on the Generals Highway, heading for Sequoia National Park. Drive 7.5 miles and turn left at the sign for Big Meadows and Horse Corral. Drive 3.5 miles to Big Meadows Guard Station.

Contact: Hume Lake Ranger District, Sequoia National Forest/Giant Sequoia National Monument, 35860 East Kings Canyon Road, Dunlap, CA 93621; 559/338-2251, fax 209/338-2131.

Big Meadows Guard Station

23. MONTECITO SEQUOIA LODGE

Montecito Sequoia Lodge is not for everybody. The place is run like a high Sierra Club Med, with a heavy emphasis on organized activities, especially for families. If you like to be left alone to do your own thing, you might find the atmosphere too obtrusive. But if you're looking for a way to keep your kids busy, active, and happy in the outdoors, you're in luck. In fact, with all the children's activities available, you might actually get some time alone with your spouse.

The lodge is located at 7,500 feet in elevation in Giant Sequoia National Monument, and bills itself as a "family vacation camp." That means in addition to all the great outdoor adventures possible in the surrounding area, there is also much to do right at the resort. Organized activities include tennis, archery, basketball, volleyball, canoeing, wa-

Off Highway 198 in Giant Sequoia National Monument

Luxury rating: 3

Recreation rating: 4

THIS CABIN RANKS . . .
Best for Families

terskiing, horseback riding, swimming, and cross-country skiing in winter.

The lodge is reached via a long driveway off the main road, so as you pull in, you feel like you are heading to your own private vacation retreat. At the driveway's end is a pretty little lake, a big lodge, and several cabins and motel-style rooms.

Many people like the simple payment plans at Montecito Sequoia Lodge. Four- and six-night package deals are available that include all activities, meals, and accommodations. In the slow, off-season months of fall and spring you can purchase accommodations-only packages.

Neither the 13 cabins nor any of the lodge rooms have kitchens; you eat all meals in the lodge dining room. Montecito Sequoia has developed a reputation for healthy, wholesome food served buffet style. One entrée at dinner is always vegetarian. Many diners take their food outside to the huge deck that overlooks the high peaks of the Great Western Divide.

The cabins at Montecito Sequoia house two to eight people. Each has a king or queen bed, two or three bunk beds, a woodburning stove, and electricity. For bathrooms and showers, you walk to the nearby bathhouse. (Private bathrooms are available only in lodge rooms, not cabins.)

In winter, visitors come to Montecito Sequoia to take advantage of excellent cross-country skiing and snowshoeing. Nearly 100 miles of groomed and backcountry trails lead from the lodge into surrounding national monument and park land. If you don't have your own equipment, you can rent everything you need, and lesson packages are available. Weather permitting, ice-skating is allowed on the lodge's small lake.

Facilities: There are 13 cabins that can accommodate up to eight people, plus 36 lodge rooms. The cabins do not have private baths; a central bathhouse is available. The cabins do not have kitchens; a restaurant is on-site.

Bedding: Linens and towels are provided.

Reservations and rates: Reservations are required. Fees range from $90 to $120 per adult per night, including all meals. (Children's rates are discounted). Rates are discounted in spring and fall. Pets are not permitted.

Directions: From Fresno, drive east on Highway 180 for 55 miles to the Big Stump Entrance Station at Kings Canyon National Park. Continue 1.5 miles and turn right on the Generals Highway, heading for Sequoia National Park. Drive 8.5 miles to the right turnoff for Montecito Sequoia Lodge. Turn right and drive a half mile to the lodge.

Contact: Montecito Sequoia Lodge, P.O. Box 858, Grant Grove, CA 93633; 559/565-3388 or 800/227-9900; website: www.montecitosequoia.com.

Montecito Sequoia Lodge

24. PEAR LAKE SKI HUT

There isn't a cross-country skier or snowshoer alive who wouldn't enjoy a stay at Sequoia National Park's Pear Lake Ski Hut. But to make the trip, you need to accomplish two things: First, secure a reservation with the Sequoia Natural History Association; second, be in good enough shape so that you can cross-country ski or snowshoe six miles, much of it uphill. The total elevation gain is 2,000 feet from the trailhead at Wolverton to the ski hut north of Pear Lake, so it's not advisable for novice skiers or snowshoers. But with a few days of training and good aerobic conditioning, even intermediates can make the trip, especially if they start early in the day.

© ANN MARIE BROWN

Off Highway 198 in Sequoia National Park

Luxury rating: 2

Recreation rating: 3

The ski hut is open to public use from mid-December to late April each year. To get a reservation, you must phone or make a written request by mid-November. A lottery is held and dates are assigned accordingly. Usually everybody gets a reservation, although not always on the precise dates they want. Holiday weekends are the hardest to reserve; weekdays are easy.

The cabin houses 10 people in bunk beds; most people go with a group of friends so they have the whole place to themselves. If your group is smaller than 10, you will probably share the hut with another group. No matter, you'll quickly make friends. If you don't, you can settle your differences with a rousing snowball fight.

The Pear Lake "hut" is an impressive stone building with huge wooden rafters that serves as a backcountry ranger station in the summer. It is heated by a wood pellet stove. Propane cooking stoves and lanterns are provided, as well as all cooking and eating utensils, and a composting toilet.

The trail to reach the lake is a spectacular day hike in summer, and an equally spectacular ski trip in winter. With your gear loaded on your back, you set out on the Lakes Trail from Wolverton Ski Area at 7,200 feet, heading east along Wolverton Creek. The trail starts climbing and keeps on climbing. The apex of your ascent is The Hump at 9,400 feet. After this high point, you have less than three miles of trail to cover, mostly downhill. You'll glide along the icy shores of Heather Lake, Emerald Lake, and Aster Lake. When you reach Pear Lake Ski Hut at six miles out, you are less than a half mile from the shores of large Pear Lake.

The Sequoia Natural History Association makes your trip easier by sending you a suggested packing list. The list includes all the winter clothing and skiing equipment you might expect, plus some important essentials like a sleeping bag (bunks are provided but no bedding), propane fuel and matches (for the stoves and lanterns), enough food for your stay plus extras for emergencies, and water purification equipment. You must filter or boil all your water. The Association also insists that skiers carry survival equipment, just in case an avalanche, whiteout, or other snow emergency should occur.

Facilities: There is one ski hut that can accommodate up to 10 people. Propane cooking facilities are provided. There is a wood pellet stove for heat and a compost toilet. No drinking water is available.

Bedding: Linens and towels are not provided; bring your own.

Reservations and rates: Reservations are required. The fee is $20 per person per night. Pets are not permitted.

Directions: From Visalia, drive east on Highway 198 for 40 miles, through the town of Three Rivers, to the Ash Mountain Entrance Station at Sequoia National Park. Continue 20 miles on the Generals Highway, past Giant Forest, to the Wolverton Ski Area turnoff on the right side of the road. The trail to Pear Lake begins at the far edge of the parking lot.

Contact: Sequoia Natural History Association, HCR 89, Box 10, Three Rivers, CA 93271-9792; 559/565-3759; website: www.sequoiahistory.org.

Pear Lake Ski Hut

25. BEARPAW HIGH SIERRA CAMP

The tent cabins at Bearpaw High Sierra Camp, elevation 7,800 feet, make the spectacular backcountry of Sequoia National Park accessible to people who don't want to backpack—but love to hike. To get there, you hike an easy, nearly level 11.5 miles through some of the most gorgeous high-country scenery you can imagine. When you arrive, you are spoiled by the opulence of tent cabins with clean beds and bedding, plus showers and homestyle meals. Not only that, but you are treated to incredible vistas of the Great Western Divide.

You don't have to carry a tent. You don't have to plan your meals in advance. You don't have to pack a camp stove or pots and pans. All you need are your clothes and whatever personal items you want to bring—cameras, books, a day pack, fishing equipment, et cetera.

Your ticket to Bearpaw High Sierra Camp is the stunning High Sierra Trail, a popular trans-Sierra route that eventually leads all the way to Mount Whitney. In this section, the path travels along the north rim of the Middle Fork Kaweah River Canyon. Although 11.5 miles may sound like a long hike, the trail has a mere 1,000-foot elevation gain.

At Bearpaw Meadow, the campground is perched on the edge of a granite gorge. Once you're settled into your cozy tent cabin, you

© ANN MARIE BROWN

*Off Highway 198 in Sequoia
National Park*

Luxury rating: 2

Recreation rating: 4

THIS CABIN RANKS . . .

Best for Hiking

can spend a day hiking to Upper and Lower Hamilton Lakes. The lakes are set in a glacially carved basin at the base of 13,000-foot peaks. Many other excellent day hikes are available; the staff at Bearpaw can point you on your way.

One of the nicest things about Bearpaw is its small size. The maximum number of guests is 18, plus two staff members who work there.

So how do you get a reservation for this high-country paradise? It isn't easy. At 7 A.M. on January 2, the park concessionaire starts taking telephone reservations for the following summer at Bearpaw. Within a couple of hours, every date for the next season is booked.

If you're not one of the lucky ones to get through, it can seem disappointing, but it doesn't have to be. Although tons of people make reservations for Bearpaw, many of them never show up. The reservation office keeps a waiting list, and as people drop out, the wait-listers get in. Since there is a 30-day cancellation policy, wait-listers are usually phoned at least 30 days in advance to see if they want to fill an empty space.

Facilities: There are six tent cabins that can accommodate two to three people. Tent cabins do not have heat or electricity, but lanterns are provided. Showers and bathrooms are located a few feet away. A backpacker's campground is also available.

Bedding: Linens and towels are provided.

Reservations and rates: Reservations and a permit are required; phone 888/252-5757 or 559/253-2199 as early as 7 A.M. on January 2 for the following summer. The fee is $150 per adult per night ($75 for children under 12), which includes breakfast and dinner. The High Sierra Camp is open from mid-June to mid-September. Pets are not permitted.

Directions: From Visalia, drive east on Highway 198 for 40 miles, through the town of Three Rivers, to the Ash Mountain Entrance Station at Sequoia National Park. Continue 16 miles on the Generals Highway to the Giant Forest area. Turn right on Crescent Meadow Road and drive 3.5 miles to the Crescent Meadow parking area. The High Sierra Trail begins near the edge of Crescent Meadow.

Contact: Delaware North Parks Services, P.O. Box 89, Sequoia National Park, CA 93262; 559/565-4070 or 888/252-5757; website: www.visitsequoia.com.

Bearpaw High Sierra Camp

26. WICKY-UP RANCH

Wicky-Up Ranch is an eclectic bed-and-breakfast and working orange ranch just 18 miles from the Ash Mountain entrance to Sequoia National Park. Its one cottage, Calico Room, is as fittingly quirky and charming as the rest of the ranch.

Off Highway 216 in Woodlake

Luxury rating: 4

Recreation rating: 3

First, some background: Monica and Jack Pizura own and operate Wicky-Up Ranch, which has been in Monica's family for five generations. Their California craftsman-style home was built in 1902 for Illinois State Senator Fred E. Harding, Monica's great-great uncle. The house is filled with antiques, Oriental rugs, and family heirlooms, each with its own story, which Monica will tell you if you ask.

The lush grounds surrounding the ranch house are a melting pot of interesting flora. Alongside the dark green acres of orange groves grow a multitude of roses, two giant deodar cedar trees, and a huge coastal live oak planted by Monica's mother. A trio of ringneck doves coo from a small aviary under the oak's wide canopy. The gardens are peppered with whimsical copper sculptures created by Jack.

The Calico Room cottage is tiny (less than 100 square feet), but adorable. It has bunk-style stacked beds; the top is a twin and the bottom is a full-size feather bed. A small bathroom with sink and toilet adjoins the main room. When it's time to clean up, guests head outside to a private patio and an intimate, enclosed outdoor shower.

Calico Room cottage is so small that kitchen facilities are out of the question. But since Wicky-Up Ranch is operated as a bed-and-breakfast, your first meal of the day is prepared in fine style. Monica whips up a three-course, gourmet candlelight breakfast for her guests, and serves it in the cedar-lined dining room of the main house. Fresh-squeezed orange juice is de rigueur, of course. The food is a delight for the eyes as well as the stomach; Monica pays strict attention to presentation as well as taste.

After breakfast, the Pizuras will take you on a jeep tour of the orange groves, if you desire. Or, you can set out to Lake Kaweah for swimming and water sports, or the Kaweah River for white-water rafting in spring. A few miles farther is the southern entrance to Sequoia National Park at Ash Mountain, and the start of the long road to the spectacular Mineral King Valley. Hikers will find a wide array of trails at either location.

Facilities: There is one cottage that can accommodate two people. There are no kitchen facilities.

Bedding: Linens and towels are provided.

Reservations and rates: Reservations are required. Fees are $100 for two people, including breakfast. Pets are sometimes permitted with prior approval.

Directions: From Visalia, drive east on Highway 198 for 25 miles to Lemon Cove. Turn left (west) on Highway 216, which becomes Avenue 344. Drive 3.2 miles; Wicky-Up Ranch is on the right.

Contact: Wicky-Up Ranch, 22702 Avenue 344, Woodlake, CA 93286; 559/564-8898; website: www.wickyup.com.

Wicky-Up Ranch

27. SEQUOIA MOTEL

Sequoia Motel is a peaceful oasis in the town of Three Rivers, with comfortable cabins and motel-style rooms. Located across the road from the White Horse Inn, a popular local restaurant, the motel features a relaxing swimming pool and colorful flower gardens.

© ANN MARIE BROWN

Off Highway 198 in Three Rivers

Luxury rating: 3

Recreation rating: 4

Cabin 5 is a favorite of couples, with its private deck shaded by the canopy of a huge canyon oak. The one-room cabin has a fireplace, complete kitchen, full bath, cable television, queen bed, and sleeper sofa.

If you need more space, Cabin 6 has two bedrooms, plus a full bath, fireplace, kitchen, and deck. Four people can sleep comfortably in its two twin beds and one queen bed.

Located just four miles from the Ash Mountain entrance to Sequoia National Park, Sequoia Motel is an obvious choice for people who want to explore the many wonders of the park. But there is also much to do in the Three Rivers area. In spring and early summer, the main activity is whitewater rafting on the Kaweah River. Guided raft trips are available from put-in points between the national park entrance and Lake Kaweah.

During the hot weather of summer, Lake Kaweah is a haven for water sports, including waterskiing, personal watercraft riding, sailing, and fishing. Boats are for rent at the Kaweah Marina. Anglers fish the rivers and streams that empty into the lake; the fishing season is open year-round in the Kaweah drainage.

When the weather cools in autumn and winter, cyclists take advantage of the quiet roads in the Three Rivers area. Both North Fork and South Fork Drives are quiet paved stretches suitable for long rides. The town of Three Rivers has bike lanes along both sides of the highway through the center of town. Plans are in the works to extend them all the way to the Sequoia National Park entrance.

Facilities: There are two cabins that can accommodate up to four people. Both have fully equipped kitchens.

Bedding: Linens and towels are provided.

Reservations and rates: Reservations are recommended. Fees are $100 to $150 per night for cabins. The resort is open year-round. Pets are not permitted.

Directions: From Visalia, drive east on Highway 198 for 40 miles, through the town of Three Rivers. Sequoia Motel is on the right at 43000 Sierra Drive (Highway 198), about two miles east of the center of town.

Contact: Sequoia Motel, P.O. Box 145, 43000 Sierra Drive, Three Rivers, CA 93271; 559/561-4453; website: www.sequoiamotel.com.

OTHER CABINS AND COTTAGES NEARBY

• Cort Cottage, P.O. Box 245, Three Rivers, CA 93271; 559/561-4671.

• Cinnamon Creek Ranch, P.O. Box 54, Three Rivers, CA 93271; 559/561-1107; website: www.cinnamoncreek.com.

Sequoia Motel

28. SEQUOIA VILLAGE INN

The cottages at Sequoia Village Inn have the three essentials for a perfect vacation: location, location, location. Situated at the Ash Mountain entrance to Sequoia National Park, they are ideally positioned for day trips into the remote southern areas of the park at Mineral King and South Fork, as well as the busier central areas of the park at Potwisha and Giant Forest.

The people who run Sequoia Village Inn have gone out of their way to make the place nice, with well-constructed buildings, private patios and verandas, and lovely gardens. The inn has five cottages, two large chalets, and one suite. Most of the cottages have full kitchens and views of either the Kaweah River or the mountains, plus special touches like clawfoot tubs, four-poster beds, and unique tilework. The large chalets are two stories high and have three bedrooms, fireplaces, full kitchens, and room for up to 12 people. A swimming pool and hot tub are on the premises.

With a one-minute drive from your cottage, you can be at the Ash Mountain entrance to Sequoia National Park. From there, your first stop should be Potwisha Campground, where you can pick up the trail to Marble Falls on the Marble Fork of the Kaweah River. March, April, and May are the best months to visit, when the foothill wildflowers bloom and the air is comfortably cool.

Off Highway 198 in Three Rivers

Luxury rating: 4

Recreation rating: 4

From the same campground, you can take a five-mile loop hike to see Monache Indian historical sites, including some pictographs painted on the side of Hospital Rock. Along the route are many swimming holes in the Middle Fork Kaweah River.

If you want to reach higher elevations and cool mountain air, just continue up the park road for another 12 winding miles to the Giant Forest area. Hike the 380 stairsteps to the top of Moro Rock and admire its dazzling views of the Great Western Divide. Then take a walk on any of a multitude of trails: Sunset Rock, Crescent Meadow, Huckleberry and Hazelwood Loop, or the Congress Trail. Up here at 6,000 feet, you're in the land of big Sequoias and cool, grassy meadows—an extreme contrast to the Three Rivers foothill country.

A longer drive from Sequoia Village Inn can take you into spectacular Mineral King in southern Sequoia National Park. It's 25 curving miles to the end of the road in Mineral King Valley, but if you get an early start on the drive and give yourself all day to hike and explore, it's worth it.

Facilities: There are five cottages, two three-bedroom chalets, and one small suite. Most have fully equipped kitchens. A swimming pool and hot tub are on-site. A restaurant is across the street.

Bedding: Linens and towels are provided.

Reservations and rates: Reservations are recommended. Fees range from $79 to $115 per night for two people to $218 to $228 per night for four people. Pets are permitted in some cottages with a $5 fee per night.

Directions: From Visalia, drive east on Highway 198 for 40 miles, through the town of Three Rivers. Six miles past Three Rivers, you'll see Sequoia Village Inn on the left. If you reach the Ash Mountain entrance station to Sequoia National Park, you've gone a quarter mile too far.

Contact: Sequoia Village Inn, 45971 Sierra Drive, P.O. Box 1014, Three Rivers, CA 93271; 559/561-3652; website: www.sequoiavillageinn.com.

OTHER CABINS AND COTTAGES NEARBY

- Buckeye Tree Lodge, 46000 Sierra Drive, Three Rivers, CA 93271; 559/561-5900; website: www.buckeyetree.com.
- The Gateway Lodge, 45978 Sierra Drive, Three Rivers, CA 93271; 559/561-4133; website: www.sequoiapark.com.

Sequoia Village Inn

29. LAKE ELOWIN RESORT

Here's one to add to the "know before you go" category: Lake Elowin isn't really a lake. It's a large, artificially constructed pond with a single island and surrounded by a grassy lawn. The "lake" is located at Lake Elowin Resort, a complex of cabins just outside Three Rivers and Sequoia National Park.

Off Highway 198 in Three Rivers

Luxury rating: 3

Recreation rating: 3

If you're the type who likes to make your own rules, you won't be happy here. Lake Elowin Resort is policy intensive, and they ask you to agree to their terms before you reserve a cabin. For most visitors, the rules make good sense: no smoking anywhere on the premises, outside or inside; no car alarms; no littering; no stereos playing outdoors; no throwing rocks in the lake. If you break any of the rules, you pay a hefty fine. Fair enough.

In case you haven't figured it out, Lake Elowin Resort isn't a party place. It's a quiet, peaceful getaway, and the managers intend to keep it that way.

Although Lake Elowin is one of the oldest resorts in Three Rivers, you wouldn't know it from their cabins—all 10 are in excellent condition. In keeping with the quiet atmosphere of the place, they don't have televisions or phones, but they do have one or two bedrooms, comfortable queen beds, and fully equipped kitchens. Only one cabin has a fireplace.

People who come to Lake Elowin Resort pass their time in a variety of ways: swimming and canoeing in the large, pretty pond (or small lake, whatever you prefer), reading on the shaded lawn areas, dipping into the Kaweah River swimming hole on the resort's property, and fishing nearby stretches of the river. Many visitors drive into the southern part of Sequoia National Park to spend the day, then return in the evening to barbecue outside their cabin (or cook inside if the mood strikes them).

Facilities: There are 10 cabins ranging in size that can accommodate up to six people. All cabins have fully equipped kitchens.

Bedding: Linens and towels are provided.

Reservations and rates: Reservations are required. Fees are $61 to $110 per night with a two-night minimum on summer weekends. The resort is open year-round. Pets are not permitted.

Directions: From Visalia, drive east on Highway 198 for 40 miles, through the town of Three Rivers. Approximately three miles east of town, turn left on Dineley Drive. Cross the bridge and turn right; the resort is a quarter mile farther on the right.

Contact: Lake Elowin Resort, Dineley Drive, Three Rivers, CA 93271; 559/561-3460; website: www.lake-elowin.com.

Lake Elowin Resort

30. PARADISE CANYON CABINS

In the summer of 2001, a new resort opened near the Mineral King entrance to Sequoia National Park, and it's unlike anything anywhere else in the Sierra. The place is called Paradise Canyon, and it may forever change the meaning of the word romance.

Off Mineral King Road near
Three Rivers

Luxury rating: 3

Recreation rating: 4

THIS CABIN RANKS . . .
Most Secluded

Only two cabins are for rent at Paradise Canyon. They are located behind a locked gate almost six miles from the town of Three Rivers, on the lonely, winding road to Mineral King. Perched on a oak-shaded slope above the East Fork of the Kaweah River, the one-bedroom units have gas fireplaces, full kitchens, and comfortable queen beds. Their best features are screened-in porches (to keep the evening mosquitoes out) and woodburning hot tubs. To heat up the water, you simply add a few logs. Sure, it takes a while, but there's no reason to hurry in Paradise.

Although the canyon setting is very remote and rustic, the cabins do have electricity generated by solar panels, and running water. (The bathroom is located in a separate building and is shared by both units.) A caretaker lives on the premises to make sure everything operates smoothly.

The entire property is 14 acres in size. A hiking trail leads from the cabins downhill to the river, arriving at a remarkably deep, inky blue swimming hole fed by a small waterfall. It's a completely private spot; the only access is by kayak during the highest flows of spring, and even then this stretch of river is considered to be unrunnable. Be sure to bring your hiking boots to negotiate the trail; it is steep and rough in places, but worth every footstep. The walk takes 10 to 15 minutes.

In addition to this fabulous swimming spot, your recreation options include the spectacular trails of Mineral King, less than an hour away on the circuitous road. But Paradise Canyon's owners strongly recommend that guests spend at least one day of their visit just relaxing on the property. Both cabins are serenaded by the music of a neighboring creek, enticing you to soak in the hot tub or read on the porch, accompanied by sweet water sounds.

The owners are marketing this lovely retreat specifically to singles or couples without children. Because of the rugged, isolated nature of the canyon, they do not allow anyone under 18. The cabins are perfectly sized for one to three people, and feature special "adult" touches, such as fine china instead of ordinary dishes.

Facilities: There are two one-bedroom cabins with fully equipped kitchens, fireplaces, and hot tubs. A shared bathroom is located in a separate building.

Bedding: Linens and towels are provided.

Reservations and rates: Reservations are required. Fees are $84 to $96 per night with a two-night minimum. The resort is open year-round. Pets are permitted with prior approval.

Directions: From Visalia, drive east on Highway 198 for 38 miles to Mineral King Road, 2.5 miles east of Three Rivers. (If you reach the Ash Mountain Entrance Station, you've gone too far.) Turn right on Mineral King Road and drive 5.8 miles to the resort on the left side of the road.

Contact: Paradise Canyon Cabins, P.O. Box 1150, 49215 Mineral King Road, Three Rivers, CA 93271; 559/561-4088; website: www.sequoiacabins.com.

Paradise Canyon Cabins

31. SILVER CITY RESORT

Silver City Resort in Mineral King is the kind of place you daydream about all winter long, when the southern Sierra is shut down by deep snow. The resort is located in the beautiful Mineral King Valley in southern Sequoia National Park. Accessible by only one road—a 25-mile, winding thoroughfare that starts in the town of Three Rivers—Mineral King requires some serious effort to reach. But it's worth it.

© ANN MARIE BROWN

Off Mineral King Road in Mineral King

Luxury rating: 3

Recreation rating: 5

THIS CABIN RANKS . . .
Best for Hiking

Silver City Resort is the only commercial enterprise in Mineral King other than two park campgrounds. A lucky few own summer homes in Mineral King, but except for them and a few dozen campers, you won't find hordes of people. The road in is too long and slow for casual visitors.

The cabins at Silver City Resort come in a wide range of sizes and configurations, from an incredibly tiny one-room cabin called the Hiker's Hut (no kitchen, no bath, no electricity) to large three-bedroom chalets with full kitchen, bathroom, outdoor deck, and woodstove. Each cabin is different, so make sure you request the amenities you want.

While staying at Silver City Resort, you will want to sample some of Mineral King's trails. Hikers looking for an easy stroll should follow the first mile of Farewell Gap Trail along the East Fork Kaweah River. Some people cast a line into the water as they walk, hoping to catch a trout or two. Another pleasant easy hike is Cold Springs Nature Trail out of Cold Springs Campground. Like

Farewell Gap Trail, the path parallels a babbling section of the Kaweah and offers fabulous views of Sawtooth Peak, Mineral Peak, and Rainbow Mountain. Hike either trail at sunset and you'll have plenty of memories to fuel your off-season Mineral King fantasies.

Hikers seeking more of a challenge can choose between several trails to spectacular high alpine lakes, including Eagle Lake (6.8 miles round-trip), Mosquito Lakes (7.4 miles round-trip), Monarch Lakes (8.4 miles round-trip), and Crystal Lake (10 miles round-trip). Each is located above 10,000 feet in elevation, so expect classic high-country scenery with plenty of stark granite and deep blue water.

After so much hiking around, you'll be grateful for the good food at Silver City's café. It's simple fare—eggs and pancakes for breakfast, burgers and sandwiches for lunch and dinner—but it's consistently fresh and delicious. The resort serves its full menu Thursday through Monday. On Tuesday and Wednesday, they offer only beverages and homemade pies, so if you're staying over midweek, make sure you bring provisions to cook in your cabin's kitchen or outside on the barbecue. The variety of pies is surprising—apple, marionberry, blueberry, and so on—but eventually you'll have to eat something else.

Facilities: There are 10 cabins and four large chalets ranging in size from studios to three bedrooms. Most have fully equipped kitchens. Some cabins have private bathrooms; a central restroom and shower area is available. A restaurant and general store are on-site.

Bedding: Linens and towels are not provided; bring your own.

Reservations and rates: Reservations are recommended. Fees range from $70 to $250 per night. Early June, late September, and October stays are discounted. The resort is open from late May through October. Pets are not permitted.

Directions: From Visalia, drive east on Highway 198 for 38 miles to Mineral King Road, 2.5 miles east of Three Rivers. (If you reach the Ash Mountain Entrance Station, you've gone too far.) Turn right on Mineral King Road and drive 25 miles to Silver City Resort on the left side of the road.

Contact: Silver City Resort, P.O. Box 56, Three Rivers, CA 93271; 559/561-3223 in summer or 805/528-2730 in winter; website: www.silvercityresort.com.

Silver City Resort

32. MOUNTAIN HOME GUARD STATION

Mountain Home Guard Station is one of four Forest Service cabins in Giant Sequoia National Monument available for public rental. These special facilities were once the residences of fire patrol officers keeping watch over the national forests, and today can be the vacation home of families or small groups.

If you want to achieve a feeling of wilderness with the comfort of a roof over your head, the Mountain Home Guard Station provides it. The cabin is 900 square feet in size and looks about the same as it did when it was built in the 1930s. Although it doesn't have electricity, it has running water and a working bathroom with hot showers. The heating system and kitchen appliances are propane. For light, you bring your own lanterns. Beds are provided for six people; if your group is larger, some people will have to sleep on the floor (or they can bring tents for outside).

© ANN MARIE BROWN

Off Highway 190 near Mountain Home State Forest

Luxury rating: 3

Recreation rating: 4

The cabin is set at 6,000 feet in elevation in a small patch of national monument land surrounded by Mountain Home State Forest. The state forest is home to impressive stands of Giant Sequoias, including the oddity Hercules Tree, which had a large room cut into its base in 1897. The guard station cabin is only four miles from two lovely waterfalls and swimming holes in the state forest—Hidden Falls and Galena Creek Falls—and two miles from the Adam and Eve Loop Trail. ("Adam" is a Giant Sequoia that is 27 feet in diameter and 240 feet tall.) The loveliest path for Sequoia viewing is the two-mile stretch of Moses Gulch Trail that runs between Shake and Moses Gulch Campgrounds.

Those eager to fish can find native rainbow, brown, and brook trout in the many miles of the North Fork of the Middle Fork of the Tule River and its tributary streams. The state forest also has three ponds that are stocked with rainbow trout. Guide service and rental horses are available at a pack station near Shake Camp.

One more note: If the Mountain Home Guard Station is booked for the nights you want, try renting one of the other guard stations in the Tule River Ranger District—Poso Station or Frog Meadow. Poso Station even comes with electricity—what luxury!

Facilities: There is one cabin that has beds for six people; up to 15 people are permitted. It has a fully equipped kitchen. There is no electricity but propane heating is available.

Bedding: Linens and towels are not provided; bring your own.

Reservations and rates: Reservations are required; it is recommended to phone at least six months in advance. The rate is $75 per night. The cabin is open from May 15 to November 15. Pets are permitted.

Directions: From Porterville, drive east on Highway 190 for 18 miles to Springville. At Springville, turn left (north) on Balch Park Road/Road 239 and drive 3.5 miles, then turn right on Bear Creek Road/Road 220. Drive 14 miles to Mountain Home State Forest Headquarters, then continue beyond it for 2.5 miles to a T-junction. Turn left; the guard station is a half mile farther.

Contact: Tule River Ranger District, Sequoia National Forest/Giant Sequoia National Monument, 32588 Highway 190, Springville, CA 93265; 559/539-2607.

Mountain Home Guard Station

33. CAMP NELSON CABINS

If you've never been here, it's hard to imagine how beautiful southern Tulare County is. I don't mean the section you see while driving Highway 99 around Visalia; I mean the landscape to the east, where the elevation rises, the temperature drops, and the Sequoias grow to enormous proportions.

Off Highway 190 near Camp Nelson

Luxury rating: 4

Recreation rating: 3

Accessing the area takes some effort; the main road is the winding Highway 190 out of Porterville and Springville. The better the scenery gets, the more twisty the road becomes, so prepare to drive slow and take your Dramamine. Your destination is the town of Camp Nelson at 5,000 feet in elevation, where a company called Mountain Real Estate will rent you a vacation cabin.

Each of Mountain Real Estate's cabins is someone's private home—vacation retreats that don't get used by their owners. The cabins vary in size and amenities, but all have fully equipped kitchens, plus fireplaces or woodburning stoves. Many have laundry facilities, televisions, and VCRs. All you need to pack are sheets, pillow cases, and towels, plus your clothes and groceries (don't forget soap, toilet paper, and trash bags).

With Camp Nelson as your base, your nearby outdoor options include the Golden Trout Wilderness to the north and a multitude of trails to the south along Highway 190. One of the best trails leads to the Needles Lookout. Via an easy 2.5-mile walk, you reach a fire tower perched precariously on a granite spire, from which you have expansive views of the Kern River Basin, Lloyd Meadow, and the Golden Trout Wilderness.

Closer to home, be sure to pay a visit to the Amos Alonzo Stagg Tree, the sixth largest Giant Sequoia in the world at 243 feet tall and 29 feet in diameter. The tree is reached by a short walk from the parking area at Alder Drive in Camp Nelson. (Alder Drive is best accessed via Redwood Drive, 2.5 miles east of Camp Nelson on Highway 190.)

As if there wasn't enough to do in Giant Sequoia National Monument, another spectacular chunk of public land is available nearby for exploration: Mountain Home Demonstration State Forest and Balch County Park. Expect to find Giant Sequoias, clean mountain air, and crystal clear streams.

Facilities: There are 12 cabins ranging in size from one to three bedrooms, all with kitchen facilities.

Bedding: Linens and towels are not provided; bring your own.

34. GOLDEN TROUT WILDERNESS PACK TRAINS CABINS

If you like being around horses, you're going to like staying in the rustic cabins at Golden Trout Wilderness Pack Trains. Run by Dan Shew and his family since 1979, the cabins are a small part of Shew's much larger horse pack trip business. Some vacationers reserve the cabins the night before an early morning start on a long horse trip into the Golden Trout Wilderness, while others come to stay for a few days and take shorter half- or full-day rides.

One thing is certain: If you aren't comfortable with the close proximity of dozens of horses, you won't be happy here. The cabins are located within a stone's throw of the corral, so be prepared for plenty of equine sounds and smells. It's part of the package.

Don't expect luxury, either. The cabins are basic, one-room jobs with no electricity. They do have private bathrooms and showers, which is fortunate, because you get awfully dusty riding horses all day. The cabins don't have kitchens; you take your meals at the main lodge, where the Shew family lives. (The nearest restaurant or store is 10 miles away in Ponderosa.) You'll eat with the Shews and the ranch crew, which turns your vacation into an authentic Western ranch experience. Dan's wife, Kelly, does most of the cooking.

Visitors who choose to go on half- or full-day horseback rides will be taken to water slides, swimming holes, secret trout

© ANN MARIE BROWN

Off Highway 190 near Quaking Aspen

Luxury rating: 2

Recreation rating: 4

THIS CABIN RANKS . . .
Best for Horseback Riding

fishing spots, and Giant Sequoia groves. A popular destination is the summit of 9,100-foot Jordan Peak. Multiday pack trips usually center around fly fishing in summer and deer hunting in autumn, but you and your family or friends can design any kind of trip you want. The Shews are happy to oblige.

If you want to bring your own horse with you, corrals are available for boarding. The pack station provides the water and hay. You and your trusty steed can spend the day loping around the wilderness and have a hot meal and a shower (for you, not your horse) awaiting in the evening.

Facilities: There are four one-room cabins that can accommodate up to four people. The cabins have no kitchens or electricity. Meals are available at the main lodge.

Bedding: Linens and towels are provided.

Reservations and rates: Reservations are recommended. Fees are $50 per night. The resort is open from late May to late October. Pets are not permitted.

Directions: From Porterville, drive east on Highway 190 for 44 miles, past Camp Nelson, to Quaking Aspen. Just before the turnoff for Quaking Aspen Campground, turn left on Forest Service Road 21S50 and drive 7.5 miles to Golden Trout Wilderness Pack Trains.

Contact: Golden Trout Wilderness Pack Trains, P.O. Box 756, Springville, CA 93265; 559/542-2816 (summer) and 559/539-2744 (winter); website: www.goldentroutpacktrains.com.

Golden Trout Wilderness Pack Trains Cabins

35. MOUNTAIN TOP BED AND BREAKFAST

Ponderosa is a small mountain community in Giant Sequoia National Monument, north of Kernville and south of Sequoia National Park and the Golden Trout Wilderness. Situated at 7,200 feet in elevation, Ponderosa is a blink-and-you'll-miss-it town. It's main enterprise is a café and saloon called Ponderosa Lodge.

Just down the road from the lodge is a place you can call your own for a few nights or a week. It's a mountain cabin that is rented out as part of a bed-and-breakfast business. Perfect for a family and longer stays, Mountain Pine Cabin has two stories; the first floor is a large studio area with full kitchen, living room, potbelly stove, and bathroom. Upstairs in the loft area is an open double bedroom (overlooking the downstairs) and an enclosed private bedroom. A barbecue and picnic table are located on the outside deck.

Although Mountain Pine Cabin is part of Mountain Top Bed and Breakfast, cabin guests don't receive a morning meal with the other bed-and-breakfast guests. Instead, you're on your own to cook in your cabin, or you

© ANN MARIE BROWN

Off Highway 190 near Quaking Aspen

Luxury rating: 3

Recreation rating: 3

can head to Ponderosa Lodge and order a plate of trout and eggs. So, if you're set on the bed-and-breakfast experience, consider staying at the main house.

The cabin is available for rent year-round. How you'll spend your time depends on what season it is. In winter, you can snowmobile, cross-country ski, or snowshoe. (Ponderosa Lodge rents equipment.) Once the snow is gone, you can fish in local streams, take a horseback ride at Golden Trout Wilderness Pack Station, go white-water rafting on the Kern River, or mountain bike on a labyrinth of Forest Service roads. Hikers should head to the spectacular grove of Sequoias on the Trail of 100 Giants. Other excellent trails include the hike to the peak of 9,300-foot Slate Mountain, the short walk to the top of granite Dome Rock, or the steep trek to see 100-foot-high Nobe Young Falls. If visiting fire lookout towers interests you, two of the finest are nearby: Jordan Peak and the Needles Lookout.

Facilities: There is one large two-bedroom cabin that can accommodate up to six people, plus two guest rooms. The cabin has a fully equipped kitchen. A small general store and restaurant are nearby.

Bedding: Linens and towels are provided.

Reservations and rates: Reservations are required. Fees are $100 per night for four people; each additional person is $10 per night. The resort is open year-round. Pets are not permitted.

Directions: From Porterville, drive east on Highway 190 for 46 miles, past Camp Nelson and Quaking Aspen Campground, to Ponderosa (two miles beyond Quaking Aspen). Turn left at Aspen Drive (by the Ponderosa Lodge); Mountain Top is a quarter mile farther on the left.

Contact: Mountain Top Bed and Breakfast, 56816 Aspen Drive, Springville, CA 93265; 559/542-2639 or 888/867-4784; website: www.rainwaterpad.com /mountaintop.

Mountain Top Bed and Breakfast

36. ROAD'S END LODGE

When you hear about a place with a name like Road's End Lodge, it makes you want to pack up the car and go straight there. Well, go ahead. This resort is as good as its name, especially if you like the idea of a cabin right alongside the "wild and scenic" Kern River.

Off Sierra Way near Kernville

Luxury rating: 3

Recreation rating: 4

If you've never been to the outdoor paradise north of Kernville and Lake Isabella, your first visit will be a stunner. Much of the lowland terrain near the Kern River is chaparral and oaks—not much different than, say, San Diego. But drive a few miles up the road and suddenly you're in a land of lush meadows and Giant Sequoias.

The Kern River is best known for river rafting and fishing, and you can do both if you visit Road's End Lodge in spring or early summer. As the season wears on and the river quiets down, activities shift to inner tubing and swimming.

First-time visitors may be confused by that fact that the road doesn't end at Road's End; in fact, it keeps going until it joins up with Highway 190 and heads west to Porterville. When the resort was built in 1922, this was the end of the road, but the forces of progress eventually had their way. Road's End Lodge was originally a pack station that took hunters into the high country at Big Meadow and Cannell Meadow, now accessible by automobile.

Although Road's End's cabins are antiques, they are well cared for. Each one is painted dark green on the outside and is lined with knotty pine and plentiful charm on the inside. All cabins have fully equipped kitchens; most have fireplaces. Half the cabins are directly on the river; the other half are across the road, a few steps away.

Although most people visit Road's End for its sandy beach and easy access to the Kern River, you can also make it a base camp for day hiking and exploring. The amount of trails located within a few miles of the resort is daunting. A few favorites: North Fork Kern River Trail (especially in springtime for wildflower viewing), Packsaddle Cave Trail (bring your flashlight and peek inside a limestone cavern), Trail of 100 Giants (an easy stroll around impressive Giant Sequoias), and any of the multitude of paths in the high country off Sherman Pass Road. Talk to the nice folks at Road's End Lodge for updated trail information.

Facilities: There are seven cabins ranging in size that can accommodate two to eight people. All cabins have fully equipped kitchens; most have fireplaces. A general store is on-site.

Bedding: Linens and towels are provided.

Reservations and rates: Reservations are recommended. Rates range from $80 to $150 per night with a two-night minimum. Pets are not permitted.

Directions: From Kernville, drive 19 miles north on Sierra Way/Road 99. Road's End Lodge is three-quarters of a mile north of the small settlement of Fairview.

Contact: Road's End Lodge, P.O. Box 2022, Kernville, CA 93238; 760/376-6562.

Road's End Lodge

37. WHISPERING PINES LODGE

If the name Whispering Pines doesn't make you want to jump out of your chair and drive to Kernville right away, try this phrase: bed-and-breakfast cottages and bungalows on the Kern River.

© ANN MARIE BROWN

Off Sierra Way near Kernville

Luxury rating: 4

Recreation rating: 4

That's the Wild and Scenic Kern River, of course, a celebrated favorite of rafters, anglers, and swimmers alike. A vacation cottage along its banks is the best way to take advantage of the Kern's many offerings.

Each of the four cottages at Whispering Pines has a river view, fireplace, king bed, full kitchen, and gas barbecue. Everything is beautifully decorated; they've spared no expense on draperies, furniture, and fabrics. Motel-style rooms are also available.

Breakfast is included in the price of your cottage, and it's more than your basic Danish and orange juice. Guests head to the dining room each morning for gourmet coffee, homemade breads and muffins, quiches, and fresh fruits. The owners go to great lengths to make things nice; they even hand out the local newspaper.

If you want to swim or fish, all you need to do is walk 100 feet from your cottage down to the river. Bring your fly-fishing gear. For more water activities, take a drive to nearby Lake Isabella, one of the largest bodies of water in Southern California, with a capacity of 11,000 surface acres of water. (The average for the year is usually 8,000 surface acres.) It is an excellent lake for windsurfing, kayaking, and waterskiing; bass fishing is also popular. Trout fishers usually stick to the Kern River, although the Department of Fish and Game plants some rainbows in Isabella.

For hikers and mountain bikers, the Cannell Meadow National Recreation Trail begins less than a mile from Whispering Pines; it is a nine-mile trail that leads from the foothills at 2,800 feet in elevation to Cannell Meadow at 7,500 feet. In spring, the lower stretches of this trail are lovely; in summer, you'll want to start at the upper end or you'll bake in the heat.

A short drive to Wofford Heights and then up Highway 155 takes you into the richly forested Greenhorn Mountains. The area offers myriad hiking trails in summer and cross-country skiing trails in winter. Hikers shouldn't miss two easy, lovely trails: Unal Trail and Sunday Peak Trail. In the winter, cross-country skiers can glide to their hearts' content at Shirley Meadows Ski Area.

Facilities: There are four one-bedroom, duplex-style cottages with fully equipped kitchens. Motel rooms are also available.

Bedding: Linens and towels are provided.

Reservations and rates: Reservations are recommended. Fees range from $119 to $159 per night for two people, including breakfast. Each additional person is $20 per night. Pets are not permitted.

Directions: From Kernville, drive north on Sierra Way/Road 99 for one mile to Whispering Pines Lodge on the left.

Contact: Whispering Pines Lodge, 13745 Sierra Way, Kernville, CA 93238; 760/376-3733 or 877/241-4100; website: www.kernvalley.com/inns.

OTHER CABINS AND COTTAGES NEARBY

• Chuck Richard's Falling Waters River Resort, 15729 Sierra Way, Kernville, CA 93238; 760/376-2242 or 888/376-2242; website: www.chuckrichards.com.

Whispering Pines Lodge

38. SIERRA GATEWAY COTTAGES

Considering that Kernville, the Kern River, and Lake Isabella are premier Southern California recreation destinations, you'd think the region would be loaded with cabin resorts. Instead, it's loaded with pedestrian-looking motels.

That's what makes Sierra Gateway Cottages special. These three newly remodeled one- and two-bedroom cottages are the real thing—not duplexes or motel units—with queen beds, full kitchens, fireplaces, patios, and gas barbecues. They're everything you need for a vacation in any season in the Kern River Valley.

Their location isn't perfect—they're set along the highway, not the Kern River. But you can walk to the river and also to the restaurants and shops of downtown Kernville. The cottages are set up on a hill next door to James Store, a busy, full-service grocery, tackle, and sporting goods store.

Given all the activity around here, the cottages are surprisingly quiet, both inside and outside on their small landscaped patios.

Off Sierra Way in Kernville

Luxury rating: 4

Recreation rating: 4

Recreation options in the Kernville area are unlimited. In spring, rafting and kayaking trips are offered on the Upper Kern for every level of ability. Numerous local companies can get you set up with the kind of trip and equipment you want. Lake Isabella, which boasts sailing, boating, windsurfing, and fishing opportunities, is only a five-minute drive away. Fishing on the Kern River is only one minute away.

Hikers can explore the trails to the immediate north on Sierra Way, or, when the summer temperature heats up, drive 20 miles north to the turnoff for Sherman Pass Road. Following Sherman Pass to Big Meadow and Horse Meadow, you can choose from many cool-air, high-country trails, including Sherman Peak Trail, Salmon Creek Trail, and Manter Meadow Loop.

Mountain bikers take their pick from beginner rides like the Greenhorn Summit Loop and Forest 90 Fire Road, or advanced single-track trails like the Whiskey Flat and Wall Street rides. Check out the Forest Service visitor center in Kernville for bike trail maps and details.

Last but not least, don't forget winter recreation in the area. Shirley Meadows ski resort is less than a half-hour away, with two double chairlifts, a family-oriented ski school, and rental program. Both skiers and snowboarders are welcome. Near Shirley Meadows are several excellent cross-country ski and snowshoe trails.

Facilities: There are three one- and two-bedroom cottages, all with fully equipped kitchens. Stores and restaurants are nearby.

Bedding: Linens and towels are provided.

Reservations and rates: Reservations are recommended. Fees are $110 per night. A two-night minimum stay is required. Weekly rates are discounted. The resort is open year-round. Pets are not permitted.

Directions: From Kernville, drive north on Sierra Way/Road 99 for a quarter mile to Sierra Gateway Cottages on the left.

Contact: Sierra Gateway Cottages, 13432 Sierra Way, Kernville, CA 93238; 760/376-2424.

Sierra Gateway Cottages

39. OAK FLAT LOOKOUT TOWER

Have you ever visited a fire lookout tower, perched high on a mountaintop amid miles of forested wild country? Have you ever stood at the lookout and gazed at the 360-degree panorama, dreaming of working as a fire scout and living alone in your mountain tower with only scenery, silence, and solitude?

© ANN MARIE BROWN

Off Highway 178 near Bakersfield

Luxury rating: 2

Recreation rating: 3

THIS CABIN RANKS . . .
Most Unusual

If the answer is yes—or if it's no, but you've always wanted to—I know the perfect place for you to spend the night. It's the Oak Flat Lookout Tower in the Greenhorn Mountains near Bakersfield. Situated at 4,910 feet in elevation, the lookout was built in 1934 and used to detect fires until 1984.

This is how to book a stay. First, phone the Greenhorn Ranger District of Sequoia National Forest to make a reservation. Summer weekends can be tough; weeknights are easy. You'll fill out some paperwork and mail in a check for $35 per night, which goes directly to maintaining the lookout tower.

Next, start packing. Remember to pack light because everything must be hauled up to the tower, which means climbing 40 narrow, steep stairs or using a manual basket pulley system. (Acrophobiacs won't be happy here; the stairs can be daunting.) The heaviest thing you carry should be bottled water; none is available at the tower.

Pack your sleeping bag and favorite pillow. (Two small beds are inside.) Flashlights and candles are a good idea, plus plenty of matches for lighting the propane appliances, which include an overhead light, heater, and stove. Bring an ice chest if you want to keep food or drinks cool (there's no refrigerator), and firewood if you want to have a campfire outside. Most important of all, take along plenty of trash bags for hauling out your garbage at the end of your stay.

Got your warm clothes for windy nights? Shorts and T-shirts for hot summer days? Hiking boots? Plenty of good food, plus cooking and eating utensils? Toilet paper for the outhouse? Okay, you're ready. The rangers at the Greenhorn District will give you a combination for the locks on the lookout road gate and tower. In winter, snow, rain, or ice can make the road impassable except for four-wheel-drive vehicles, but most of the year a passenger car is fine. Remember that you are 15 miles from the nearest pay phone or services, so if you have a need to stay in touch with the outside world, bring along a cell phone.

Passing the time on your visit is easy: Just sit and admire the view of the Kern River Valley. If you need some exercise, the Badger Gap Trail begins at the tower and heads downhill through sagebrush and oaks. It's a full 10 miles to its junction with Kern River Trail near Highway 178.

Facilities: The lookout tower can accommodate up to four people. Propane cooking and heating facilities are provided. There is no drinking water.

Bedding: Linens and towels are not provided.

Reservations and rates: Reservations and a permit are required. The fee is $35 per night. Young children are not advised. Pets are permitted.

Directions: From Bakersfield, drive east on Highway 178 for 12 miles to Rancheria Road. Drive 15 miles north on Rancheria Road (the pavement turns to dirt and gravel) to Forest Service Road 27S20. Turn right and drive a half mile (stay right at the fork) to the locked gate; open it and then continue the last quarter mile to the lookout.

Contact: Greenhorn Ranger District, Sequoia National Forest, 3801 Pegasus Drive, Bakersfield, CA 93308; 661/391-6088.

Oak Flat Lookout Tower

40. RANKIN RANCH

Off Highway 58 near Caliente

Luxury rating: 4

Recreation rating: 4

THIS CABIN RANKS . . .
Best for Families
Best for Horseback Riding

Rankin Ranch is a taste of old California—the era of cowboys, cattle ranching, hay rides, and horseshoes. It is situated at 3,500 feet in elevation in Walker Basin, roughly midway between Bakersfield and Tehachapi. The land surrounding the ranch is a classic high mountain valley, with a mix of wide open meadows and forest. If you think this sounds like a good place to saddle up and ride into the sunset, you're right.

A man named Walker Rankin founded the original cattle ranch here in 1863, and the place has stayed in the family ever since. It is one of the oldest and largest family-owned ranches in California. Rankin family members still live on the 31,000 acres and raise Herefords.

The Rankins have also used their land to build a successful guest ranch business. For nearly 40 years, vacationers have come to Rankin Ranch to ride horses, fish, hike, and live the ranch life for a few days. It's especially popular with families; a long schedule of children's activities takes place daily.

The best season to visit may be spring, when Rankin Ranch offers its lowest rates of the year and the wildflowers bloom in Walker Basin. From late March to May, the mountain slopes and high meadows come alive with color. It's a sight to behold.

The ranch has seven duplex-style cabins that are on the modern side, with carpeting and wood paneling. Families rent both sides of the duplex and open the adjoining doors. (Couples will end up with half a duplex.) The fee for a night at the ranch includes three big meals in the dining room and all the horseback riding you can stand, plus a wide range of other activities: trout fishing in little Julia Lake, horseshoe tournaments, bingo, tennis, swimming, volleyball, hay rides, and so on. You pay nothing extra for anything, including the organized children's programs, so you know in advance exactly what your vacation will cost.

Even if you've never been on a horse before, you'll have a good time at Rankin Ranch. Free riding instruction is provided, and each horse is carefully selected for each rider's abilities. Before long, even novices are riding out of the corral to check on the cattle or help bale the hay.

Facilities: There are seven cabins that can accommodate a total of 30 to 45 people; none have kitchen facilities. Meals are provided.

Bedding: Linens and towels are provided.

Reservations and rates: Reservations are required. Fees range from $135 to $170 per person per night, and include three full meals a day, horseback riding privileges, and all activities. Children under 12 stay for reduced rates. Discounts are available in April, May, and September. The ranch is open from April to September. Pets are not permitted.

Directions: From I-5 just south of the I-5/Highway 99 split, take the Lake Isabella/Lamont/Arvin exit. Drive 15 miles north on Wheeler Ridge Road, then turn right (east) on Highway 223 (Bear Mountain Boulevard) and drive 16 miles. At the Highway 223 junction with Highway 58, drive east on Highway 58 for one mile and take the Caliente cutoff. Drive through Caliente and continue 2.5 miles until the road forks. Take the unsigned left fork up the hill; it's nine miles to Rankin Ranch from the fork.

Contact: Rankin Ranch, P.O. Box 36-HP, Caliente, CA 93518; 661/867-2511; website: www.rankinranch.com.

Rankin Ranch

CHAPTER 6

Death Valley and the Deserts

*T*he Death Valley and the Deserts region encompasses three of California's most spectacular national parks: Death Valley, Joshua Tree, and Mojave, plus the world famous oasis of Palm Springs and surrounding palm-lined villages of Desert Hot Springs and Twentynine Palms.

Although Death Valley, Joshua Tree, and Mojave are all considered "desert parks," each is distinctly different. Death Valley is the largest U.S. national park outside of Alaska. Although its name is foreboding, the park comprises a vast landscape of desert beauty, from soaring sand dunes and mountain ranges to below-sea-level salt flats. In summer, the park is the hottest place in North America—greater than 120°F is common—but in winter, temperatures are cool and mild.

Death Valley is home to the lowest point in elevation in the Western hemisphere: Badwater, at 282 feet below sea level. In stark contrast, it's also home to Telescope Peak, elevation 11,048 feet, which is snow-covered six months of the year.

You must plan ahead before making a trip to Death Valley. Accommodations, services, and towns are few and far between. Only three lodgings are available within the massive park's borders, and of those, only Furnace Creek Ranch has cabins.

In contrast to Death Valley's remoteness, Joshua Tree National Park is surrounded by small cities that offer a variety of lodging choices, including historic adobe bungalows at 29 Palms Inn and a stately stone mansion with cottages at Roughley Manor. One of the West's most unusual towns is found near Joshua Tree— Pioneertown, built in the early 1940s as a permanent Western "stage" for filming movies. A stay at Rimrock Ranch Cabins will give you the chance to explore this real but unreal Western town.

Once you're in the park, civilization is left behind. Joshua Tree is best known for its wide desert plains covered with strange looking Joshua trees, amazing rock formations and boulder piles, rugged mountains, and gold mining ruins. The park is situated where the high Mojave Desert meets the low Colorado Desert, producing a wide variety of desert flora. Because much of the park is higher than 4,000 feet in elevation, the hiking and recreating season is somewhat longer than at Death Valley. Still, the most comfortable weather usually occurs from October to May; summer temperatures frequently soar past 100 degrees.

Only 50 miles to the north, Mojave National Preserve is located where the Mojave, Great Basin, and Sonoran Deserts join. As a result of this convergence, Mojave contains a wide diversity of plant and animal life, as well as interesting geological features. These include Cima Dome, a granite batholith covered with a dense forest of Joshua trees, and the volcanic rock cliffs of Hole-in-the-Wall. The 500-foot-tall Kelso Dunes, second highest in California after Death Valley's Eureka Dunes, are another of the preserve's attractions.

Like Joshua Tree, Mojave National Preserve is mostly high desert terrain, with elevations ranging from 2,000 feet to 5,000 feet. Although summers can be hot, December to February is frequently windy and cold; higher elevations of the park are sometimes dusted in snow. There are no services to be found anywhere in the park; the closest cabins or cottages are located in Randsburg at the historic Cottage Hotel.

Last but not least, the Death Valley and Deserts region includes the desert's most famous city, Palm Springs. This oasis was originally the home of the Agua Caliente band of the Cahuilla Indians, who still own major portions of the town's land. Not unlike today's Palm Springs visitors, the Agua Caliente worshipped the pure water flowing down the desert canyons, the natural hot springs, and the wind-sheltering curve of the San Jacinto Mountains.

Incorporated as a city in 1938, Palm Springs gained (and has never lost) an aura of glamour as a favorite retreat of movie stars and international celebrities. So many luminaries—from Ginger Rogers to Dinah Shore—made the desert their home that it is impossible to name them all. The stylish red tile roofs and sparkling swimming pools of Palm Springs' cottage resorts reflect the glittering history of the area.

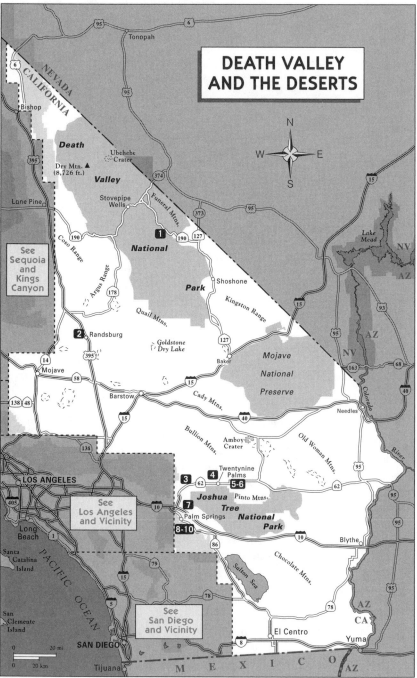

DEATH VALLEY AND THE DESERTS

N
W E
S

NEVADA

CALIFORNIA

Death

Dry Mtn. ▲
(8,726 ft.)

Ubehebe
Crater

Valley

Stovepipe
Wells

Funeral Mtns.

Bishop

Lone Pine

**See
Sequoia
and
Kings
Canyon**

Coso Range

Argus Range

National

1

Shoshone

Kingston Range

Park

Quail Mtns.

2 Randsburg

Goldstone
Dry Lake

Baker

Mojave

National

Lake
Mead

NV

AZ

AZ

NV

Preserve

Mojave

Barstow

Cady Mtns.

Colorado

Needles

River

Bullion Mtns.

Amboy
Crater

Old Woman Mtns.

LOS ANGELES

**See
Los Angeles
and Vicinity**

3 **4**

Twentynine
Palms

5-6

Joshua

Pinto Mtns.

Tree

7

Palm Springs

National

Park

8-10

Long
Beach

Santa
Catalina
Island

PACIFIC OCEAN

Blythe

Chocolate Mtns.

AZ

CA

San
Clemente
Island

**See
San Diego
and Vicinity**

Salton
Sea

El Centro

Yuma

SAN DIEGO

0   20 mi
0   20 km

Tijuana

M E X I C O

AZ

© AVALON TRAVEL PUBLISHING, INC.

CHAPTER 6
DEATH VALLEY AND THE DESERTS

1. FURNACE CREEK RANCH

Don't confuse Death Valley's Furnace Creek Ranch with Death Valley's Furnace Creek Inn. The Inn is everything the Ranch is not. The Inn stands for elegance; the Ranch stands for economy. The Inn defines service; the Ranch defines serviceable.

Off Highway 190 in Death Valley

Luxury rating: 3

Recreation rating: 4

But if you're on a budget and want to avoid staying in a cheap motel in Pahrump, Nevada, the cabins at Furnace Creek Ranch will serve you well. Located just one mile from the park's Furnace Creek Visitor Center, the ranch's cabins are perfectly situated for exploring Death Valley.

Furnace Creek Ranch is an entire little town, much like Curry Village in Yosemite National Park. Once the crew quarters for the Borax Mining Company, today Furnace Creek Ranch has a post office, general store, three restaurants, motel and cabins, golf course, horseback riding facilities, saloon, and the Borax Museum. The ranch's claim to fame, besides its Borax mining history, is that it has "the world's lowest golf course" at 214 feet below sea level. How's that for a novelty?

The cabins are side-by-side duplexes, fairly modern and pedestrian in appearance, but adequate. They have telephones and televisions complete with pay-per-view movies and Nintendo; this contributes to their motel-like ambience. Still, the cabins are quiet and peaceful, considering their density. Because they do not have kitchens, guests eat at the ranch café or neighboring steakhouse. Both seem overpriced, but the food is adequate.

It matters little if the cabins don't bowl you over, because you won't do much besides sleep and shower in them. There is a ton of exploring to do in Death Valley, and because its landscape is so vast, you spend a lot of time just driving from place to place. One excellent day trip is to head north to Scotty's Castle (60 miles) to tour a fascinating 1930s desert mansion. Afterwards, drive a few miles farther to Ubehebe Crater, then either hike down into its depths or follow its rim trail to two smaller volcanic craters.

The ambitious can drive another 40 miles west to see Eureka Sand Dunes, the tallest sand dunes in California at 680 feet. The drive is hell—a bumpy dirt road all the way—but the sand dunes are fabulous. Another day can be spent closer to the Furnace Creek area, hiking trails in Golden Canyon, Mosaic Canyon, the Keane Wonder Mine, and Salt Creek. Yet another day can be spent driving south in the park to visit Badwater, Wildrose Peak, and the Charcoal Kilns. Like I said, there's a lot to do.

Facilities: There are 24 duplex cabins that can accommodate up to four people, plus numerous motel rooms. None of the accommodations have kitchens. Several restaurants and stores are on-site.

Bedding: Linens and towels are provided.

Reservations and rates: Reservations are recommended. Fees range from $95 to $135 per night. Pets are not permitted.

Directions: From Barstow, drive east on I-15 for 60 miles to Baker and Highway 127. Turn north on Highway 127 and drive 80 miles to Death Valley Junction. Turn west (left) on Highway 190 and drive 30 miles, past the Furnace Creek Inn, to Furnace Creek Ranch on the left.

From U.S. 395 at Olancha, take Highway 190 east for 80 miles, past Stovepipe Wells Village. Turn right and drive 14 miles to Furnace Creek Ranch.

Contact: Furnace Creek Ranch, P.O. Box 1, Death Valley, CA 92328; 760/786-2345; website: www.furnacecreekresort.com.

OTHER CABINS AND COTTAGES NEARBY

• Delight's Hot Spa, P.O. Box 368, Tecopa, CA 92389; 760/852-4343 or 800/854-5007.

Furnace Creek Ranch

2. THE COTTAGE HOTEL

Do you feel like getting away? Far, far away where nobody would ever think to look for you? The Cottage Hotel in Randsburg might be the place.

The town, population 80, calls itself "a living ghost town." It's located south of Ridgecrest, northwest of Barstow, and northeast of Mojave. If you're getting a mental picture of dried-out cow skulls and vultures circling overhead, you're pretty close.

Even so, the Cottage Hotel at Randsburg is a wonderful place. A centerpiece of this historic gold mining town, the Cottage Hotel was completely rebuilt and reopened in 1994. In its previous lives, it survived three fires, several flu epidemics, and a bevy of rough-and-tumble customers. Highlighted by cactus gardens and vintage oddities like an antique switchboard, the hotel displays photo albums and historic papers documenting the area's past.

The Cottage Hotel has only one cottage, plus four bed-and-breakfast rooms decorated in Gold Rush–era style. Located next door to the hotel, the cottage is just large enough for

© ANN MARIE BROWN

Off U.S. 395 in Randsburg

Luxury rating: 3

Recreation rating: 3

a couple or small family, with one bedroom, one bath, a living room, kitchen, and barbecue deck.

In addition to relaxing in the serenity of this way-out-there location in the Mojave Desert, you'll probably want to do some exploring. Several ghost towns are nearby: Garlock, Balarat, Skidoo, and Cerro Gordo. A few miles to the south and east is the Rainbow Basin Natural Area, run by the Bureau of Land Management. Take a driving tour through its colorful desert canyons, or park at Owl Canyon Campground and hike to the base of Velvet Peak.

Or, drive northeast to Trona Pinnacles Natural Landmark and walk around its more than 500 giant tufa spires, which poke upward from the earth as high as 140 feet. It's one of the strangest landscapes in California. For more desert exploring, Red Rock Canyon State Park is nearby, plus the Desert Tortoise Natural Area. For the best chance of seeing a tortoise, show up in spring, when the elusive creatures leave their burrows to munch on wildflowers.

Facilities: There is one cottage that can accommodate up to four people. It has a fully equipped kitchen. A general store and restaurant are on-site.

Bedding: Linens and towels are provided.

Reservations and rates: Reservations are recommended. Fees are $75 for two people, plus $10 for each additional person. Pets are not permitted.

Directions: From Kramer Junction at U.S. 395 and Highway 58, drive north on U.S. 395 for 26 miles to Johannesburg. Turn left and drive one mile to Randsburg and the Cottage Hotel.

Contact: The Cottage Hotel, 130 Butte Avenue, Randsburg, CA 93554; 760/374-2285 or 888/268-4622; website: www.randsburg.com.

The Cottage Hotel

3. RIMROCK RANCH CABINS

The name Pioneertown sounds like a section of Disneyland, not a real town. But Pioneertown is real, and it's found north of Joshua Tree National Park near Desert Hot Springs and Yucca Valley.

Off Highway 62 in Pioneertown

Luxury rating: 3

Recreation rating: 3

THIS CABIN RANKS . . .
Most Unusual

Pioneertown not only sounds like Disneyland, it looks like Disneyland. The town was constructed by Gene Autry and Roy Rogers in the early 1940s as a permanent Western "stage" for filming movies (and later television serials). Classics such as *The Shootout, Cisco Kid,* and *Annie Oakley* were made in Pioneertown; the OK Corral is located here.

Today, the railroad-tie and adobe structures are inhabited by real people who own and operate a post office, bowling alley, motel, and the honky-tonk Pioneer Palace, where a four-generation family serves up good food, live music, and Western entertainment. Gunfights are staged on Mane Street (not Main Street) every Sunday afternoon.

If you want to see this strangely surreal Old West town, your best bet is to book a stay at Rimrock Ranch. The ranch was built in 1947 as the first homestead in the Rimrock high desert area. Set at 4,500 feet in elevation, it's just at the start of the snow line, so the temperature is 15 to 20 degrees cooler than in nearby Joshua Tree. This makes Rimrock ideal for summer visits to the park. You can spend all day hiking or rock climbing in the desert heat, then retreat to the cool tranquillity of your mountain cabin.

The ranch has four barn-red cabins with green roofs, each furnished with antiques and Western-style decor (no surprises here). If you like knotty pine interiors, you'll like this place. Most everything is vintage, except that the largest cabin has an espresso machine in addition to its Wedgewood stove. Every cabin has a fully equipped kitchen and private patio with outdoor fireplace. You'll bathe in, and drink, natural mineral water from the ranch's well. A hot tub and hand-built barbecue pit are shared among the cabin guests, as well as a large stargazing observation deck and swimming pool.

Rimrock Ranch borders on Pipes Canyon Wilderness Preserve, where you can take advantage of hiking, biking, and rock climbing opportunities. The myriad trails of Joshua Tree are only a short drive away. In addition, Big Morongo Canyon Preserve is easily accessible off Highway 62; more than 235 bird species have been identified at the preserve.

Facilities: There are four cabins that can accommodate up to four people. All have fully equipped kitchens.

Bedding: Linens and towels are provided.

Reservations and rates: Reservations are required. Fees are $75 to $145 per night for two people, plus $20 for each additional person (up to four). Summer rates are discounted. Pets are permitted with a $10 fee and a $25 deposit.

Directions: From Banning on I-10, drive east for 17 miles to the Highway 62 exit. Turn northeast on Highway 62 and drive 25 miles to Yucca Valley. Turn left (north) on Pioneertown Road and drive five miles to Pioneertown. Continue through town for four more miles (stay on the paved road) to Rimrock Ranch on the left.

Contact: Rimrock Ranch Cabins, P.O. Box 313, Pioneertown, CA 92268; 760/228-1297; website: www.rimrockranchcabins.com.

Rimrock Ranch Cabins

4. MOJAVE ROCK RANCH

My first experience at Mojave Rock Ranch was a little unworldly. As I drove in, the place looked deserted except for a 1930s Chevy truck in mint condition. In a corral by the parking lot, a donkey stood watching me with unconcealed curiosity. A big water tank behind the corral bore the sign "Mojave Rock Ranch—Established Way Back," so I figured I must be in the right place.

Off Highway 62 near Joshua Tree

Luxury rating: 4

Recreation rating: 3

THIS CABIN RANKS . . .
Best in the Desert
Most Secluded

Strains of Vivaldi played from outside speakers as I approached the ranch's front door. The grounds were landscaped with remarkable precision and beauty, using only desert plants. Pieces of sculpture, colorful paintings, fabulous stone work, and barrel cactus popped up in every available space.

I have since learned the score at Mojave Rock Ranch: The owners know exactly what they are doing. They have strategically created a secluded desert getaway with attention paid to every detail. The ranch is artistic, funky, and tastefully elegant at the same time.

The four two-bedroom cabins are available for rent on a daily, weekly, or monthly basis. The Ranch features a sleeping porch with a 180-degree view. The Bungalow has an exquisite goldfish pond and water garden made from 1,000 bottles. The Homesteader has lots of windows and French doors that overlook the desert scenery, plus a turn-of-the-century wagon parked in its yard. The Casita features built-in sitting alcoves and a pond and water garden made out of a canoe.

A fully equipped kitchen is provided in all cabins, as well as a fireplace or woodstove, barbecue grill, hammock, and just about everything else you can think of. Most guests stay longer than the required two nights; this is the kind of place where you want to settle in for a while and pretend that it's home. (It will take you several days just to check out the varied, eclectic decor.)

While you're exploring the wonders of Mojave Rock Ranch, you should also make time to visit nearby Joshua Tree National Park. Because the ranch is situated near the western end of the large park, Black Rock Canyon is a logical starting point. From Black Rock, you can hike six miles round-trip to Warren Peak, elevation 5,103 feet, or 10 miles round-trip to Eureka Peak, elevation 5,518 feet. (You can also drive to Eureka Peak, but it's more fun to hike it.) From the summits, you gain great views of Mount San Jacinto and Mount San Gorgonio, both crowned in snow all winter.

It's also an easy jaunt to the park's west entrance station at Park Boulevard. From there, you can access the trails to Hidden Valley, Barker Dam, Lost Horse Mine, and Ryan Mountain. Any or all of these short hikes are well worth the effort.

Facilities: There are four two-bedroom cabins that can accommodate up to four people. All have fully equipped kitchens.

Bedding: Linens and towels are provided.

Reservations and rates: Reservations are required. Fees range from $275 to $325 per night for one to four people; weekly rates are discounted. A two-night minimum stay is required. Pets are permitted with a $10 fee per night, but they are not allowed inside the buildings (an enclosed dog area and dog house are provided with each cabin).

Directions: From Banning on I-10, drive east for 17 miles to the Highway 62 exit. Turn northeast on Highway 62 and drive 30 miles to the town of Joshua Tree. Turn left (north) on Sunfair Road. (If you reach Copper Mountain College on Highway 62, you've gone too far.) Drive six miles on Sunfair Road, then turn right by the wagon wheel that is signed 2015. Drive a half mile to the ranch.

Contact: Mojave Rock Ranch, P.O. Box 552, Joshua Tree, CA 92252; 760/366-8455; website: www.mojaverockranch.com.

Mojave Rock Ranch

5. 29 PALMS INN

If you don't consider yourself to be an admirer of desert landscapes, a stay at 29 Palms Inn will convert you. Located just outside of the border of Joshua Tree National Park, 29 Palms is funky, charming, and the ideal base camp for enjoying the surrounding desert.

© ANN MARIE BROWN

Off Highway 62 in Twentynine Palms

Luxury rating: 4

Recreation rating: 4

THIS CABIN RANKS . . .
Best in the Desert

The inn has been around since 1928 and owned by the same family for five generations. It has 16 cabins, varying from adobe bungalows to old wood-frame buildings. Some of the cabins are duplexes, but they are private and quiet, with thick walls and fenced-in patios. Some units have fireplaces, some have woodstoves, and some don't have either, so be sure to ask for what you want. Only two buildings have kitchens; these are the three-bedroom Guest House and the one-bedroom Irene's Historic Adobe.

If you don't get a kitchen unit when you reserve, you won't be missing much. A complimentary continental breakfast is provided each morning. For lunch and dinner, you can eat at 29 Palms Inn's restaurant, which serves wonderful food in a friendly, casual atmosphere. The sourdough bread is to die for.

Other charms of 29 Palms Inn include a duck pond surrounded by pomegranate trees, an enclosed gazebo that shelters a large whirlpool tub, a big swimming pool, and a multitude of hand-carved signs scattered about the grounds bearing quirky messages. I won't give away what they say; you'll have to see for yourself.

When you're not in your 29 Palms cabin, you'll be out exploring Joshua Tree National Park. The best trails near the inn are those leading to Forty-nine Palms Oasis, Ryan Mountain, and Lost Horse Mine. If you have time, head to the Cottonwood Spring area in the south part of the park, where a terrific eight-mile round-trip trail leads to Lost Palms Oasis. If you don't want to hike that far, take the shorter left fork to Mastodon Peak and scramble to the top of its rocky pinnacle.

The main Joshua Tree visitor center is located about two miles from 29 Palms Inn on Utah Trail Road. Rangers there can provide you with all the information you need for visiting the park.

Facilities: There are 16 cabins ranging in size from studios to three bedrooms. Two cabins have kitchens. A restaurant is on-site.

Bedding: Linens and towels are provided.

Reservations and rates: Reservations are recommended. Fees range from $80 to $285 per night. Discounted rates are offered from June 15 to September 15, and midweek year-round. Pets are permitted in some cabins for a $10 fee.

Directions: From Banning on I-10, drive east for 17 miles to the Highway 62 exit. Turn northeast on Highway 62 and drive 45 miles to the town of Twentynine Palms. Continue east to the far end of town and National Park Drive (one block east of Adobe Road). Turn right on National Park Drive, drive a quarter mile and turn right on Inn Avenue. You'll enter the grounds of 29 Palms Inn immediately.

Contact: 29 Palms Inn, 73950 Inn Avenue, Twentynine Palms, CA 92277; 760/367-3505; website: www.29palmsinn.com.

29 Palms Inn

6. ROUGHLEY MANOR INN

When Bill and Elizabeth Campbell first settled in Twentynine Palms in 1928, they constructed a humble homestead from native materials. Not long thereafter, the Campbells inherited some big bucks, and they quickly decided it would be nicer to have a three-story stone manor house with leaded windows, five fireplaces, and Vermont maple floors. Who can blame them?

The Roughley Manor today is owned by Jan and Gary Peters, who have furnished the stately house with their antique collection. In addition to its nine guest rooms, the manor also has four cottages with private baths and kitchenettes. The buildings sit on 25 beautifully land-scaped acres with a rose garden, palm and cypress trees, a hot tub under a gazebo, five-tier fountain, and extensive stone walkways and patios. The overall effect is quite elegant.

Of the four cottages, Pinto and Sunrise are a duplex. Both have queen-size four-poster beds and fireplaces. The separate Cottage has a sitting room, bedroom with queen bed, and an antique tub in the bathroom. Farmhouse has a breakfast bar that separates the living room from the kitchenette, and an antique four-poster bed.

© ANN MARIE BROWN

Off Highway 62 in
Twentynine Palms

Luxury rating: 5

Recreation rating: 3

Roughley Manor is operated as a bed-and-breakfast, and the morning meal is downright decadent. Jan Peters' twice-baked potatoes topped with eggs and bacon are legendary. Evening tea and dessert is served nightly at 6:30.

The manor is located only a couple miles from the Oasis Visitor Center and northern entrance to Joshua Tree National Park. If it's your first trip, be sure to drive to the overlook at Keys View, elevation 5,185 feet. On a clear day, the vista takes in Mount San Gorgonio, Mount San Jacinto, the Coachella Valley, and the Salton Sea. On a really clear day, Signal Mountain in Mexico, more than 90 miles away, can be seen. Take the short walk from the overlook to the top of Inspiration Peak, just to the north of Keys View.

Many more hiking trails are found nearby, including the four-mile round-trip to Lost Horse Mine and its well-preserved gold stamp mill, and the three-mile round-trip to the summit of Ryan Mountain.

Facilities: There are four one-bedroom cottages, plus nine guest rooms. The cottages have kitchenettes (microwave and refrigerator).

Bedding: Linens and towels are provided.

Reservations and rates: Reservations are recommended. Fees are $125 to $150 per night for two people, which includes breakfast. Pets are not permitted.

Directions: From Banning on I-10, drive east for 17 miles to the Highway 62 exit. Turn northeast on Highway 62 and drive 45 miles to the town of Twentynine Palms. Continue east to the far end of town and Utah Trail. Turn left (north) on Utah Trail and drive a half mile to Joe Davis Road. Turn right and drive a half mile to Roughley Manor on the left.

Contact: Roughley Manor Inn, 74744 Joe Davis Road, Twentynine Palms, CA 92277; 760/367-3238; website: www.roughleymanor.com.

Roughley Manor Inn

7. TWO BUNCH PALMS

Two Bunch Palms is a 56-acre playground in the hot sun of Desert Hot Springs. Two Bunch Palms is a serious health spa, offering mud baths, massages, skin treatments, and the like. It's also a hot springs oasis, where water rushes out of the ground at more than 150°F and flows into an assortment of beautiful rock pools. And even more, it's a country club with tennis and racquetball courts, artificially constructed lakes, lush landscaping, and a gourmet restaurant.

Off I-10 in Desert Hot Springs

Luxury rating: 5

Recreation rating: 3

THIS CABIN RANKS . . .
Most Luxurious
Best in the Desert

The variety of accommodations at Two Bunch Palms is as diverse as the resort itself. There are modern, spacious casitas and villas, luxury "spa suites," older bungalows with Victorian antiques and Art Deco accessories, and even the House on the Hill, a very secluded two-bedroom house with dramatic desert and mountain views. Plus there are smaller, less-expensive guest rooms.

Far and away the most interesting lodging is the Rock House. As the story goes, in 1928 the Miami police gave Al Capone 24 hours to get out of town. The increasingly paranoid Capone wanted a hideaway where any enemy could be spotted for miles around; he chose Two Bunch Palms. He built the first permanent structures at the oasis: an enclave of bungalows made of solid rock, complete with stained glass windows and a sentry turret. He and his gangster buddies supposedly hid out at Two Bunch Palms until the early 1930s, and then one day, perhaps out of fear of being discovered, everyone just got up and walked away. Not long after, Capone was sentenced to federal prison in Georgia.

Capone's Rock House is in the heart of Two Bunch Palms, alongside its "grotto," where rock-lined mineral water pools are shaded by towering palm trees. The main activity at the resort is soaking in its many pools. Bicycles are available if you'd like to ride around the grounds, and walking and running trails crisscross the property.

Two Bunch Palms is not a budget-minded place, but it becomes substantially more affordable from June to September, and also in the first three weeks of December. The best rates are available in July and August; ask about their combined resort and spa packages, which include taxes and gratuities.

Facilities: There are 45 guest rooms, suites, villas, and bungalows, ranging in size from studios to three bedrooms. Some have fully equipped kitchens. A restaurant is on-site.

Bedding: Linens and towels are provided.

Reservations and rates: Reservations are required. Fees are $335 to $645 per night for villas and $175 to $295 per night for guest rooms. Substantial discounts are available in summer. Children under 18 are not permitted. Pets are not permitted.

Directions: From I-10 in Banning, drive east for 23 miles and take the Palm Drive/Desert Hot Springs exit. Drive north on Palm Drive for five miles. Turn right (east) on Two Bunch Palms Trail and drive one mile to the gated entrance to Two Bunch Palms, on the right.

Contact: Two Bunch Palms, 67425 Two Bunch Palms Trail, Desert Hot Springs, CA 92240; 760/329-8791 or 800/472-4334; website: www.twobunchpalms.com.

Two Bunch Palms

8. KORAKIA PENSIONE

Korakia Pensione is Palm Springs at its most stylish. The bed-and-breakfast inn consists of two adjacent historic villas, each encompassing a passel of bungalows, guest houses, gardens, and pools. Its beautifully appointed accommodations have been written up in *Travel & Leisure, Condé Nast Traveler, Architectural Digest,* and *The New York Times.*

© ANN MARIE BROWN

Off Highway 111 in Palm Springs

Luxury rating: 4

Recreation rating: 3

Korakia's freestanding bungalows are located in what is called the Mediterranean villa, across the street from the main inn, or Moroccan villa. Both villas were built in the 1920s. Decorative details are perfect in every way: handmade feather beds, wood accents, antique furnishings, white-washed walls, and stone and tile floors. My favorite units are the South Pool Bungalow, a one-bedroom with a Japanese stone bath, and the North Pool Bungalow with eight glass doors opening out from its living room to the pool. The grounds of the villas consist of 1.5 acres of fruit trees, mosaic tile fountains, stone waterfalls, and bougainvillea.

For all this luxury, prices at Korakia are fairly reasonable. A gourmet continental breakfast is included in the price, and kitchens are available in most units.

It's unlikely, but if you are willing to drag yourself away from the sparkling swimming pools of this oasis, you can visit the nearby shops, restaurants, and attractions of Palm Springs. Most of the downtown is within walking distance.

A short drive will take you to newly opened Tahquitz Canyon. Named for an Agua Caliente shaman who abused his powers and was banished from his tribe, Tahquitz Canyon is a spectacular outdoor museum of desert flora and fauna. Entry is by guided hike only; preserve rangers lead groups on an easy, two-mile trek through the canyon to

199-studio-
2Mei
?nonsmoking en.
?bed site n.
AAA

the base of its 65-foot waterfall. Tahquitz's other treasures include plentiful bird life, Native American rock art, and lush stands of desert lavender, mesquite, and creosote.

If you seek a longer, more solitary desert adventure, head over to neighboring Murray Canyon, where you can hike unescorted. A delight for photographers, the colorful canyon is filled with nearly 1,000 leafy Washingtonia fan palms, 100-foot-high red rock outcrops, a multitude of rotund barrel cactus, and a series of small waterfalls, called the Seven Sisters, at two miles out. Bighorn sheep are often spotted standing guard on the high canyon walls.

Facilities: There are 20 guest houses, bungalows, studios, and rooms, ranging in size from studios to two bedrooms. Most have fully equipped kitchens.

Bedding: Linens and towels are provided.

Reservations and rates: Reservations are recommended. Fees range from $149 to $395 per night, including a continental breakfast. Pets are not permitted.

Directions: From I-10 in Banning, drive east for 12 miles and take the Highway 111 exit for Palm Springs. Drive southeast for 10 miles; Highway 111 becomes Palm Canyon Drive. Turn right on Arenas and head west four blocks. Turn left on Patencio; Korakia is on the left.

Contact: Korakia Pensione, 257 South Patencio Road, Palm Springs, CA 92262; 760/864-6411; website: www.korakia.com.

Korakia Pensione

$89 -hotel- 29,30,31, 1
$99 studio 30,31,1
$99

9. CASA CODY COUNTRY INN

Casa Cody, the oldest operating hotel in Palm Springs, is a wonderful historic hideaway. Although it is located in the midst of Palm Springs Village, Casa Cody offers far more seclusion than other neighboring lodgings. Once you pass through its gates, you feel as if you've entered your own private desert compound.

The most impressive (and private) unit at Casa Cody is its 1910 two-bedroom adobe villa, where Charlie Chaplin once stayed. The villa has open-beamed ceilings, tile and wood floors, and extensive rock work in its kitchen and bath—counters, shower, and tub. It's tempting to move right in and never leave.

Even the smaller cottages have private patios, fireplaces, fully equipped kitchens, cable television, and private phones. Casa Cody's decor is Southwestern in style, bringing to mind the colorful resorts of Santa Fe. Its grounds are a mix of flowering vines and shrubs, and huge citrus and fig trees. In season, you can pick your own grapefruit. Two swimming pools and a hot tub are also on the property.

No trip to Palm Springs is complete without a ride on the world-famous Aerial Tramway, and no tram ride is complete without a hike at its high ter-

© ANN MARIE BROWN

Off Highway 111 in Palm Springs

Luxury rating: 4

Recreation rating: 3

minus. During the 15-minute, two-mile ride, you are whooshed from the Palm Springs' desert floor at 2,643 feet in elevation to Mount San Jacinto State Park at 8,516 feet. Palm trees suddenly transform into conifers and the air temperature drops 30 degrees.

At the top, hiking opportunities abound. A good introductory hike is the four-mile round-trip to Round Valley. The trail meanders past huge granite boulders, old-growth white firs, and Jeffrey pines to a pretty alpine meadow. There's nothing quite like the experience of walking among desert cactus in the morning, then hiking among mountain conifers in the afternoon.

The ambitious can get an early start on long summer days and head for the summit of 10,804-foot San Jacinto Peak, a 12-mile round-trip. Just be sure to make it back in time for the last tram of the day, or bring your backpacking gear.

If you ride the Aerial Tramway from November to April, you have a good chance for a winter wonderland at the top. Cross-country skis and snowshoes are available for rent; visitors glide around the snow-covered hiking trails.

Facilities: There are 23 guest houses, bungalows, and rooms, ranging in size from studios to two bedrooms. Most have fully equipped kitchens.

Bedding: Linens and towels are provided.

Reservations and rates: Reservations are recommended. Fees range from $109 to $349 per night in winter, and $69 to $229 per night in summer, including a continental breakfast. Pets are permitted with a $10 fee.

Directions: From I-10 in Banning, drive east for 12 miles and take the Highway 111 exit for Palm Springs. Drive southeast for 10 miles; Highway 111 becomes Palm Canyon Drive. Turn right on Tahquitz Canyon Way, drive two blocks, then turn left on Cahuilla. Casa Cody is on the right.

Contact: Casa Cody Country Inn, 175 South Cahuilla Road, Palm Springs, CA 92262; 760/320-9346; website: www.casacody.com.

Casa Cody Country Inn

10. ORCHID TREE INN

The Orchid Tree Inn is quintessential Palm Springs: a 1930s desert garden retreat with a cluster of red-tile-roofed Spanish bungalows set amid swimming pools, palm trees, cactus gardens, citrus trees, and bougainvillea. Once seven separate smaller properties, the inn now has a total of 50 units,

© ANN MARIE BROWN

Off Highway 111 in Palm Springs

Luxury rating: 4

Recreation rating: 3

including 10 one-bedroom bungalows large enough for a small family, plus three swimming pools and two hot pools.

In season (November to April), a complimentary breakfast is served daily. The rest of the year, you're on your own to cook in your bungalow, or walk a few blocks into downtown Palm Springs to order your eggs at a restaurant.

Orchid Tree is only a short walk from many of Palm Springs' attractions, including the Palm Springs Desert Museum and Cahuilla Indian Museum. Within a couple miles are the Palm Springs Aerial Tramway (ride to the top and hike in the cool shade of conifers at Mount San Jacinto State Park) and the Agua Caliente Indian Reservation (explore the waterfalls and desert flora and fauna of spectacular Murray, Andreas, Palm, or Tahquitz Canyons). Smoke Tree Stables is nearby for those who prefer to take a guided horseback ride through the desert. Bicycle rentals are available in town, and Bighorn Bicycle Adventures leads guided tours.

One of the most unusual local attractions is the giant wind farm at the northern entrance to Palm Springs. Palm Springs Windmill Tours takes visitors on a 90-minute electric cart ride through thousands of 80- to 300-foot-tall wind turbines. During the tour, you learn how windmills make electricity, why some blades are turning while others stand still, and why the popularity of wind farms is increasing.

And as if there weren't enough to do right in Palm Springs, a one-hour drive will take you to Joshua Tree National Park, Anza-Borrego Desert State Park, or Idyllwild in San Bernardino National Forest.

Facilities: There are 50 rooms, suites, and bungalows that can accommodate up to four people. All have fully equipped kitchens.

Bedding: Linens and towels are provided.

Reservations and rates: Reservations are recommended. Fees range from $109 to $249 per night in winter, and $69 to $189 per night in summer. Pets are not permitted.

Directions: From I-10 in Banning, drive east for 12 miles and take the Highway 111 exit for Palm Springs. Drive southeast for 10 miles; Highway 111 becomes Palm Canyon Drive. Turn right on Baristo; the inn is on the right at the corner of Baristo and South Belardo.

Contact: Orchid Tree Inn, 261 South Belardo Road, Palm Springs, CA 92262; 760/325-2791 or 800/733-3435; website: www.orchidtree.com.

Orchid Tree Inn

INDEX

Silver City Resort: 221–222
Silver Lake Resort: 140–141
Silver Strand State Beach: 106
Simpson House Inn: 24–25
Slate Mountain: 227
Sleepy Hollow Cabins: 46–47
skiing: Angelus Oaks 63, 64, 65; Big Bear Lake (the town) 57, 58, 60, 61; Descanso 97; Fawnskin 54; Giant Sequoia National Monument 211; Green Valley Lake 53; Julian 93, 94, 95; June Lake 141, 143, 144, 145, 146, 147; Kernville 230, 231; Lake Arrowhead (the town) 50; Lakeshore 193, 195; Lee Vining 128, 130; Mammoth Lakes 156, 157, 160, 167, 170; Mount Baldy 44, 45; Mount Laguna 100; Palm Springs 251; Pinecrest 116,117; Pine Mountain Club 33; Running Springs 51; Sequoia National Park 212–213; Shaver Lake 189, 190; Springville 227; Strawberry 115; Twin Peaks 48; Wawona 153; Wrightwood 42; Yosemite 139, 151, 152
Smoketree Resort: 59
Snowcrest Lodge: 44–45
snowshoeing: Giant Sequoia National Monument 211; June Lake 144, 146; Kernville 231; Lakeshore 193, 195; Mammoth Lakes 160; Palm Springs 251; Pinecrest 117; Pine Mountain Club 33; Sequoia National Park 212–213; Shaver Lake 190; Springville 227; Yosemite West 151
Solvang: 16–19
South Lake: 202, 203
Springville: 226–227
Stagecoach Trails Resort: 96–97
Stanislaus National Forest: 114, 115
Stanislaus River: 115
Stonewall Peak: 97
Strawberry: 114–116
Strawberry Creek Inn: 78
Sunset Inn Yosemite Guest Cabins: 131
surfing: Cayucos 11; Malibu 40; Montecito 29–30; Pismo Beach 15; San Diego 101, 102; Santa Barbara 25

swimming: Angelus Oaks 63, 64, 65; Avalon 67, 68; Bass Lake 184; Big Bear Lake (the town) 55–56, 57, 58, 59, 60, 61; Big Pine 204; Bishop 169, 172, 200, 202, 203; Borrego Springs 91; Bradley 6, 7; Bridgeport 119, 120, 122, 123, 124, 125; Caliente 234; Camp Nelson 224; Cayucos 11, 13; Crestline 46; Crowley Lake 168; Death Valley 240; Descanso 97; Desert Hot Springs 248; Fairview 228; Fawnskin 54; Fish Camp 154, 156; Giant Sequoia National Monument 210, 211, 223; Goleta 19; Grant Grove Village 207; Green Valley Lake 53; Groveland 131, 132; Hollywood 41; Idyllwild 76, 77, 79; Julian 92, 93, 94, 95, 96; June Lake 140, 141, 143, 144, 145, 147; Kernville 229, 231; Kings Canyon National Park 208; Laguna Beach 72, 74; Lake Arrowhead (the town) 49, 50; Lakeshore 191, 192, 194, 195, 198, 199; Lee Vining 127, 128, 130; Long Beach 69–70; Malibu 40; Mammoth Lakes 86, 148, 157, 160, 161, 163, 164, 165, 167, 170; Manhattan Beach 187; Midpines 149; Mineral King 221; Mono Hot Springs 197; Montecito 29–30; Mount Baldy 43, 45; Mount Laguna 99, 100; Newport Beach 71; Oakhurst 183; Ojai 31; Palm Springs 249, 250, 251, 252; Pine Mountain Club 33; Pinecrest 116, 118; Pioneertown 243; Pismo Beach 15; Quaking Aspen 225–226; Rancho Santa Fe 87; Running Springs 51; San Diego 101, 102, 104; Sanger 206; Santa Barbara 21, 22, 23, 25, 26, 27, 28; Santa Ysabel 89; Sequoia National Park 214; Shaver Lake 188, 190; Solvang 18; Springville 227; Strawberry 114, 115; Three Rivers 216, 217, 219, 220; Twentynine Palms 245; Valley Center 75; Ventura 32; Warner Springs 90; Wawona 153; Wishon 187; Woodlake 215; Wrightwood 42; Yosemite 134, 135, 136, 137; Yosemite West 151

ABOUT THE AUTHOR

Ann Marie Brown is the author of nine books on California recreation, including *California Waterfalls, Day-Hiking California's National Parks, Foghorn Outdoors: California Hiking* (with Tom Stienstra), and *Easy Hiking in Southern California.*

© BILL RHOADES

Notes

Notes

Notes

Notes

**AVALON
TRAVEL**
publishing

How far will our travel guides take you? As far as you want.

Discover a rhumba-fueled nightspot in Old Havana, explore prehistoric tombs in Ireland, hike beneath California's centuries-old redwoods, or embark on a classic road trip along Route 66. Our guidebooks deliver solidly researched, trip-tested information—minus any generic froth—to help globetrotters or weekend warriors create an adventure uniquely their own.

And we're not just about the printed page. Public television viewers are tuning in to Rick Steves' new travel series, *Rick Steves' Europe*. On the Web, readers can cruise the virtual black top with *Road Trip USA* author Jamie Jensen and learn travel industry secrets from Edward Hasbrouck of *The Practical Nomad*.

In print. On TV. On the Internet.

We supply the information. The rest is up to you.

Avalon Travel Publishing

Something for everyone

www.travelmatters.com

Avalon Travel Publishing guides are available at your favorite book or travel store.

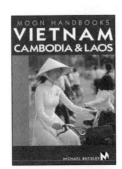

MOON HANDBOOKS provide comprehensive

coverage of a region's arts, history, land, people, and social issues in addition to detailed practical listings for accommodations, food, outdoor recreation, and entertainment. Moon Handbooks allow complete immersion in a region's culture—ideal for travelers who want to combine sightseeing with insight for an extraordinary travel experience in destinations throughout North America, Hawaii, Latin America, the Caribbean, Asia, and the Pacific.

WWW.MOON.COM

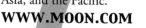

shows you where to travel and how to travel—all while getting the most value for your dollar. His Back Door travel philosophy is about making friends, having fun, and avoiding tourist rip-offs.

Rick

has been traveling to Europe for more than 25 years and is the author of 22 guidebooks, which have sold more than a million copies. He also hosts the award-winning public television series *Rick Steves' Europe*.

WWW.RICKSTEVES.COM

ROAD TRIP USA

Getting there is half the fun, and Road Trip USA guides are your ticket to driving adventure. Taking you off the interstates and onto less-traveled, two-lane highways, each guide is filled with fascinating trivia, historical information, photographs, facts about regional writers, and details on where to sleep and eat—all contributing to your exploration of the American road.

"[Books] so full of the pleasures of the American road, you can smell the upholstery."
~**BBC radio**
WWW.ROADTRIPUSA.COM

FOGHORN OUTDOORS guides are for campers, hikers, boaters, anglers, bikers, and golfers of all levels of daring and skill. Each guide focuses on a specific U.S. region and contains site descriptions and ratings, driving directions, facilities and fees information, and easy-to-read maps that leave only the task of deciding where to go.

"Foghorn Outdoors has established an ecological conservation standard unmatched by any other publisher." ~**Sierra Club**

WWW.FOGHORN.COM

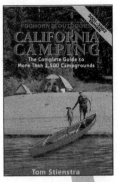

TRAVEL SMART guidebooks are accessible, route-based driving guides focusing on regions throughout the United States and Canada. Special interest tours provide the most practical routes for family fun, outdoor activities, or regional history for a trip of anywhere from two to 22 days. Travel Smarts take the guesswork out of planning a trip by recommending only the most interesting places to eat, stay, and visit.

"One of the few travel series that rates sightseeing attractions. That's a handy feature. It helps to have some guidance so that every minute counts." ~San Diego Union-Tribune

CiTY·SMaRT™ guides are written by local authors with hometown perspectives who have personally selected the best places to eat, shop, sightsee, and simply hang out. The honest, lively, and opinionated advice is perfect for business travelers looking to relax with the locals or for longtime residents looking for something new to do Saturday night.

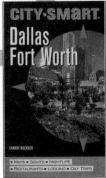

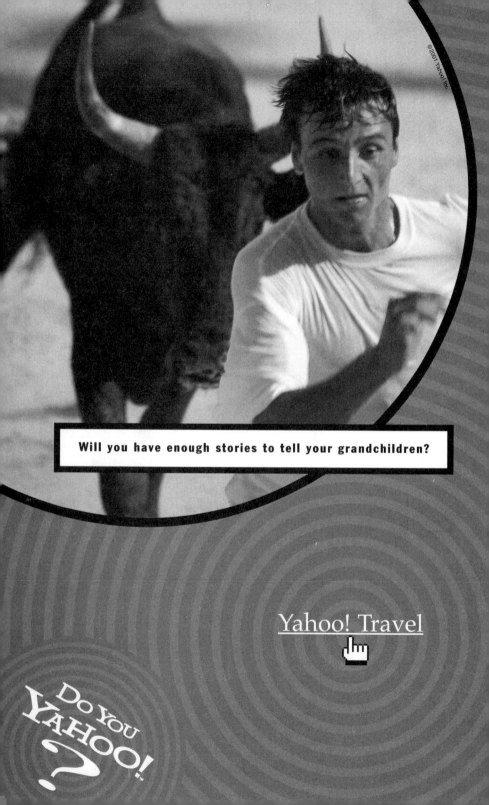

Will you have enough stories to tell your grandchildren?

Yahoo! Travel

Do You Yahoo!?